D1085037

The Rhetoric of Conservatism

The Rhetoric of Conservatism:
The Virginia Convention of 1829-30
and the Conservative Tradition in the South
by Dickson D. Bruce, Jr.

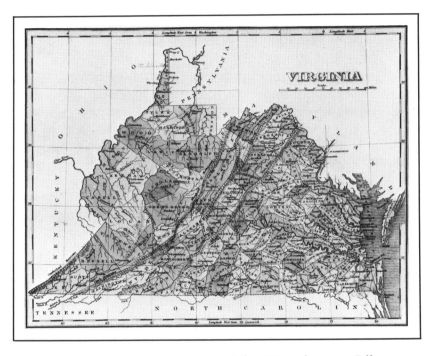

The Huntington Library
San Marino, California
1982

Library of Congress Cataloging in Publication Data

Bruce, Dickson D., 1946-
    The rhetoric of conservatism.

    Includes bibliographical references and index.
    1. Virginia—Constitutional history. 2. Virginia—Politics and
government—1775-1865. 3. Virginia. Constitutional Convention (1829-
1830) 4. Conservatism—Virginia—History. I. Title.
JK3925 1829.B78   1982   320.5'2'09755   82-9224
ISBN 0-87328-121-7   AACR2

TABLE OF CONTENTS

For my parents

PREFACE

This book grows out of a general interest in questions of how political language and political beliefs work and of how one can understand their meaning. These are not easy questions, but they are important. The words politicians use often have meanings and associations that are anything but obvious and that are based, to a great degree, on the setting in which the words are spoken. At the same time, what politicians say may be no less significant in determining the course of political action than are more clearly defined economic or social interests. Indeed, it is not difficult to find instances in American history in which language has been used to mobilize beliefs leading people to act in ways that, by any reasonable calculation, are contrary to their own material interests. This adds a complexity to political history that is worth trying to understand.

The history of the southern United States has provided many instances in which one can see language operating with such power. The Virginia Convention of 1829-30, on which this book focuses, was a small episode of this sort—one manageably studied with some depth—but the force of words has characterized much about southern politics, at its broadest level, since at least the American Revolution. It may be an exaggeration to claim, as some historians have, that southern orators started the Civil War, but southern orators have achieved great influence in state and national politics. And it is neither an exaggeration nor particularly new to note that the most popular southern orators have not often used their influence for the benefit of the people from whom they have drawn the strongest and most consistent support. Anyone with an interest in the workings of political language and ideology can find much to study in the history of the American

South, including that of Virginia during the early nineteenth century.

Early national Virginia has additional interest, given the state's special place in American political history during that period. Home of some of America's most noted democratic theorists, birthplace of Presidents, and the most southerly state to discuss with some seriousness the emancipation of its slaves, it was also a state dominated by an elitist political system supported by a strong conservative credo. Because of this combination of factors, the Virginia conservatism put forward in 1830 bore important relationships to past ideological currents in America, just as it would occupy a significant place in the development of southern proslavery conservatism prior to the Civil War. This book examines those relationships, and seeks to show the meaning of Virginia conservatism on the basis of its ties to political circumstances and to the cultural and social characteristics of the state.

The basic research for this study was undertaken in 1975, when I was a Fellow of the Huntington Library in San Marino, California. It is based mainly on work in the Library's holdings—especially of published Virginia materials—and its direction was strongly influenced by discussions with other scholars from a variety of fields who were then in residence there. Research in the Huntington Library was supplemented by work in the manuscript holdings of the Earl G. Swem Library of the College of William and Mary, the Virginia State Library, and the Virginia Historical Society. I am grateful to staff members of all those institutions for their assistance.

The expenses incident to this work were met, in part, as a result of financial support from the Huntington Library, from the University of California, Irvine, Academic Senate Committee on Research, the School of Social Sciences, and the Program in Comparative Culture.

I have received much valuable advice in writing this study, from a number of people. I am particularly grateful to Jim Flink, Pete Clecak, and Dickran Tashjian for taking time to read the entire manuscript, and to Michael Johnson and

Richard Frank for commenting on portions of it.

Finally, my wife Mary and daughter Emily were, as ever, supportive.

LIST OF ILLUSTRATIONS

INTRODUCTION

The development of a conservative ideology in the antebellum South has mainly been studied in recent years with two key assumptions in mind. One is that the ideology was primarily a product of the nineteenth century, representing a "great reaction" to the growing democratic tendencies in American society—including the South—during the period. The other is that, however coherent the claims of antebellum southern ideologues, what they were really concerned about was sectionalism and, ultimately, slavery. William Sumner Jenkins's contention that during the nineteenth century "the Southern mind was absorbed in making a defense of slavery" to the exclusion of all else[1] remains something of a guiding assumption for the study of antebellum thought in the region.

To an extent, the assumption is accurate, and one should not be surprised that this is so. The complex interplay of external pressures with economic and "racial" needs made slavery the central focus for southern thinking, almost inevitably. Nevertheless, it is not correct to treat antebellum southern conservatism as if it were simply synonymous with the proslavery argument nor, for that matter, as if it sprang up only in the nineteenth century and in response to immediate dangers. Rather, the main tenets of the proslavery argument were part of a more broadly focused conservative ideology that was relatively old by the time southern ideologues sought to apply it to the institution's defense. The conservative tradition in the South dated far back into the nineteenth century—indeed, to Revolutionary times—and the proslavery argument was, ultimately, an application of that tradition to the specific demands of defending slavery.

This study is an exploration of the foundations of southern

conservative ideology, and focuses on one episode in the region's history, the Virginia Convention of 1829-30, which would revise the state's 1776 constitution. In this convention, slavery was only implicitly at issue, the dominant concerns being suffrage reform and reapportionment of the legislature. While it would be possible to see slavery as an underlying issue for the debates in convention, the arguments for and against revision were stated in terms of the most general political concerns. Because of this, the debates in the convention—particularly the arguments against revision—provide a good picture of the larger context out of which southern thought would develop in the later antebellum period. Accordingly, most of this book focuses on the convention, exploring the ideological sources of the conservative argument against change as well as the relationships of that argument to culture and to social values, and then concludes with a more detailed account of the development of proslavery in the later antebellum period.

To understand the issues presented in 1829-30, one must first look, briefly, at the more general setting within which those issues developed. The key issue was that of inequality in the political system, of who could and who could not participate in political affairs. Inequality and its foundation were open questions in Virginia between the American Revolution and the Convention of 1829-30—just as the nature of a justifiable inequality was a fundamental issue in proslavery arguments—and several factors conspired to make them so. One was the Virginia social, political, and economic system, a system in which the rightness of inequality in every sphere was strongly asserted by those who were advantaged. A second factor that made inequality an issue was that of economic and demographic change, such that the old system fit less and less well with social and economic developments in Virginia life. Third, Virginians of all levels were confronted by the ideological changes, grounded in the rhetoric of the American Revolution, which made existing forms of inequality seem unjust to many people. These issues took their shape in the setting of Virginia's political system as it had developed during the colonial period and as it had survived into the early years of the nineteenth century.

Virginia's colonial oligarchic system prior to 1776 is too familiar to need a full description here. Suffice it to say that Virginia, which would become the center of so much Revolutionary fervor, was hardly distinguished by rampant democracy in its own politics. Although it would be an exaggeration to describe the state as an "aristocracy,"[2] the fact remains that power was concentrated in the hands of a few Virginians, and heredity had much to do with its distribution.

The dominance of Virginia politics by a few families has been thoroughly documented. Referring to themselves on occasion as the "gentry" or even as "aristocrats," these Virginians relied to a great extent on family background and connections in order to determine a man's political standing. A few families dominated the major political posts, and power was passed from generation to generation along family lines.[3] Wealth supplemented name as a source of power and influence.

Political dominance brought its own rewards to Virginians during the colonial and early national periods, some practical, others psychological. Not least of these latter benefits was the approximation of the Virginia system to what was perceived as the aristocratic structure of English society. Jack P. Greene has demonstrated the power of English norms in colonial American life, and this was nowhere more apparent than in Virginia.[4] Borrowing English social categories to describe themselves, Virginia "gentlemen" modeled much in their lives, including their politics, on what they took to be the English example. But economic benefits were there, as well, particularly in a society where the ownership and distribution of land had much to do with economic life. Political influence and economic influence went closely together in colonial Virginia: elite status would not have been easy to give up.

The Virginia elite put its system on the firm economic foundation of real property. Until the Constitution of 1830, freehold suffrage was the law in Virginia, and this would become a major issue in the debates which culminated in the Virginia Convention of 1829-30. The definition of a freehold was liberalized during the colonial and early national periods, but the concept of property as a prerequisite to political participation remained intact. Ideologically, as an element in the understanding of political rights, the concept was important. Practically, the effect was to maintain limited participation in the political process. Julian Chandler estimated that up to three-fourths of white adult males were disfranchised prior to 1830,[5] although the figure may be high. But, add to this the unrepresentative character of a government in which legislative apportionment was based on geography rather than population, favoring the older eastern counties, and the undemocratic nature of Virginia politics is clear. To be sure, there was a measure of complexity about these matters. D. Alan Williams, for instance, has suggested that in the colonial period political participation, including office-holding, by small landowners was extensive. Robert E. and B. Katherine Brown, in the most extensive critique of the traditional view of Virginia politics, have also tried to show that there was a degree of openness in the system, asserting that small landowners, in particular, could exercise a good deal of influence in Virginia political life.[6] Nevertheless, for men of the period, both restricted suffrage and skewed apportionment seemed important bulwarks for a system of government by the few. Political power always rested in the hands of a minority of what was already a minority of Virginians. Although new men might enter the system, their entrance and mobility were fully controlled by those who held the reins of government.[7] As Virginian George Tucker wrote in 1837, "a strong aristocratical spirit" prevailed in the politics of colonial Virginia, and it would carry forward into political practices during the early history of the state.[8]

And here, of course, was the real crux of the matter. It was not simply that the political system was closed to outsiders, nor was it that an industrious man could not rise even to the highest level. It was that mobility was tightly controlled by an

xiv

established elite throughout the colonial period and into the nineteenth century, and this control had one expression in an ideology that asserted family, wealth, and a particular style of life as prerequisites for political power.[9] Virginia's leaders saw themselves as a breed apart, as men who had a special fitness to govern, and they asserted the view that social and political stability demanded their presence. Theirs was, as J. R. Pole has aptly described it, a government of the few "with the acquiescence–or without the manifest dissent–of the governed."[10]

It was against this colonial background that one may view political events in Virginia during the period from the Revolution through the Convention of 1829-30. The Constitution of 1776 had preserved the colonial system virtually intact. Suffrage requirements were left alone, with but little discussion, when the document was instituted, and both the House of Delegates and the newly added Senate reflected the eastern domination of Virginia politics in their apportionment.[11] After about 1800, however, strong agitation for reform began to rock the state, as many Virginians sought to call a constitutional convention to revise the 1776 document in order to make it more democratic and fairer to all of Virginia's major sections. From the opening of the nineteenth century, conservative elite Virginians were forced to develop an overt ideological defense of their system, one intended to counter the arguments for democracy. The process would culminate in the Convention of 1829-30, producing a new constitution for the state. While this new constitution would exhibit some changes in regard to suffrage and apportionment, it represented, nevertheless, an important conservative victory, or so most observers agreed at the time. Because of this, the conservative arguments in debate may be seen as an important early statement of an antidemocratic ideology that could work in the South, one which would come to dominate southern political thought up to at least the time of the Civil War.

The main themes in this Virginia conservative ideology would hold together with great consistency. First, as the product of an effort to defend the existing system against efforts to change it, Virginia conservatism emphasized the importance of political and social stability while at the same time asserting how fragile any apparently stable system really was. Along with this, conservatives would stress that any change, no matter how seemingly trivial, was ultimately unpredictable, setting loose forces which no one could clearly anticipate or control. Second, this was a conservatism that placed social obligations over individual fulfillment as an acceptable motivation for political action. Virginia conservatives professed to reject a competitive, individualistic morality in favor of one in which every citizen would seek to subordinate his own desires to the accomplishment of public good. From this, conservatives would argue for the necessity of social and political hierarchy even as they would assert that rights had to be based on such a social fact as property rather than on a view of the individual as a sovereign, responsible being. Third, and related to both the above points, Virginia conservatism stressed human finitude. At best, conservatives would argue, human beings are very imperfect; their dreams of progress, chimerical and utopian. At worst, humans are willful and corrupt, making the key task of government not the encouragement of human fulfillment but the control of human passion. Conservatives relied on this view not only for their rejection of individualism but also in support of their openly antidemocratic sentiments and their disapproval of the principles upon which much of reform was based.

As most students of American ideas will recognize, such an ideology was not uniquely Virginia. One sees elements of it in American Revolutionary rhetoric, but one sees it even more clearly in other, earlier American debates between conservatives and democrats, those which occurred during the late eighteenth and early nineteenth centuries. Virginia was not the first American state in which democratic reformers attacked the elitist forms of government which had been set up at the close of the American revolution, nor was it the first state in which conservatives had sought to respond, ideologically, to demands for more democracy in political life.

xvi

This conflict had marked much of early American political life, beginning with the "critical period" between 1776 and the adoption of the Federal Constitution—a document which was itself an effort to protect "the worthy against the licentious,"[12] and later, in the evolution of the party system, in the conflict between conservative Federalists and the more democratic Republican party.[13] Indeed, much that Virginia conservatives said in the Convention of 1829-30 could have come straight out of Federalist rhetoric, and it is not difficult to place them squarely in that older conservative tradition.

However, to place Virginia conservative ideology in tradition is not to explain fully what it was about. The key issues which conservative and reform ideologies both sought to address were quite sharply drawn in this convention, as were the political alignments on the basis of which debate took place. The Virginia dispute over constitutional reform was essentially a regional one: western Virginia was the locus of the reform sentiment which conservatives from the east were forced to combat. But regional divisions covered a concatenation of other differences among Virginians in the early nineteenth century, including those of religion, livelihood, and political and cultural backgrounds and traditions. The Convention of 1829-30 brought all these differences into a single arena for conflict, and looking at the arguments used by both sides allows one to see how Virginia's nineteenth-century leaders drew upon rather tangible aspects of their own society and culture as they sought to achieve political goals.

The point is important because it stresses that, while conservative ideology had clear roots in the American political tradition—indeed, such roots would have contributed to its strength—it had to fit closely with the requirements set by constitutional debate, including the need to answer reform arguments and to address certain well-defined constituencies among convention delegates and among the state's voters. Why, in the Virginia setting of 1829, would an ideological approach to issues seem so viable, and why would a particular ideology seem so pertinent? As historian Merrill Peterson has noted, the Virginia Convention of 1829-30 was "unexcelled" as an ideological encounter, "the last gasp," as he has called it, "of Jeffersonian America's passion for political disputation."[14] But what aspects of the early national Virginia context contributed to the debate's taking such a form? Focusing on ideas, then, this study nonetheless tries to understand those ideas in context, in terms of what conservatives themselves thought their arguments could do to defeat the proponents on constitutional reform.

Accordingly, the approach to ideology which this study makes is one that can best be described as rhetorical, in that it seeks to define ideas in terms of the very specific purposes and intents of those who used them. But a major issue, given such an approach, is not only that of conservative intent but also, and perhaps more importantly, that of political acceptability—how a political argument could be made which was acceptable to its audience and, hence, which made support of conservative aims seem reasonable and justifiable. Conservatives not only wanted to make a particular case in their debate with reformers, after all, but they wanted to put that case forward in the most effective, persuasive way they could. This meant that those to whom they sought to appeal had to find the presentation of a conservative ideology to be an acceptable presentation in the context of Virginia political life.

Such an emphasis on the acceptability of its political arguments implies that one must address two underlying issues in order to understand the meaning of Virginia conservatism in 1829-30. One of these has to do with the standards conservatives themselves used to evaluate the acceptability of a political argument. Such standards would provide a major set of guidelines according to which conservative arguments would be framed, influencing conservatives as they chose certain points to emphasize in debate and in their selection of some political ideas over others in the fight against reform. Just as one cannot understand conservative ideology without knowing something of what it was intended to do, neither can one understand much of both its form and substance without an appreciation for the views conservatives held about politi-

xviii

cal language and the limits they observed in order to make their own arguments acceptable. Hence, one must examine their norms for political language and, too, the theories and methods of rhetoric which seemed important to them.

In addition, Virginia conservatism, to be acceptable, also had to be believable. Thus, it had to cohere, as does any ideology, with more general assumptions about human nature and society. The kinds of regional differences that contributed to political alignments on constitutional questions may have been obvious, but conservative arguments went well beyond an appeal to such interests. In support of the main themes of their ideology, conservatives depended heavily on certain conceptions about "fundamental truths" of human nature and society. These "truths" were essentially cultural matters, products of the formal and informal processes of enculturation to which people in the society were exposed. Without such support, conservative arguments would have appeared farfetched, even irrational.

And, indeed, there was much in Virginians' cultural lives that would have disposed them to appreciate conservative appeals to a sense of social and political fragility, to a rejection of individualism, and to an acknowledgement of human finitude. The professed morality of Virginia's conservative elite—found in their letters to each other, in their diaries, and in popular essays—made such notions as those of human weakness, the unpredictability of all areas of life, the importance of community, and the impossibility of achieving moral perfection virtual articles of faith, and these were notions which clearly supported the main points of conservative ideology, making it seem credible. One finds these notions expressed in many contexts, including religion, social life, and even physical existence, and they were learned from several sources, both social and intellectual. But they provided the essential cultural background without which political conservatism would have little power in the battle over constitutional reform.

This book is organized in a way that should make clear the depth of the connections between conservative ideology and culture. Chapters one and two try to account for the immediate stimulus to conservative ideological development, the movement for constitutional reform in early nineteenth-century Virginia. Chapter one surveys the major issues and events which led up to the Convention of 1829-30. It shows how the reform movement developed, the ways in which reform and conservative positions were shaped over time, and the basic sources for division that existed among Virginians during the period. Chapter two is an account of the convention itself, examining its composition and the kinds of strategies by which both sides, but especially conservatives, sought to win necessary votes among the delegates. Chapter three traces the main outlines of the conservative arguments in the convention debates.

Beginning with chapter four, the analysis moves below the surface of the arguments to understand why the conservative case took the form it did. This chapter looks mainly at the political culture of early national Virginia's elite, at their normative ideas about how politics should take place. The strategies conservatives evolved for confronting reform developed within the framework of this political culture, because it defined the limits on acceptable public political action and argument for them. Hence, too, this chapter explores the important influence of ideas about rhetoric and political language, as such, on the conservative case.

More general cultural matters are addressed in chapter five. Here, one sees in more detail those "fundamental truths" upon which Virginia conservatism rested, and the sources from which Virginians could learn those truths, especially in their reading, in social life, and in religion. In addition, this chapter relates the cultural foundations of conservatism to more specific alignments that organized Virginians on the issue of constitutional reform.

Finally, the book concludes with an examination of the ties between the conservatism of 1829-30 and the more narrow but prominent rhetoric of the proslavery argument in chapter six, and a brief epilogue examines the relevance of antebellum conservatism to that of later times.

NOTES–INTRODUCTION

1. William Sumner Jenkins, *Pro-Slavery Thought in the Old South* (1935; reprint ed., Gloucester, Mass.: Peter Smith, 1960), vii.

2. Thomas P. Abernethy makes this point in *The South in the New Nation, 1789-1819* (Baton Rouge: Louisiana State Univ. Press, 1961), 442.

3. Charles S. Sydnor, *American Revolutionaries in the Making: Political Practices in Washington's Virginia* (New York: Free Press, 1965), pp. 60-61, 63, 65.

4. Jack P. Greene, "Search for Identity: An Interpretation of the Meaning of Selected Patterns of Social Response in Eighteenth Century America," *Journal of Social History* 3 (1969-70): 205.

5. Julian A. C. Chandler, *The History of Suffrage in Virginia* (Baltimore: The Johns Hopkins Press, 1901), p. 22.

6. D. Alan Williams, "The Small Farmer in Eighteenth-Century Virginia Politics," *Agricultural History* 43 (1969), 99; R. E. and B. K. Brown, *Virginia, 1705-1786: Democracy or Aristocracy?* (East Lansing: Michigan State Univ. Press, 1964), pp. 11, 132.

7. See the figures in Jack P. Greene, "Foundations of Political Power in the Virginia House of Burgesses, 1720-1776," *William and Mary Quarterly* 3d ser. 16 (1959).

8. George Tucker, *The Life of Thomas Jefferson, Third President of the United States*, 2 vols. (Philadelphia: Carey, Lea and Blanchard, 1837), 1: 220.

9. Sydnor, *American Revolutionaries*, passim.

10. John R. Pole, "Representation and Authority in Virginia From Revolution to Reform," *Journal of Southern History* 24 (1958): 17.

11. Chandler, *History of Suffrage*, p. 16; Chandler, *Representation in Virginia* (Baltimore: The Johns Hopkins Press, 1896), pp. 18-19; Richard R. Beeman, *Patrick Henry: A Biography* (New York: McGraw-Hill, 1974), p. 104.

12. See Gordon S. Wood, *The Creation of the American Republic, 1776-1787* (1969; paperback ed. New York: Norton, 1972), esp. chapters 11-12. The quotation, from John Dickinson, is on p. 475.

13. John Zvesper, *Political Philosophy and Rhetoric: A Study of the Origins of American Party Politics* (Cambridge: Cambridge Univ. Press, 1977), chap. 2.

14. Merrill D. Peterson, *Democracy, Liberty, and Property: The State Constitutional Conventions of the 1820s* (Indianapolis: Bobbs-Merrill, 1966), p. 271.

CHAPTER ONE

The Movement for Constitutional Change in Virginia: Background to the Convention of 1829-30

Virginia was a changing society in the years from 1776 to 1829. The changes that were taking place caused many of the state's citizens to conclude that the plan of government, created at the height of agitation for independence from Britain, was unsatisfactory for governing the commonwealth's affairs. While it may have been appropriate for the aristocratic setting of colonial Virginia, it had little relevance to the democratic republic that many believed independence had brought. And it was wholly out of touch with the kind of state Virginia had become. In particular, Virginia was no longer to be identified solely with its Tidewater past. The balance of population had moved steadily westward since the close of the Revolution, and the society had come to be divided into four great and fairly distinct regions. These were the East, or Tidewater, extending from the Atlantic coast to the Fall Line on the rivers; the Piedmont, extending westward from the Fall Line to the Blue Ridge mountains; the Valley, lying between the Blue Ridge and the Alleghenies; and the trans-Allegheny West.[1] That Virginia was so divided had much to do with the growth of the reform movement in the state.

The Virginia Constitution of 1776 had locked in eastern domination of the state's politics and government, primarily by means of the system of apportionment and the suffrage requirements it provided. The system of apportionment was

1

based on county representation. Each county in the state was permitted to send two representatives to the House of Delegates, and the Senate was based on twenty-four districts, represented by one member each, and created by grouping existing counties together. The problem with this would become increasingly clear with the westward movement of Virginia's population after the American Revolution, for the West was the region of greatest growth. C. H. Young, writing in 1901, showed, for example, that while the western part of the state was growing by 36.2% as late as the decade between 1820 and 1829, the East grew by only about 2%, continuing a trend that had existed for four decades.[2] Still, because legislative apportionment was by county rather than by population, older eastern areas with established counties could maintain a hold on state government, despite western growth, and westerners were dependent upon an eastern-dominated legislature's willingness to create new counties if they were to receive any increase in representation at all. Since the legislature was the seat of power in the state, as it had been in the colony of Virginia, the issue of representation was an important one, and much of the reform effort would be focused on making population, and especially the white, non-slave population the basis for legislative apportionment.

But suffrage requirements, too, helped to preserve eastern domination of the state's affairs. Virginia's was a freehold suffrage. In order to vote in the state, under the Constitution of 1776, one had to be white, male, and owner of 100 acres of uncultivated land without a house, or 25 acres of improved land with a house, or a house and lot in town. Under this requirement, eastern counties fared better than did those in the West. According to Robert Paul Sutton, who has estimated the level of disfranchisement in Virginia's four main regions for 1828, just prior to the Convention of 1829-30, the average percentage of white adult males disfranchised in the East was only about 27 percent, as opposed to an average of about 44 percent in the West and 49 percent in the Valley. In the Piedmont, about 35 percent of adult white males were

2

disfranchised.[3] Clearly, changes in suffrage leading to the enfranchisement of all white adult males, along with apportionment reform, would contribute greatly to western strength in state politics.

Simple equity was, then, one argument for revising the state's constitution in order to bring political practices into line with social conditions. Westerners were citizens and taxpayers, and had reason to believe that they had a right to complain about the level of representation they were receiving in Richmond. As Augustine Smith commented on the situation in 1809, eighty freeholders along the James River might have the same representation that "twelve times their number" in other counties enjoyed, and this was hardly an equitable state of affairs.[4]

Beyond that, however, there were important substantive reasons why achieving equity in the state government should have been of concern to people in the West and why, by contrast, eastern Virginians should have sought to keep things pretty much as they were. Some of these reasons were economic. Westerners had long felt that economic policies promulgated by the state government discriminated against their section, and with some justification. For one thing, the West had developed very differently from the East, economically. While the older region remained wedded to plantation agriculture for its economic base, the West was developing a more diversified economy. In addition to farming a variety of crops, including wheat and other grains, westerners engaged profitably in manufacture, especially in iron and textiles, and in a thriving trade in wool. Eastern leaders at both the state and national levels showed little sympathy for western economic concerns. Thus, for example, the West had a strong interest in protective tariffs on both iron and wool, but eastern leaders consistently opposed the imposition of such tariffs, blocking legislative support for them and helping to prevent their passage in Congress.[5]

A similar division between the sections occurred over banking policy. The West, a developing region with a need

3

for credit, fought hard for the extension of state-chartered banks to their region, while the East and Piedmont stood steadfastly opposed to such extensions. Although two branches of the Bank of Virginia were chartered at Wheeling and Winchester in 1817, these did little to ease western concerns, because they remained strictly under the control of the Bank of Virginia at Richmond,[6] which kept tight reins on the money available to fill western needs. There is no doubt that this banking policy had much to do with western efforts to redress the inequalities built into the state's plan of government. Indeed, much of a major effort toward constitutional reform in 1816 was most immediately inspired by western opposition to the passage of a state banking law "more effectually to prevent the circulation of notes emitted by unchartered banks," a measure which would strengthen Richmond's control over the state's economic life.[7]

But the biggest source for economic and political divisions between the east and west in Virginia was the issue of internal improvements, particularly as western population grew and the region's economy began to thrive. Western farmers and manufacturers had a real need to get their products to eastern markets, but transportation systems to the east were largely undeveloped and could only be developed with state or federal support. Western leaders were, thus, strong proponents of internal improvement schemes at both the state and federal levels, but often felt themselves blocked by eastern interests. In 1812, for example, the state Assembly appointed a commission to suggest plans for the improvement of navigation on the western rivers, a commission which made substantial recommendations and suggested that federal aid be secured for their construction. The commission's report was, in this case, adopted by the Assembly but it was on a united vote of western against eastern legislators.[8] And it was a short-lived victory.

In general, state-funded internal improvements for the West, even if approved of in principle, were discouraged in fact. Improvements along the James and Kanawha rivers, for

4

example, were to have provided a major link between east and west in Virginia, but the Assembly did little to aid their progress, for some time showing a disposition to abandon them altogether. Appropriations were continually defeated for a Chesapeake and Ohio canal, which also would have been of great value to the West. With the coming of the railroads in the 1820s, eastern opposition to western interests simply prevented the construction of any lines which might have seemed to serve the west at eastern expense, further adding to the western view that easterners were dedicated to maintaining a stranglehold on western economic life. The internal improvements question was a key factor in leading westerners to want to alter the plan of government and to gain a greater voice in Virginia's affairs, a fact noted by reformers and conservatives alike in discussions of reform.[9]

But exacerbating these specific issues was the fact that, as Thomas Jefferson once noted, different parts of the state were simply developing in very different ways.[10] Both the Tidewater and the Piedmont, as plantation-based regions, maintained the kind of social organization which one identifies with the slaveholding South, for they were economies in which land and slaves were clearly concentrated in a few hands, and in which there were great extremes of wealth and poverty. The Piedmont did, however, suffer politically given the traditional eastern domination of the state. The West, extending from the western counties of the Piedmont, through the Valley, and including all the trans-Allegheny region, and with its more diversified economy and its lesser dependence on slavery, was also marked by the relative absence of the extremes of wealth and poverty which characterized regions dominated by plantation agriculture.[11] In certain ways, then, eastern and western Virginia, at loggerheads over economic and political issues, were also very different societies, because the demographic and economic differences separating them also had important social and cultural implications.

Charles H. Ambler, in his classic study of sectionalism in

5

Virginia, described the ways in which ethnic and religious differences as well as differences in regional composition insured that the westward advance of the Tidewater's "peculiar institutions" would be interrupted by "a new society, naturally hostile to things Virginian" in the Blue Ridge area, even during the colonial period.[12] At that time, people whose religion was evangelical and who held more democratic views of society and politics had dominated the settlement of the western part of Virginia, and they had little appreciation for the "aristocratical" political institutions or the established Anglicanism of Virginia's Tidewater elite. This, in itself, contributed to the tensions that would exist between East and West after independence and on into the nineteenth century.

One can see something of this cultural tension early in the state's history in the battle to disestablish the Episcopal Church in Virginia. Prior to the Revolution, the Anglican Church—which would adopt the name "Episcopal" with independence—was an established church, supported by taxes and tied to the political apparatus of the colony by law. Membership on the parish vestry had political as well as spiritual importance to Virginia's ruling elite, if, indeed, spiritual importance it had. However, with the growth of Presbyterianism in the eighteenth century, particularly after the Great Awakening, this colonial religious establishment underwent increasing challenge, and the challenge would be strengthened by the rhetoric and ideals of the American Revolution. The challenges themselves were never without class dimensions, moreover, as Presbyterians and other evangelicals, notably the Baptists and, later, the Methodists, drew most of their strength through democratic messages that attracted adherence from outside Virginia's political and social elite.[13]

The issue would come to a head in Virginia in 1784, when the state legislature began a debate on a series of bills designed for the support of religion, a debate in which sectional divisions within the state were to play an important part. Among other issues discussed were a general assess-

6

ment for the support of religion and an "incorporation bill" which would, among other things, secure to the Episcopal Church perpetual title in the glebes and other property of the old establishment. At one level, the debates on these issues pitted evangelical denominations against the traditional, and Episcopalian, leadership of the state. At another, the issue was sectional. The East, where the Episcopal Church was strong, also favored both assessment and incorporation. The West, by contrast, strongly opposed these measures, and this was the section of Virginia in which Presbyterianism was the dominant religion.[14] Such a sectional division, as Norman Risjord has argued, had mainly to do with the number of dissenters individual legislators could number among their constituents,[15] and it emphasizes the extent to which the religiously diverse western population, its religious life having developed apart from the Tidewater establishment, found itself at odds with the older region in religious concerns.

But this difference in religious ideas betokened a more general difference in social outlook separating east and west. As H. J. Eckenrode noted, there was a great deal of dissimilarity between the tradition-minded, hierarchically based society of eastern Virginia and the democratic ideals and individualism that accompanied evangelical religion. Westerners had long harbored democratic sentiments. They had been dissatisfied with a Revolution which, to many, had not gone far enough toward establishing democracy, and, upon its close, they would continue to work for a more democratic order, whether it was in the area of religion or in that of politics.[16] Indeed, it is not irrelevant that, in the Virginia debates on the adoption of the Federal Constitution, in 1788, some of the staunchest anti-federalist opposition would be expressed by men from that western region which would become Kentucky, opposition based chiefly on the view that the proposed document was dangerously antidemocratic.[17] The roots of the conflict between conservatives and democratic reformers went well back into Virginia history and were well established long before the Convention of 1829-30 itself.

7

How then, did the reform movement develop out of the sectional conflict that characterized Virginia politics during the early national period? What kinds of directions did it take, and how were the issues defined in ways that determined the course of constitutional debate in the state? To understand the growth of reform, one must look backward to see how the state's initial plan of government, the Constitution of 1776, was devised and how its provisions produced dissatisfaction in regard to the twin sectional issues of suffrage and apportionment.

Virginia's Constitution of 1776 was, above all, a conservative document. Formed at the height of revolutionary agitation and framed by the same convention which resolved independence, it was a document which, as Richard Beeman has said, "most closely resembled the old colonial charter, with only the power of the King, Privy Council, and Royal Governor stripped away."[18] Insofar as it was a constitution intended to preserve the basic outlines of colonial Virginia politics and government, an intention hardly missed by the framers or subsequent generations, the constitution has been ably characterized by Beeman's description. At the same time, though, Virginians who composed the document had not found the task entirely smooth. Although no records of the debates in the 1776 convention were kept, the best evidence indicates that discussions were frequently tense, especially in regard to writing a plan of government.

The delegates who arrived in Williamsburg in the spring of 1776 after a hard-fought election campaign were, by and large, men who had had many years of experience in governing Virginia. Campaigning had been bitter during the months prior to the convention, but it had not involved many men from outside that small group of leaders which had long dominated Virginia's political affairs. Indeed, by background, experience, and status, the convention's delegates comprised a rather homogeneous group of "planter-aristocrats" who had relied on ties of occupation, kinship, friendship, and connections to make their ways through Virginia's

8

colonial political system. The campaign itself had been one of personality rather than substance—voters had been asked to choose between men rather than between their stances on the specific issues at hand. But very few of the delegates were outsiders to Virginia's traditional governing elite.[19]

The key issues to come before the 1776 convention, as delegates and their constituents alike understood, were independence from Great Britain, which the delegates would resolve on May 15, and, as one county had instructed its delegates, to "plan out that form of government which may the most effectually secure to us the enjoyment of our civil and religious rights and privileges, to the last of our posterity." This latter action the convention voted to undertake at the same time it resolved independence and, accordingly, a committee under the leadership of Archibald Cary was appointed to draw up a Declaration of Rights and a plan of government, a written constitution for Virginia. After much debate and some amendment, both were passed unanimously.[20]

It is unfortunate that no records were kept of convention debates. What we know of the outlines of the discussion can come only from the letters and accounts of delegates, or from looking at various draft documents considered by the Cary committee. All this material does show, however, that despite a basic homogeneity of the delegates to the convention, there was a strong division between a group of conservatives—including Robert Carter Nicholas and Carter Braxton—who, having reluctantly approved independence, wanted to consolidate elite power in Virginia, and those more liberal leaders who desired independence and desired, also, to broaden slightly participation in government. This conflict informed the final document.

On the liberal side, it is generally accepted, was the Virginia Declaration of Rights, drafted by George Mason. Debated for about two weeks, the Declaration of Rights was intended to state certain inalienable, fundamental rights which could not be taken away by constitution or statute. Mason was hardly a wild-eyed radical himself. He was a conservative Vir-

9

ginia planter who, like others, had absorbed some of the Whiggish rhetoric of the day, which he embodied in his document. The first sentence brought conflict to the convention: "All men," Mason had written, "are born equally free and independent, and have certain inherent natural rights, of which they cannot, by any compact, deprive their posterity." Other clauses sparked discussion, notably that on religion, but Mason's first sentence went to the heart of Virginia political ideas and caused the greatest split between the old conservatives and their more radical colleagues.[21]

Slavery seems to have had something to do with conservative objections to Mason's first sentence, especially with Robert Carter Nicholas's often-quoted remark that the phrase "born equally free" was a "forerunner...of convulsion." Slaves had somehow to be defined out of any "equal freedom" that might exist in society.[22] The body settled on the more general phrase "by nature free and independent," which, because it allowed for conventional inequality, avoided any embarassing conclusions. Other changes in wording and organization were also made, all indicative of the conflict between that "certain set of aristocrats" Thomas Ludwell Lee execrated in a well-known letter, and the more liberal delegates, including Mason, Patrick Henry, and their allies.[23] If one effect was to spell out certain important rights, another was to produce a document in which rights were not in conflict with politics as usual. In particular, the final Declaration emphasized the protection of property even more than Mason's draft. The resulting document, as Robert L. Hilldrup suggested, was to consist of value generalizations, drawn on English law, which were open to the sorts of restrictions necessary to leave old ways intact.[24]

If the Declaration of Rights caused much debate, the formation of a plan of government was an even hotter question, although accounts of the discussion which took place are, to say the least, conflicting. Edmund Randolph, an observer whose account has been a standard for many years, painted a picture of harmony which was not entirely true. For

10

him, the constitution was only a little short of a triumph for moderation, created by men who were not "absorbed in their inveteracy against Great Britain," but who, instead, "confessed their want of perfect information." Though he noted that a "fluctuation between old prepossessions and recent hatred" undermined as thorough a consideration of the British constitution as might have been desired, Randolph's main conclusion was that "custom and habit, revolting against the pruning knife of reformation, transplanted into the constitution of Virginia many valuable things, which perhaps might have been discarded, had they not previously appeared in Virginia garb."[25] Randolph did not deny the existence of divisions among the delegates, but he nevertheless felt that they were subordinate to the unity of purpose that guided the delegates in their work.

In any case, the Constitution of 1776 demonstrated little basic change from the colonial system which had, for so long, supported Virginia's elite. Indeed, if anything, it strengthened the hold of the elite on the new state's affairs. The governor, for example, was to be appointed by the legislature and, chosen annually, would be essentially its creature. The legislature had traditionally been the seat of power in the colony, and it would continue to be in the state. Similarly, the county court system, long a major fixture in the Virginia system, was preserved. And, again, legislative apportionment, which would be a key issue in the reform movement, continued to be by county, just as the freehold requirement for suffrage remained in force.

Indeed, neither apportionment nor suffrage seems to have occasioned a great deal of debate, although there was some controversy on the suffrage question. The freehold qualification was accepted as "natural" according to Randolph, and he could not recall that "a hint was uttered in contravention of this principle."[26] In fact, the principle was strengthened by a clause in the Declaration of Rights guaranteeing suffrage to "all men having sufficient evidence of permanent common interest with, and attachment to, the community,"[27] a phrase

11

which everyone took to mean property-holding—but it hardly went undiscussed. Some delegates, including Mason, apparently felt that existing qualifications were too high and needed significant liberalization.

In general, Virginia's property qualifications had never been so well established even in colonial times as Randolph's account implied. Even Julian A. C. Chandler, whose classic studies of Virginia politics strongly emphasized the elitism of the state's system, stressed the extent to which freehold qualifications had undergone challenges during the colonial era. In some cases, as when the House of Burgesses sought to lower the property requirement from 100 to 50 uncultivated areas, the British sovereign held things in check. Here, of course, the main advantage would have gone not to the lower classes, but to those among the gentry who owned unimproved tracts in several counties, since, during that period, one could vote in any county where he held land. Beyond that, however, there was, according to Chandler, a fairly clear pattern of nonfreeholder voting in Virginia throughout the colonial period, and elections were often contested on the ground of illegal votes—something that would continue after independence, too. Virginians could hardly have considered the freehold qualification "natural," however much they sought to keep it in force.[28]

At the time of the 1776 Convention, suffrage requirements demanded the actual ownership of real property. While no one in convention anticipated later reformers by suggesting white adult male suffrage for Virginia, the draft constitution Mason presented to the Cary committee would have extended suffrage to holders of leases having "an unexpired term of seven years, and to every Housekeeper who hath resided for one year past, in the county, and hath been the father of three children in this country." Whatever quantitative effect the proposal might have had is hard to gauge, but its conceptual one is fairly important, for Mason was involved in redefining what it would mean to have "permanent common interest with, and attachment to the

12

community." Should the extension have been approved, it would have meant that one's stake in society was to be based less on his holding of property than on evidence of his having made a voluntary commitment to citizenship—such as choosing to settle and raise a family. Mason's proposal was not entirely unprecedented, since some Virginia towns had been using similar suffrage requirements for some time, but it was not a proposal which conservatives were willing to adopt on a large scale.

In this disagreement, however, one may see the core of a major issue which would divide conservative and reform spokesmen in the debates on constitutional reform. For Mason and his supporters, the locus for citizenship and political rights was to be placed in the person—the individual who, by his actions, demonstrated his commitment to the community. For the conservative opponents of Mason's plan, individual choice was less important than the tangible, enforced commitment to society which property itself created. Question of choice and assent were, in this view, irrelevant and unreliable insofar as matters pertaining to citizenship or rights were concerned. This issue of whether rights had to do with person or with property would provide a key ideological division between conservative and reform positions in the debates culminating in the Convention of 1829-30.[29]

Mason's proposal was not approved, and one cannot be certain how extensively it was discussed. The main attention of the convention was on the organization of government, for which several plans were presented. These ranged from the almost monarchical plan proposed by Carter Braxton, who would have installed a governor and council appointed for life, to that of "Democraticus" (probably Patrick Henry), who urged annual elections and frequent rotation of officeholders.[30] Even here, however, the resulting constitution made minimal changes in the existing system. Perhaps, as Robert Hilldrup has suggested, the crisis of wartime, the failure of radicals to unify, and the feeling of a need for cooperation—coupled with, as Randolph implied, a com-

13

fortable familiarity with existing institutions—made the 1776 plan seem to be one with which men could live.[31] After all, the convention was itself composed almost entirely of men used to the prerogatives of government and accustomed to the existing mechanisms of politicking, so that it is not surprising they should have chosen to continue things pretty much as they had been. None of them seems to have anticipated that the constitution he and his colleagues approved would provide a touchstone for debate for the next half-century and more.

Nevertheless, criticism of the document began almost upon its adoption, and the earliest critics were themselves part of Virginia's governing elite. The most prominent and vocal of these was Thomas Jefferson. He had been in Philadelphia attending the Continental Congress at the time of the 1776 constitution's creation, but Jefferson was keenly interested in the plan his home state should adopt. He even sent a proposed constitution to the convention, though it was not to be a factor in the discussions which took place. Not as democratic as some of his subsequent proposals for reform, this proposed constitution was more liberal than either Mason's draft or the plan finally approved. In particular, Jefferson's proposal would have gone somewhat further in liberalizing suffrage requirements, reducing the definition of a freehold to one-quarter acre in town or 25 acres in the country, and granting suffrage to all who had paid "scot and lot to the government in the last two years."[32] Conservative in holding to the freehold principle, or at least to the payment of taxes as a requirement for voting, Jefferson was nonetheless willing to reduce the requirement significantly.

One notes Jefferson's draft because, for the rest of his life, Jefferson would be one of the most persistent critics of the Constitution of 1776, and he would be recognized as such by conservatives and reformers alike. Questions of suffrage and apportionment were major aspects of Jefferson's attack, though they were by no means the only ones, because the provisions of the constitution on both questions were con-

14

trary to his strongest opinions on society and government. He launched his attack most notably, of course, in his *Notes on the State of Virginia*, where he argued that both aspects were unjust: suffrage, because many who paid taxes and had defended the state in the militia were excluded; apportionment, because of the unequal weight given to the East. He would incorporate these views into a 1783 draft constitution for Virginia in which he set suffrage requirements, in lieu of an unspecified amount of real property, to include one year residency or enrollment in the militia. Apportionment was to be based on the number of electors, by county. Jefferson's arguments would be repeated frequently during the campaign for revision.[33]

In later years, as agitation for a convention grew stronger, Jefferson remained on the side of reform. Owing conservative intransigence to "fears of the people" which were irrelevant in the American setting, Jefferson continually asserted the need to place Virginia's government on a firmer foundation. And, in an 1816 letter to John Taylor, he reiterated his view that those who had to fight ought to be allowed to vote. By that year, certainly, he was able to see a broadened suffrage as an indispensible requirement for republican institutions, and he would hold to this view for the rest of his life.[34]

In general, defenders of the constitution, especially before 1800, chose to deal only briefly with Jefferson's views on suffrage. James Madison, in commenting on Jefferson's 1783 draft, argued—albeit lukewarmly—for the value of freehold qualifications and searched for a middle course that acknowledged rights of person as well as of property.[35] St. George Tucker, whose works presented by far the most lucid and systematic defenses of the 1776 Constitution, had a keen awareness of the document's shortcomings. For Tucker, however, property as well as person had to be considered the basis for a political order, and he developed a rather complicated system of taking that into account. Developing a formula which would base representation on population, slaveownership, and land taxes taken together, Tucker also concluded that the East was not overrepresented in Virginia's legislature and, he would argue, the same principle whereby representation should be apportioned—population, slaveholding, and taxes, taken together—could also be used to determine suffrage. Tucker's calculus, one might note, would be continuously used by conservatives, even up to the time of the convention.[36] "Person-hood," alone was not enough for political participation, even if one did have to serve in the militia.

Not surprisingly, Jefferson was part of a decided minority during the eighteenth century. In 1784, following a petition from Augusta County, an effort to institute some reforms in the constitution reached the legislature. Madison was one who addressed the body, arguing for an equality of representation and noting ambiguities in regard to suffrage (chiefly on the issue of whether Roman Catholics could vote). He reported to Jefferson a general fear of a convention with full powers.[37] Five years later, another motion proposing a convention was put before the House of Delegates, pointing to a need to correct errors "great in number and fatal in their influence." Focusing mainly on the organization of government, this motion also cited unequal representation created by the state's legislative apportionment. The motion met with a decidedly hostile reception.[38] Finally, in the 1790s, several efforts would be made to revise the Constitution in order to broaden suffrage and correct the inequities of apportionment. On a clearly regional vote in 1797, the issue was, for a time, put to rest.[39]

Still, for all their lack of success, these early efforts to change the constitution were important, for they reveal much about the ways in which both the reform movement and the conservative response developed during the early national period. The earliest cases for reform were made primarily from experience, on the ground that, as a 1789 resolution put it, "time has now revealed its errors," and the 1776 Constitution needed redoing. Indeed, so convinced were reformers that their sense of the "errors" was widely under-

16

stood that it became a matter of form in the 1790s to say that
the defects were "too obvious to require Enumeration or
criticism"; the phrase became a commonplace in the printed
petitions Virginians submitted to the legislature requesting
revision. And the constitution's "errors" were mostly practical
in character, focusing on such matters as the length of legislative sessions, the lack of any provision for amendment, and,
of course, legislative apportionment.[40]

Despite the moderate tone and practical intent of these
early reform efforts, however, opponents responded in a way
that was to be a trademark of conservatism throughout the
period. In 1784, the leading opponent of constitutional revision was Patrick Henry, whose "violent opposition" seems to
have been based mainly on his dislike for calling a convention
of any sort, and most likely, on his general antipathy toward
Madison and Jefferson, the two leading advocates of reform.[41] The legislative debates on the issue have not survived, but Madison's summary of the event, written to Jefferson, tells the tale. The issue became defined rather quickly as
a contest between a small group which favored a convention
with full powers and those who favored no change at all. The
group favoring a middle course—"a great number," according to Madison—"were not disposed to be active even for such
a qualified plan."[42] One can guess what must have happened
on the floor of the House. Conservatives defined the question in such a way that one was either for total change or for
leaving things alone. No middle ground would have been
possible.

One must speculate about what happened in 1784. But,
that is not really necessary for understanding debates on the
same issue five years later. At that time, when the resolution
to call a convention was presented before the legislature, emphasizing the Constitution's practical problems, an amendment to the resolution was offered striking everything after
the word "resolved"—the actual recommendation for a
convention—and referring to criticisms contained in the resolution's preamble with the following words: "That the fore-

17

going statement contains principles repugnant to Republican Government, and dangerous to the freedom of this country, and therefore ought not to meet with the approbation of this House, or be recommended to the consideration of the people."[43] Opposition in 1789, as it had been in 1784, was violent and tended to focus not on the main issues raised by reformers but, rather, on the alleged danger any proposal for reform posed to the safety of Virginia's government.

Eighteenth-century opponents of change anticipated the later rhetorical history of reform in Virginia. Forcing reformers to justify the possibility of even moderate change, conservatives did nothing so much as to force a radicalization of reform. Ignoring the specifics of the case, conservatives directed attention away from such matters as legislative sessions or even the simple inequity of the existing plan for apportionment and toward a discussion of the system as a whole. Should the entire constitution, that is to say, be preserved, or should it be changed? Stated this way, the issue could only become polarized, and that is precisely what happened.

One form of evidence of this polarization may be found in the legislative petitions, which displayed increasing truculence as the eighteenth century drew to a close. Thus, a 1796 petition from Berkeley County, after asserting the right of the people to alter their form of government, leveled strong charges of "aristocracy" against a Virginia leadership that sought to prevent change, just as Augusta petitioners in 1794 had charged such resistance to men "influenced from interest and unworthy motives."[44] The language indicates the extent to which those who desired reform were coming to feel frustrated by the state's political system and its established leadership. Successful conservative opposition to change, in other words, must have made reformers see that a more thoroughgoing constitutional reform would be needed if Virginia were ever to have a more equitable political system.

The increasing belligerence of reform demands was complemented by a noticeable difference in the way the case for

18

reform was made. If the earliest efforts focussed on practical problems, as time passed it became far more common for reformers to hold the entire Virginia plan of government up to the light of first and fundamental principles, thereby to find Virginia's political system sadly defective. The Declaration of Rights, reformers pointed out, had asserted that "all men are by nature equally free and independent," and under that standard, no one could justify the eastern-oriented, elitist-structured government provided by the Constitution of 1776.[45]

This shift in the focus of reform language had a decided effect on the substance as well as the tenor of reform demands. As J. R. Pole has pointed out, apart from minor practical questions, the main concern which united all proponents of constitutional reform in Virginia was always that of representation rather than suffrage. Indeed, among the earliest reformers were those plantation owners from outside the Tidewater who favored changing the system but who could hardly have been called democrats.[46] Moreover, and no less significantly, dissatisfaction over apportionment developed strength far earlier than it did over suffrage, and Pole, for instance, is right when he notes a failure on the part of Virginia's nonfreeholders to agitate the issue. The earliest legislative petitions simply made no mention of suffrage, and it was not until the early nineteenth century that western Virginians, in particular, would begin to assert strongly the antirepublican character of a system that would tax men and call them to the militia without giving them the right to vote.[47]

That suffrage and representation should have become linked may reflect, in part, only one more manifestation of the sectional character of reform issues, since the eastern counties fared better under Virginia's suffrage restrictions than did those of the West. But ideological factors, too, could only have contributed to the linking of suffrage and apportionment reforms, especially as reformers began to compare the entire constitution with fundamental principles of natural equality. How, after all, could one complain on grounds of

19

principle about unequal representation when some men—
also possessed of natural rights—had no representation at
all?[48] Having chosen to recur to fundamental principles and
to derive policy from those principles, reformers put themselves in such a position that they could not very well push for
changing the basis of representation without an accompany-
ing reform in the prerequisites for suffrage.

One does not want to lay too much to rhetoric. Political
considerations had much to do with reform calculations and,
in addition, other states in the union had been adopting
white manhood suffrage for years, older states and newly
admitted ones alike. Still, it is important to note that, most
likely driven by the ruling elite's intransigence, Virginia reformers chose to make their case through an appeal to fundamental principles, rather than from simple experience,
and this tactic would have major consequences both for their
own position and for the conservative response. The contest
would be between those who wanted no change and those
who would put Virginia's government on a wholly new basis,
and reform rhetoric increasingly reinforced that of the
conservatives in advancing this point of view. By the early
years of the nineteenth century, these strategies for addressing the issue of reform were quite well set.

Why, then, did conservatives finally acquiesce to reform
demands for a convention? Ultimately, it must have been a
response to popular pressure. Reformers were able to organize enough people, from everywhere outside the Tidewater, to make it clear to even the staunchest conservative
that the movement for change could not be resisted. Fairly
early in the nineteenth century, reformers, after years of
frustration by conservative opposition to revision, had begun
to look for popular support, expressed outside the normal
channels of legislative petition, of their efforts to bring about
constitutional change. Their most significant attempts in this
regard were two conventions held at Staunton, one in 1816
and another in 1825, each leading to memorials calling for a

general convention. These Staunton meetings failed to achieve their objectives immediately, but both had major roles in forcing the legislature finally to act on bringing a convention about.

The Staunton Convention of 1816 included delegates from every part of Virginia except the Tidewater, and directed its attention almost entirely to the question of representation and to revision of the constitution so as to provide for subsequent amendment, a provision lacking in the Revolutionary document. Proceedings of the convention show some disagreement among the delegates, but the resulting memorial to the legislature was overwhelmingly approved, by a vote of sixty-one to seven. The seven dissenters were not opposed to revision but only to a convention with unlimited powers.[49] Chapman Johnson, who was to be active in 1829-30, spoke for the dissenters when he demurred from anything other than a limited convention, restricted to specific issues, for fear of committing "the whole constitution, with its consecrated principles, to untried hands."[50] This was a position, however, to which few conservatives or democrats were by that time willing to listen. Indeed, conservatives responded predictably, as when William Branch Giles, looking at the whole reform effort in 1817, declared that it could only lead to "the entire immolation" of the fundamental character of the 1776 Constitution, equating reform quite explicitly with revolution.[51]

Still, the Staunton memorial was forwarded to the General Assembly, and a form for legislative petition in support of the memorial was recommended to the people. Reform leaders were optimistic about their chances for success. Debates on the question in the legislature were, of course, quite hot, but before Christmas the House agreed to hold a referendum on the issue. Should a majority of the electors, under existing suffrage rules, agree to a convention, one would be called.[52] The matter then went to the Senate, and there it met with problems. Questions of whether the convention should be

21

limited to specific amendments, of who should be qualified to vote for delegates, and, ultimately, of revision itself, all occupied the attention of the state's upper house.

Virginia still had an eastern-dominated legislature in 1817, and in the Senate the East had the votes. The West had no convention. Not that westerners went away empty-handed. Conservatives were unwilling to permit a convention, but they were willing to try to compromise, in the interest of quieting reform agitation. Under the leadership of Littleton W. Tazewell, conservatives agreed to equalize senatorial districts on the basis of white population in exchange for a western agreement to equalize land taxes. Conservatives hoped, as William Wickham wrote to Tazewell in May, "that enough was done at the last session to quiet the Western counties and to prevent any mischief at the next."[53]

The second Staunton Convention, in 1825, made more demands. Calling for a convention to change the basis of representation, this meeting also addressed the question of suffrage. While the convention's resolution stopped short of demanding "universal" suffrage, it did declare that a freehold should not be the only acceptable "evidence of permanent common interest with, and attachment to the community." Some delegates, notably David Sheffy of Augusta, still supported freehold restrictions, but the resolution was adopted by the convention and sent to the Assembly.[54]

In this session, too, debates and activities were furious, both inside and outside the legislative halls. Newspapers were filled with charges of "aristocracy" and of radicalism, and supporters and opponents of reform held meetings throughout the state, trying to gain popular support. Pro- and anti-convention petitions flooded the Assembly which met at the end of 1825. A bill to call a referendum on the subject lost by four votes.[55] It would be brought up again, and then again. Finally, in the legislative session of 1827-28, a referendum was approved. The voters called for a convention by a margin of 5000 votes.[56] In the session of 1828-29, the legislature was faced with the need to act on a convention bill.

22

The questions of suffrage and representation which would come before the convention were discussed well in advance in the debates over what form that convention should take. The former question was, essentially, one of principle: Could a constitution, which would define the limits of suffrage, be properly framed if all the people in the state–really, all the white adult males–were not represented in the convention? A memorial from Loudon County objected strongly to confining the electors for delegates to freeholders on the ground that, in any compact, no one should be subject to any restriction without his consent,[57] and this was the basic argument in the case. The argument was a strong one and, according to conservative John Wickham, actually had some effect, even on the "Friends to Freehold Suffrage."[58] In the end, however, the restriction was maintained.

The more difficult issue was that of representation. Western legislators saw, quite plainly, that if the convention were apportioned in a manner similar to that governing the existing legislature, reform would stand no chance. Easterners, for obvious reasons, feared that any departure from that scheme could seriously undercut their strength. The issue here was a simple one of who would control the convention, and neither side wanted to give way too easily. Reformers argued that representation should be on the basis of white population. Conservatives, by contrast, rejected the white population basis, arguing instead for either the "Federal Ratio," which would have counted slaves in the manner defined by the Federal Constitution, or for the county basis, which would have favored the East. The division here was a large one, and neither side had reason to adopt the other's point of view.[59]

Principle, almost everyone including the conservatives recognized, was with the West, but, as Robert Powell wrote to Waller Holladay, "the actual condition of things" demanded something else.[60] Powell and his fellow conservatives had two main concerns. First, there was a genuine fear of any scheme that might produce a western majority in the convention. At

23

the same time, however, conservatives saw a real difference between the two sections in one regard—the presence of slaves. Whatever system was adopted had, as Wickham wrote, to protect the "just rights" of the "slaveholding part of the State."[61] Here was a real difference in sectional interests which conservatives felt had to be recognized in any representation scheme that was adopted. In the end, a compromise was struck, and delegates were chosen by senatorial districts, with four delegates to come from each district. It was favorable to the East, but it was a scheme with which westerners could live since, after the reapportionment of 1816, the West was more fairly represented in the upper than in the lower house.

The decision was an important one for the organizing of the convention. It was no less important for what it led the various parties to say about themselves and their opponents. Despite the appearance of compromise on representation, the Assembly debates had contributed to a real hardening of positions and views, and this would provide the immediate background for the convention itself. Compromise, in this instance, had grown mainly out of fears each side had for the other. Irving Brant, in his biography of James Madison, has written of the "hysteria" in eastern Virginia over the threat of the convention,[62] and his characterization does not exaggerate the feelings many conservatives expressed.

James Rawlings, observing the scene from Richmond in 1828, wrote of his own opposition to the convention, but hoped for "liberality" from those who shared his point of view. He was not, however, optimistic: "I fear that we shall not get out of the affair with half the good feelings that we entered it."[63] His fears seem to have been justified. The heat with which debates took place was startling. It became common currency with reformers to accuse conservatives of having aristocratic pretensions and of conspiring to destroy all human rights. Reformers were not the only ones to use warm words. Personal attacks and withering sarcasm took prominent places in conservative oratory. Easterners may have ac-

24

cused reform leaders of demagoguery, as they often did, but westerners also found eastern remarks to be "both inflammatory and exciting towards the good people of the western part of the State."[64] The tone of discussion suggests reason enough for young conservative Hugh Grigsby's comment to Littleton Tazewell's son John that "political magnanimity is but an empty thing."[65]

Just as critical to conservatives, however, was their very strong belief that the convention, whoever controlled it, could not help but undermine their hold on the state. "Eastern ascendancy, so far as the tide water country is concerned, is destroyed," was Grigsby's sad comment on the passage of the convention bill, and he was not alone in having this feeling.[66] The convention was required to create a document which would then be submitted to a popular vote for ratification. Because the majority of voters throughout the state had to approve it, the convention could not produce a constitution that was too plainly "eastern." Conservatives had ample reason to fear the power of others. At the same time, however, there were events around them that augmented their worries about the West, and even about others in the East outside their political orbit.

For one thing, nonfreeholders, excluded from the convention, were still making demands to be heard. One of their spokesmen proclaimed that the anticonvention forces would be "most righteously punished" by nonfreeholders for their continuing intransigence, and one group in Richmond went so far as to set up alternative polls in order to try to get nonfreeholders' views across to the delegates.[67] But it was the power of the West that worried conservatives most, particularly as that power was expressed in threats by westerners to go outside the legislature if its demands were not met.

Threats of independent western action, even of secession, played an important role in the legislative debates of 1828-29. Taking republican theory to its logical conclusion, several westerners under Philip Doddridge's leadership proclaimed the right of the people—the majority having approved a

25

convention—to "organize a convention upon their own principles" and to form a constitution of their liking.[68] It was more than youth that led conservative Hugh Grigsby to speculate on the outcome of such an event. The eastern counties would never participate, and a decidedly "western" constitution would surely result. "The will of the majority must govern," he predicted, "or *civil war ensue.*"[69] For Grigsby, at least, this possibility was reason enough to compromise on the question of representation, and others probably shared his view. In any event, the convention bill was finally passed in February, 1829, and the convention itself was scheduled to open the following fall.

26

NOTES – CHAPTER ONE

1. Charles Henry Ambler, *Sectionalism in Virginia from 1776 to 1861* (1910; reprint ed., New York: Russell and Russell, 1964), pp. 1-3.

2. C.H. Young, "Virginia Constitutional Convention of 1829," *John P. Branch Historical Papers* 1 (1901), 100-110.

3. Robert Paul Sutton, "The Virginia Constitutional Convention of 1829-30: A Profile Analysis of Late Jeffersonian Virginia," (Ph.D. dissertation, Univ. of Virginia, 1967), pp. 259-61.

4. Augustine C. Smith to Samuel Myers, August 16, 1809, William and Mary College Archives, Earl G. Swen Library, College of William and Mary, Williamsburg, Virginia.

5. Ambler, *Sectionalism*, pp. 118-121.

6. Sutton, "Virginia Constitutional Convention," pp. 12-13.

7. *Charleston (Va.) Farmer's Repository*, April 17, May 8, 1816.

8. Ambler, *Sectionalism*, pp. 97-98.

9. Ibid., pp. 122-27; The view was advanced in, for example, "The Constitution of '76," by a member of the Staunton Convention (Richmond [?], 1825 [?]), 22.

10. Thomas Jefferson, *Notes on the State of Virginia*, ed. William Peden (Chapel Hill: Univ. of North Carolina Press, 1955), pp. 118-19.

11. Jackson T. Main, "The Distribution of Property in Post-Revolutionary Virginia," *Mississippi Valley Historical Review* 41 (1954): 253-56.

12. Ambler, *Sectionalism*, p. 13.

13. H.J. Eckenrode, *Separation of Church and State in Virginia: A Study in the Development of the Revolution* (1910; reprint ed., New York: DaCapo, 1971), p. 34.

14. Ibid., pp. 78, 87.

15. Norman K. Risjord, *Chesapeake Politics, 1781-1800* (New York: Columbia Univ. Press, 1978), pp. 207-208.

16. Eckenrode, *Separation of Church and State*, pp. 75-76, 98.

17. Ambler, *Sectionalism*, p. 59.

18. Richard R. Beeman, *Patrick Henry: A Biography* (New York: McGraw-Hill, 1974), p. 104.

19. Robert Leroy Hillrup, "The Virginia Convention of 1776: A Study in Revolutionary Politics" (Ph.D. diss., Univ. of Virginia, 1935), 136; *Virginia Gazette*, May 10, 1776; Hugh Blair Grigsby, *The Virginia Convention of 1776* (Richmond: J. W. Randolph, 1855), pp. 18-19.

20. Ibid.

21. Mason's draft is printed side by side with that finally adopted in James Madison, *The Writings of James Madison, Comprising His Public Papers and Private Correspondence*, ed. Gaillard Hunt, 9 vols. (New York: Putnam, 1900-1910), 1: 35-40.

22. Beeman, *Patrick Henry*, p. 101.

23. Kate Mason Rowland, *The Life of George Mason, 1725-1792, including His Speeches, Public Papers, and Correspondence*, 2 vols. (New York: Putnam, 1892), 1: 240.

24. Hilldrup, "The Virginia Convention of 1776," pp. 187, 209.

25. Edmund Randolph, *History of Virginia*, ed. Arthur H. Shaffer (Charlottesville: Univ. Press of Virginia, 1970), p. 255.

26. Ibid., p. 256.

27. Madison, *Writings*, ed. Hunt, 1, p. 237.

28. Julian A. C. Chandler, *The History of Suffrage in Virginia* (Baltimore: The Johns Hopkins Press, 1901), pp. 13, 23; Charles S. Sydnor, *American Revolutionaries in the Making: Political Practices in Washington's Virginia* (1952; New York: Free Press, 1965), p. 36; John R. Pole, "Representation and Authority in Virginia from Revolution to Reform," *Journal of Southern History* 24 (1958): 21, 31-32.

29. Chandler, ibid., pp. 12-13; Madison, *Writings*, ed. Hunt, I, p. 44. And see, on this issue, James H. Kettner, *The Development of American Citizenship, 1608-1870* (Chapel Hill: Univ. of North Carolina Press, 1978), pp. 106-107.

30. *Virginia Gazette* (Dixon and Hunter), June 15, 1776; *Virginia Gazette* (Purdie), June 7, 1776.

31. Hilldrup, "Virginia Convention of 1776," 300.

32. Thomas Jefferson, *The Writings of Thomas Jefferson*, ed. Paul Leicester Ford, 10 vols. (New York: Putnam's, 1892-99), 2: 14.

33. Jefferson, *Notes*, 118, 119; Jefferson, *The Papers of Thomas Jefferson*, ed. Julian P. Boyd (Princeton: Princeton Univ. Press, 1950-), 6, p. 296. See, also, Dumas Malone, *Jefferson and His Time*, 5 vols. (Boston: Little, Brown, 1948-74), I:239.

34. Jefferson, *Writings*, ed. Ford, 10: 306.

35. Madison, *Writings*, ed. Hunt, 5: 286-87.

36. St. George Tucker, "Sketch of a Letter to the Reverend William Bentley–Salem," June 30, 1797, pp. 46-48, in unnumbered ms. notebook (box 62), Tucker-Coleman collection; Tucker, ed., *Blackstone's Commentaries: With Notes of Reference, to the Constitution and Laws, of the Federal Government of the United States; and of the Commonwealth of Virginia*, 5 vols. (Philadelphia: William Young Birch and Abraham Small, 1803), I: 96-106. For a later version of the argument, see Thomas R. Joynes, *Letter from Tho. R. Joynes of Accomack, to Major Oliver Logan* (Snow-Hill, Md.: G. Keatinge, [1829]).

37. Madison, *Writings*, ed. Hunt, pp. 55n., 58.

38. Journal, House of Delegates, December 8, 1789, pp. 108-109.

39. Risjord, *Chesapeake Politics*, pp. 501-503.

40. Journal, House of Delegates, December 8, 1789, p. 108; Petition to the Assembly from a number of inhabitants of Augusta County, 1794, copy in Stuart family papers, Virginia Historical Society; Legislative petitions of Hampshire County, December 9, 1797, Shenandoah County, December 9, 1802, Virginia Legislative Petitions.

41. Madison, *Writings*, ed. Hunt, 2: 58; Beeman, *Patrick Henry*, pp. 116-17.

42. Madison, ibid.

43. Journal, House of Delegates, December 8, 1789, p. 110.

44. Legislative petition of Berkeley County, November 18, 1796, Virginia Legislative Petitions; Petition from Augusta County, 1794, in Stuart family papers.

28

45. See, for example, legislative petitions from Pittsylvania County, December 30, 1807, Brooke County, December 12, 1815, Hampshire County, November 19, 1816, Virginia Legislative Petitions.

46. See, e.g., Henry to Thomas Massie, July 24, 1816, Massie family papers, Virginia Historical Society, Richmond.

47. Pole, "Representation and Authority," 25, 28. See, for example, the legislative petition from Augusta County, November 12, 1795 and by contrast from Brooke County, December 12, 1815, Virginia Legislative Petitions, Legislative Department, Archives Branch, Virginia State Library, Richmond.

48. Letter to the *Virginia Argus* reprinted in the *Petersburg Intelligencer,* August 4, 1801; *Charleston Farmer's Repository,* February 5, 1817; September 25, 1816.

49. *Niles' Weekly Register* 11 (1816): 17-23.

50. Ibid.

51. *Richmond Enquirer,* February 15, 1817.

52. *Richmond Enquirer,* January 25, 1817.

53. Ambler, *Sectionalism,* p. 96; Hugh Blair Grigsby, Diary, October 4-October 31, 1829, entry for October 16, 1829, Hugh Blair Grigsby papers, Virginia Historical Society; William F. Wickham to Littleton W. Tazewell, May 2, 1817, Tazewell family papers, Personal Papers collection, Archives Branch, Virginia State Library.

54. *Richmond Enquirer,* August 2, 1825.

55. William H. Gaines, Jr., " 'The Sense of the People,' " *Virginia Cavalcade* 19 (1969): 29-30.

56. Claude H. Hall, *Abel Parker Upshur: Conservative Virginian, 1790-1844* (Madison: State Historical Society of Wisconsin, 1964), p. 47.

57. Memorial of the Non-freeholders and Freeholders of Loudon to the Convention, 1829, Convention papers, Virginia State Library.

58. John Wickham to Littleton W. Tazewell, December 21, 1828, Tazewell family papers.

59. For a good summary, see the *Richmond Daily Whig,* January, 1829.

60. Robert D. Powell to Waller Holiday [*sic*], December 23, 1828, Holladay family papers, Virginia Historical Society.

61. John Wickham to Tazewell; Powell to Holiday.

62. Irving Brant, *James Madison,* 6 vols. (Indianapolis: Bobbs-Merrill, 1941-61), 6: 467.

63. James Rawlings to Waller Holladay, April 21, 1828, Holladay family papers.

64. William W. Mahon to John Dundore, February 8, 1829, John Dundore papers, Virginia Historical Society.

65. Hugh Blair Grigsby to John Tazewell, February 3, 1829, Tazewell papers.

66. Ibid.

67. *Richmond Daily Whig,* March 30, 1829, February 16, 1829.

68. Powell to Holiday, December 23, 1828.

69. Hugh Blair Grigsby to Littleton W. Tazewell, December 5, 1828, Tazewell family papers; see Pole, "Representation and Authority," 44-45.

29

CHAPTER TWO

Patricians, Planters, and Democrats: The Convention of 1829-30

The convention at which conservatives would have to confront directly the challenge of reform was called to order in Richmond on October 5, 1829. The months prior to that date were, however, busy ones for the leaders of the state's conservative and reform factions. Some Virginians, recognizing the importance of the debates on the floor, worked hard preparing their arguments in advance of the meetings. John R. Cooke, who would represent Frederick County, filled portions of his diary with historical facts about suffrage and apportionment in Virginia from 1619 to 1776, preparing to show that there was ample precedent for change in both practices.[1] Benjamin Watkins Leigh, who would be the most eloquent opponent of reform, wrote to William Branch Giles asking Giles to look over a sketch "of the points which I ought chiefly to keep in view during the approaching convention," and requesting his comments and criticisms.[2] The debates, as such, were to be taken quite seriously.

No less serious, of course, had been the question of personnel. Hard-fought elections for seats in the convention were held at the May-June sessions of Virginia's county courts. Newspapers were filled with position papers from those who stood for election and local committees for and against reform sought to place their favored candidates on the floor.[3] Once the elections were over, politicking continued in earnest as men on each side sought to marshal allies

31

for the fight that would occur. By September 30, almost a week before the convention opened, the young observer Hugh Blair Grigsby could predict, with some accuracy, that the convention's main speakers would be Philip Doddridge, Littleton W. Tazewell, Leigh, Giles, Robert Taylor, Charles Fenton Mercer, Chapman Johnson, and Briscoe Baldwin.[4] And it soon became apparent that the two sides were not far apart in either rhetorical or numerical strength.

The Convention of 1829-30 was an exciting political show. In part, its attraction may be explained by the caliber of men elected to serve as delegates. Among them were two ex-presidents of the United States, James Madison and James Monroe; the chief justice of the United States Supreme Court, John Marshall; Governor William Branch Giles; two United States senators, John Tyler and Littleton W. Tazewell; not to mention such spectacular orators as John Randolph, Philip Doddridge, and Benjamin Watkins Leigh.[5] But the prestige of some of the delegates was not the only public attraction of the convention; no less important was the great friction among them, the fact that the convention brought together men representing sections of a severely divided state, producing a conflict that was as lively as it was serious.

The very opening of the convention was something of an omen for the shape the meetings would take. The first order of business was the election of a president, and former President Monroe, one of the several elder statesmen gracing the event, was chosen. He was led to the chair by Madison and Marshall. Monroe was not a happy choice, and by the next day, reform and conservative delegates alike were sorry for having made it.[6] Part of the problem seems to have been Monroe's age, but as Hugh Blair Grigsby pointed out in his 1854 history of the convention, there was also a problem of style. Here was a convention that found itself charged with making a constitution, the first such meeting, formally, in Virginia's history. The 1776 Convention had had the luxury of doing little more than transplanting a colonial system to an independent state; the Federal Convention of 1788, of which

32

Monroe had been a member, simply had to ratify or reject "a constitution ready made." This convention, however, would bring together severely conflicting opinions and interests, and out of that conflict, delegates would have to hammer out an acceptable document. The aged Monroe, used to an order older than the one which had been developing in Virginia over the past several decades, was no man for the task,[7] and he would ultimately be replaced in the chair by Philip Barbour. Monroe was not alone. Even Madison, astute as he had always been, was like a fish out of water in the difficult meetings of 1829-30.[8]

One should not underestimate the stormy atmosphere. It could not have been further from "a convention constituted by a representation of different portions of the same community consulting for the good of all, and aiming to blend in harmonious concert the interest of each part with the prosperity of the whole" that one conservative had hoped for earlier in the year.[9] Differences were too sharp for that, as both sides had entered the affair viewing it as a power struggle.[10] Even so, most observers, and delegates too, were still strongly impressed by the degree of disharmony which marked the proceedings. By early December, many were noticing, as did delegate William F. Gordon, that "so much bad temper has been exhibited" as to cause real problems for the assembly, and others would note the touchy character of the proceedings as time went along.[11] The convention lasted longer than some delegates had expected,[12] and that, plus the difficulty of its job, certainly increased the tension in which issues were discussed.

Perhaps a measure of the atmosphere in which deliberation had to take place lies in the treatment accorded Robert B. Taylor, of Norfolk, the only eastern delegate consistently to favor reform. Admired by some for his devotion to principle and to conscience, Taylor was frequently and bitterly excoriated on the convention floor by eastern conservatives. By November, even the normally fair-minded if conservative Hugh Blair Grigsby would speak spitefully of Taylor's "trea-

33

son to the East." Here, conservatives talked as though the lines were so sharply drawn that principles could clash or be compromised, but never reconciled, and to a great extent, they maintained this point of view as they went about the convention's business. Taylor, for his part, resigned his seat on November 11, to be replaced by the much more regionally loyal Grigsby.[13]

Much of the reason that tensions remained so high was that, not only were the main conservative and reform camps sharply divided, but neither side had a clear majority of the delegates. Grigsby, looking back on the convention a quarter-century later, would remark that many men were elected whose positions were unknown despite all the politicking for seats,[14] and there were other delegates who, from the beginning had favored some form of compromise on issues of constitutional reform. The effect of such delegates would be readily apparent in the voting on major issues to come before the body, which would emphasize how hard it was for either side to control the convention's affairs. These delegates in the middle were important, and they were unpredictable.

The voting which took place in convention on issues involving democratic reform would reveal the existence of two substantial blocs of conservatives and reformers, including 42 men who voted conservatively at least eighty percent of the time, and 39 men who voted for reform with the same frequency. Led on the conservative side by such men as Benjamin Watkins Leigh, Littleton W. Tazewell, and John Randolph of Roanoke, and on the reform side by Philip Doddridge, Charles Fenton Mercer, and Alexander Campbell, these blocs of delegates would remain strong and cohesive throughout the convention's life. But attaining a majority on a question before the body required the votes of at least 49 of the 96 delegates, so that each side needed to pick up additional votes from the fifteen men who, during the convention, would not demonstrate such strong ties with either group. For conservatives, this would mean depending on at least some support from nine delegates, in particular,

34

who, as their votes would indicate, had conservative tendencies, but whose readiness to side with the conservative bloc on any given issue was never certain. These nine men, who would vote conservatively from one-half to three-quarters of the time, included Madison, the Eastern Shore representatives Thomas Joynes, Thomas Bayly, and Abel P. Upshur, Jeffersonian William F. Gordon, physician Thomas Massie, Jr., Chapman Johnson, Joseph Martin, and John B. Clopton. Conservatives could look nowhere else in the convention for any real support, since even the weakest reformers—men such as Philip C. Pendleton, John R. Cooke, and four other less resolute reformers—would side with conservatives on fewer than one-quarter of the votes (see Table 1).[15]

What, then, were these "moderates," as one may call them, like? Above all, they were fairly independent men, insofar as voting was concerned. There was no "moderate bloc" in the Convention of 1829-30 analogous to the conservative and reform blocs of delegates. These moderates would vote together with only about as much frequency as they would vote with the staunch conservatives. In a few cases, the degree to which they sided with conservatives was clearly a matter of specific issues. Thus, Eastern Shore delegates Joynes, Bayly, and Upshur were all conservative on apportionment but all in the reform camp on suffrage. Chapman Johnson, by contrast, was with the reformers on apportionment and with the conservatives on suffrage. And, among the nine, several had long expressed mixed feelings on reform questions. Massie, working as a physician in Ohio earlier in the century, had sent home several angry letters denigrating the effects of "universal" suffrage on the political and social order of that state.[16] Upshur was one of the most prominent speakers on the conservative side during the convention debates, however much his voting record would belie his words. Madison, of course, with long ties to Virginia's governing elite, had always lacked enthusiasm for liberalizing suffrage, despite having worked for some other reforms in the past. Johnson, too, had

35

TABLE 1

Delegates to the Virginia Convention of 1829-30, by orientation

Conservatives (voting conservatively on 80% + of issues)

Mark Alexander	John Marshall
John S. Barbour	John Y. Mason
Philip P. Barbour	Richard B. Morris
Fleming Bates	Augustine Neale
Samuel Branch	Philip N. Nicholas
William H. Brodnax	William K. Perrin
Augustine Claiborne	James Pleasants
John C. Coalter	Joseph Prentis
George C. Dromgoole	John Randolph
James M. Garnett	John Roan, Jr.
William B. Giles	Alexander Rose
William O. Goode	John Scott
John W. Green	Robert Stanard
Hugh B. Grigsby	Samuel Taylor
Waller Holladay	William P. Taylor
John W. Jones	Littleton W. Tazewell
Benjamin Watkins Leigh	George Townes
William Leigh	James Trezvant
Richard Logan	John Tyler
George Loyall	John B. Urquhart
John Macrae	Richard N. Venable

Moderates (voting conservatively on 50-79% of issues)

Thomas M. Bayly	James Madison
John B. Clopton	Joseph Martin
William F. Gordon	Thomas Massie, Jr.
Chapman Johnson	Abel P. Upshur
Thomas R. Joynes	

36

Moderate Reformers (voting with reform on 70-79% of issues)

Briscoe Baldwin
William Campbell
John R. Cooke

Thomas Griggs
Philip C. Pendleton
Lucas Thompson

Reformers (voting in favor of reform on 80% + of issues)

William Anderson
John Baxter
Andrew Beirne
Elisha Boyd
William Byars
Benjamin Cabell
Alexander Campbell
Edward Campbell
Henley Chapman
Samuel Claytor
Gordon Cloyd
Samuel Coffman
Philip Doddridge
William Donaldson
Edwin S. Duncan
William H. Fitzhugh
John B. George
Peachy Harrison
Richard Henderson
John O. Laidley

James M. Mason
John P. Mathews
William McCoy
C. F. Mercer
Fleming Miller
Andrew M'Millan
Samuel Moore
Charles Morgan
William Naylor
William Oglesby
_____ Osborne
Alfred H. Powell
James Saunders
Adam See
William Smith
Archibald Stuart
Lewis Summers
Jacob Williamson
Eugenius Wilson

a long history of reform activity, although, in 1816, he had been one of those present at Staunton who had balked at the call for a constitutional convention with full powers. These were delegates, then, who brought mixed views to the convention, and they showed this by their voting.

But in many ways, especially in terms of background and interests, these nine delegates were very much like even the strongest conservatives. Like the conservatives, for example, they were mainly from the East and the Piedmont, as Table 2 indicates. All the conservatives were from those two regions of the state; and of the nine moderate delegates, only one, Chapman Johnson, came from anywhere as far west as the Valley–which would explain his reform views on apportionment. Of the other eight, four were from the Piedmont–Gordon, Massie, Martin, and Madison–and the other four were from the East. Given the sectional nature of the constitutional dispute in Virginia, the kinds of regional affiliations shown by this table are not surprising, and the high statistical correlation between region and voting indicates the extent to which sectionalism continued to influence that dispute in the convention itself.

TABLE 2

Region and Voting

Region	Conservatives	Moderates	Moderate Reformers	Reformers
East	32	4	0	0
Piedmont	10	4	2	9
Valley	0	1	3	16
West	0	0	1	14

$\chi^2 = 72.946$
$p = .001$

38

In addition, and related to the fact that both the East and Piedmont were strongly influenced by the plantation economy, conservative and moderate delegations were alike in being dominated by planters. Almost eighty percent of the conservatives were planters, and so were eight of the nine moderates, as Table 3 shows. By contrast, planters were outnumbered by lawyers among reformers, and there were almost as many merchants. There was, between conservatives and moderates, a community of interest in planting and slavery that was not shared by the more occupationally diverse body of reformers, and conservatives could appeal to this in trying to hold the moderate delegates to their side.

TABLE 3

Occupation and Voting

Occupation	Conservatives	Moderates	Moderate Reformers	Reformers
Planter	33	8	1	9
Lawyer	8	1	4	12
Farmer	0	0	0	2
Merchant	0	0	1	8
Other	0	0	0	6
Unknown	1	0	0	2

$\chi^2 = 42.879$
p = .001

*chi-square computed on the basis of known occupations, n = 93

Less tangible, but no less important, were several factors which united conservatives and moderates as, by and large, members of Virginia's traditional elite. Indeed, if one recognizes that elite status in Virginia political life was represented by the holding of statewide or national office–since these tended to remain under elite control–as opposed to having

39

only local prominence, and if one adds to that the existence of close ties of kinship with Virginia's first families, then, as Table 4 shows, conservative and moderate delegates tended to have elite status to a far greater degree than did the delegates who favored reform. This was also manifested in regard to other attributes. Thus, as Table 5 indicates, conservative and moderate delegations were overwhelmingly Episcopalian, while reform groups were dominated by Presbyterians and showed strong representation from other evangelical denominations, indicative of the extent to which the battle was joined between Virginia's traditional leaders and men of very different social and cultural backgrounds. Similarly, as Table 6 indicates, conservative and moderate delegates tended to be more highly educated than did those who favored reform—although, here, the data are not so full as they are in regard to other factors. There were, then, real differences between the two sides which would have tended to set moderates, like conservatives, apart from reform.[17]

TABLE 4

Political Past and Voting

Past	Conservatives	Moderates	Moderate Reformers	Reformers
Strong ties to tradition elite	28	9	4	16
Weak ties to tradition elite	14	0	2	23

$\chi^2 = 12.857$
$p = .01$

40

TABLE 5

Religion and Voting

Religion	Conservatives	Moderates	Moderate Reformers	Reformers
Episcopalian	24	8	1	5
Presbyterian	4	1	2	17
Evangelical	2	0	2	7
Other	2	0	0	4
Unknown*	10	0	1	6

$\chi^2 = 34.010$
$p = .001$

*chi-square computed on the basis of known religious affiliation, $N = 79$

TABLE 6

Education and Voting

Education	Conservatives	Moderates	Moderate Reformers	Reformers
College	24	6	1	8
No college	11	3	2	14
Unknown*	7	0	3	17

$\chi^2 = 6.659$
$p = .05$

*chi-square computed on the delegates with known educational background, $N = 69$

One gains a good sense of what these differences meant by looking at the lives of those who were most prominent in the convention's main groups. Hugh Blair Grigsby had rightly predicted that certain men would dominate the convention's affairs, both in leading the debate on the floor and in the

41

Hugh Blair Grigsby

negotiations that would ultimately lead to a revised constitution, although the names he cited were not entirely correct. Among those who did stand out were Benjamin Watkins Leigh, John Randolph, Abel P. Upshur, William F. Gordon, Alexander Campbell, and Philip Doddridge. Each of these men frequently addressed the delegates, and each made major contributions to the tone and substance of the convention debate.

Chief among the conservative leaders was Benjamin Watkins Leigh. In many ways, Leigh was typical of the kind of men chosen by the eastern districts to represent their interests in the convention. Born in Chesterfield County in 1781 – the same county he would represent in the convention – Leigh was the son of a William-and-Mary- and Edinburgh-educated Anglican clergyman. His mother was the granddaughter of Archibald Cary, who had played such an important role in the Virginia Convention of 1776. Leigh himself studied at William and Mary, where, incidentally, he once delivered an address "on the natural equality of man with respect to rights,"[18] and where, too, he became close to other young Virginians who would one day enter the state's leadership. Among his closest friends were Chapman Johnson, Henry St. George Tucker, and Robert Stanard.[19] Tucker was the son of St. George Tucker, perhaps the most significant thinker in early national Virginia, and he would be, too, a delegate to the Staunton Convention of 1816. Stanard and Johnson would both be delegates to the Convention of 1829-30, where Stanard would participate in the conservative cause while Johnson played an important role among moderates.

Leigh made his mark in Virginia affairs first, mainly as a lawyer. He began the practice of law in Petersburg in 1802 and gained a reputation from his first case by obtaining the acquittal of a boy who was prosecuted for killing his step-father in the act of beating his mother.[20] In 1819, he was selected to compile the state's Code, and, according to one eulogist, "was believed to be better acquainted with the his-

43

Benjamin Watkins Leigh

tory of Virginia legislation, from the foundation of the colony, than any other person in the Convention."[21] Other public commissions followed this effort. In 1822 he represented the state in Kentucky in a dispute over lands, and in 1833, he was sent to South Carolina in an effort to secure that state's withdrawal of nullification. Although he held only a few elective offices—he was in the House of Delegates from 1811 to 1813 and in the United States Senate from 1834 to 1836—Leigh had close ties to the political leadership of his state. He died in 1849.[22]

It was as an orator that Leigh was most noted, and people came to the convention to see him. His was a cultivated and calculated oratory, and he seems to have given a great deal of thought to it. Young Hugh Blair Grigsby described Leigh as a man of great eloquence, but aware of his defects, which he acknowledged "with a generous spirit."[23] He was, by all accounts, a striking man, one who, according to his eulogist, William H. Macfarland, was "gazed upon, followed, admired, for the grace and attraction of his person."[24] This, despite the fact that Leigh wore a thick-soled shoe on one foot because his leg was injured in an accident and "never recovered its proper length." According to one admirer, "This defect, instead of impairing the ease and grace of his general carriage, rather heightened their effect, and contributed to render him, what he undoubtedly was at that time, a man of uncommonly striking appearance."[25] Handsome, well-connected, and of good background, Leigh was well suited to lead Virginia's conservative side.

Something similar may be said of conservatism's more eccentric spokesman, John Randolph of Roanoke. Randolph was the convention's real celebrity, mainly because of his oratorical gifts. Even the *Richmond Daily Whig,* a long-time advocate of constitutional reform, would remark favorably of Randolph in this regard, saying, "You may dislike his person, and abhor every particular sentiment he utters, but you cannot withhold admiration from the excellence of his oratory, or fail to drink up every word he says." Mindful of the news-

John Randolph

paper's usual position on reform, however, the writer of this piece added, "We wish we could speak as commendingly of the spirit of Mr. Randolph's speech, as of its manner."[26] But, indeed, Randolph was a major drawing card for this very public convention. According to one observer, "The anxiety to hear him, among all classes of persons, strangers as well as citizens, amounted almost to phrenzy." At the session during which it was believed Randolph would make his first address to the convention, "a crowd thronged to the capitol, such as we never saw before, and never expect to see again. Ladies were absolutely packed into the galleries and the spare seats in the hall." He disappointed the audience on that occasion by remaining silent, but when Randolph actually did rise to speak, before a relatively empty hall, the crowd was said to pour in "like the waters of the ocean, when the dyke gives away."[27]

The man who caused so much commotion was related to some of Virginia's most distinguished families. Born in Prince George County in 1773, Randolph was the great-grandson of William Randolph and the nephew of Theodorick Bland, two of colonial Virginia's leading citizens, and he was a student of the distinguished St. George Tucker. He attended college, briefly, at William and Mary—where he fought a duel—and entered public life in Virginia in 1799 when he was elected to Congress. His career in Congress was long and prominent as a leader of the strict conservative faction that opposed many of Jefferson's policies, and of the southern sectionalists during the 1820s—which led him to the dueling ground against Henry Clay. Following the Convention of 1829-30, Randolph would serve as Andrew Jackson's minister to Russia, a post he held actively for only about a month. Then, his health and psyche degenerating, he died in 1833.[28]

Randolph's public image never failed to attract attention, and it enhanced his presence as an orator. In many ways he exaggerated as he dramatized the popular image of the Virginia aristocrat. Given to strong language and bursts of temper, even his dress was, as one observer noted, "that of the old Virginia gentleman. He wore white top boots with drab or buckskin shortclothes, and sometimes gaiters, and, though neat, he was generally plain in his appearance, and had not ambition to conform to any prevalent fashion." Having a voice often described as "feminine" or even "shrill," Randolph had, nevertheless, a gift for words, for manner, and for presence that virtually everyone could appreciate. He would speak often, and forcefully, on the floor of the convention.[29]

Abel P. Upshur occupied a strange place in the Convention of 1829-30. On the basis of his speeches to the convention, he would have to be ranked with Leigh and Randolph as one of the three leading conservative spokesmen. Indeed, the three of them together accounted for almost half of the major conservative speeches before the body. Still, much of Upshur's voting behavior belied his words. A delegate from Accomack, on Virginia's Eastern Shore, Upshur was among the staunchest of conservatives on questions of apportionment reform. On those of suffrage, however, his record was one of the most democratic. His was, then, for all he had to say in the convention, a somewhat less than firm conservatism.

Upshur's Eastern Shore home was, itself, on the periphery of eastern society. Its people were separated from the mainland by the Chesapeake Bay, so that anyone who hoped to make his way into the elite was forced, as Upshur's biographer, Claude H. Hall, has said, to cross over to the mainland and to escape the provincial insularity of his home region. Upshur was one who did so with some success.[30]

Abel P. Upshur was born in Accomack in 1790. The son of a prosperous planter and local leader, Upshur was the descendant of Arthur Upshur, who had settled on the Eastern Shore in the mid-seventeenth century. In the years after Arthur Upshur's arrival, he and his descendants built up extensive holdings in the region and achieved major political and social influence. Abel Upshur's own father was a Federalist member of the state legislature. Abel studied at

48

Abel P. Upshur

Princeton—from which he was expelled for participating in a student riot—and attended Yale, though he did not graduate. He read law in the office of William Wirt, in Richmond, and was a practicing lawyer in Richmond thereafter. He represented Accomack in the House of Delegates in 1812-1813 and again from 1825 to 1827. In 1816, he was elected Commonwealth's Attorney for Richmond, and from 1826 to 1841 he was a member of the state's supreme court. Upshur's career came to an end in 1844 when, serving as secretary of state during the administration of President John Tyler, he was killed by the explosion of a gun on board the battleship *Princeton*.[31]

That Upshur should have achieved such success in American politics is testimony to his own ambition, as well as to his good fortune in having the opportunity to begin his career under the tutelage of Wirt. According to Claude H. Hall, Wirt sought to make his charges into cultivated gentlemen as well as excellent attorneys, and to that end gathered around him a circle of the most noted, literary-minded Virginians, including John Randolph and Littleton W. Tazewell, both of whom would be prominent conservatives in the Convention of 1829-30. Upshur seems to have fit the part well, for he became known as a brilliant conversationalist and an amiable companion. According to one contemporary, Upshur's manners were "those of the polished and engaging gentleman—and his whole character one of the most amiable I have ever known."[32]

It is difficult to know why, belying his words, Upshur should have been so reform minded on the issue of suffrage. To be sure, his Accomack County had voted very heavily in favor of a convention in the 1828 referendum, and perhaps he shared the view of his Accomack colleague Thomas Bayly that citizens of his peninsular home, where they were "plowing the ocean" and not the land, were unfairly penalized and underrepresented because of the freehold requirement.[33] In any case, he seems not to have felt called upon to make his position clear before the delegates, nor can one find

50

William F. Gordon

any comment on his behavior from other people. Nonetheless, his voting was one example of the kind of unpredictable behavior with which conservatives had to contend if they were to contain reform.

A moderate delegate with somewhat clearer motives was William F. Gordon, who represented Jefferson's own Albemarle County in the Piedmont. Gordon was born in nearby Orange County, and he and his family had close social ties with Jefferson and Madison, who came from the same area. Gordon himself followed Jefferson in questioning the Virginia system of tying government to property. He was, nevertheless, as his biographer described him, "an aristocrat by descent and by family ties and social association."[34] He would speak frequently in the Convention of 1829-30, and he was noted in the state for his oratorical ability, but he would be even more important as the originator of a compromise plan for apportionment, the plan which would eventually be adopted by the convention.

Born in 1787, Gordon was the grandson of an Irish immigrant who had settled in Virginia in 1727.[35] His maternal grandmother was a first cousin of Benjamin Harrison, a signer of the Declaration of Independence and governor of Virginia. Gordon's father, James, had himself been a political and social intimate of some of Virginia's leading men, and, along with James Madison, had represented Orange County in the Virginia Federal Convention of 1788, where he had been a strong supporter of the proposed United States Constitution. Although William F. Gordon would not attend college, he did receive an education through local schools, among them Dr. James Gordon Waddell's Spring Hill academy, from which he received a good background in the classics, including Greek and Latin letters. He read law in the office of General Benjamin Botts, one of the state's leading lawyers, and in 1809 set up a practice in Charlottesville. In 1812, at the age of twenty-five, Gordon was appointed Commonwealth's Attorney for Albemarle County, and from that position made the acquaintance of a number of Virginia's leading figures, including Dabney Carr, a nephew of Jefferson, Joseph M. Monroe, a brother of the president, and John S. Barbour, who would be a conservative delegate to the Convention of 1829-30.

In the years leading up to the convention, Gordon had already made a mark in Virginia politics. A member of the House of Delegates from 1819 to 1829, Gordon played a prominent role in the legislative development of Jefferson's plans for the University of Virginia. From 1829 to 1835, Gordon would serve as a member of Congress from Virginia, where, although an opponent of nullification, he maintained a consistent position as a states-rights Democrat. After being defeated for reelection to Congress in 1834, Gordon would not hold public office again, but he remained active in the political affairs of Virginia and the South until his death in 1858, and even served as a delegate from Virginia to the Nashville Convention of 1850, a gathering of Southerners who hoped to organize resistance to what they saw as mounting federal encroachment upon the rights of the South and slavery.[36] Like other moderates, then, Gordon's closest political, social, and cultural ties were with the conservative camp—he was often in company of such conservative figures as Hugh Grigsby and Littleton W. Tazewell during the convention itself—and these would strongly influence his role in the convention, even as he worked for changes in the Virginia system of government.

The two most vocal leaders of the democratic cause were both from the same county of Virginia, from Brooke in the far northwest. These leaders were Alexander Campbell and Philip Doddridge, and both had careers that were very different from those of Virginia's conservatives and moderates. Of the two, Campbell is the best known outside the context of the convention, for he played an important role in American religious history as a founder of the Disciples of Christ.

Alexander Campbell was born in Ireland in 1788, son of the minister Thomas Campbell, and he lived there or in Scotland until 1809, attending the University of Glasgow for one

53

Alexander Campbell

year.[37] With his father, he moved to Pennsylvania in 1809, and, in 1810, entered the ministry. By 1811, he had begun to question many of the beliefs which he had long held, and to take those steps which, culminating in the creation of the Disciples as a separate denomination, would make him a leading figure in the religious controversies of the day. At the same time, and however active he was as a religious con-troversialist—attacking, especially, those practices which he believed to hamper the unity of believers—Campbell had lit-tle experience in politics. Indeed, his service as a delegate to the Convention of 1829-30 represented his only formal expe-rience in politics, and this occurred, according to an early his-torian of the Disciples, only "at the earnest solicitation of the people of West Virginia, and with a special pledge from his friends that he not be required to take the stump."[38] He was, nevertheless, an extremely articulate spokesman for political reform, as he would be for the religious goals to which he devoted the bulk of his time. Campbell died in 1866.

One reason for his ability to put the reform case with some eloquence was that, though he was not a political man, Camp-bell was familiar with the kinds of democratic principles and sentiments upon which that case had come to rest. The Disci-ples of Christ was nothing if not a democratically oriented religious body. Beginning out of a sense of wrongness of doc-trinal divisions among Christians, the Disciples, under Campbell's leadership, raised the Bible to a central place in the believer's life and, more, stressed the ability of every be-liever to understand and interpret the scripture for himself. In keeping with this, and despite his own education, Camp-bell worked hard to break down whatever lines existed between the clergy and the people. He opposed formal min-isterial titles and formal ministerial education because both, he felt, tended to raise the clergy above the laity; and he scorned ministerial costume, as well.[39] As he wrote in advising young preachers of his denomination, "You must endeavor to introduce that state of things which will make every man and woman in the christian ranks a preacher in word and deed."[40] For Campbell, the church was to be, truly, a gathering of equal believers.

His democratic views of Christian practice carried over, more generally, into his politics. Although Campbell was able to reconcile himself to slavery, he placed great emphasis on the natural rights of every individual, and he made no effort to divorce his political views from his religion. Thus, writing in his own *Christian Baptist* magazine in August, 1829–and, perhaps, thinking of the approaching convention–Campbell would argue, "Whatever the natural rights of men are, they belong to all men naturally; consequently, the natural rights of men are equal rights." He would add that there could be no defense for attempting to withhold rights from some men: "To give others what belongs to them, is a duty we owe them; to withhold from them what belongs to them, is a sin."[41] Such words anticipated a major part of his argument in the convention itself, and must have been a comfort to those who had chosen him their representative.

Philip Doddridge, a lawyer and politician, was born in Pennsylvania in 1773, the son of a farmer. Raised on a farm, he had little formal education, although he did attend a school in Brooke County when he moved there at the age of seventeen. He studied law locally, and began his practice in 1797. He was successful as an attorney and entered state politics in 1815, as a member of the House of Delegates. In 1828, he was elected to Congress, remaining a member until his death in 1832.[42]

Doddridge was a thoroughly western man. Not only were his origins more western than Virginian, but, as a young lawyer, his practice was a western one, extending as much toward Ohio and western Pennsylvania as toward Richmond.[43] When he entered the legislature in 1815, it was as an aggressive partisan of the West, and he began almost immediately to push for a convention to revise the state constitution.[44] He opposed eastern society in other ways, as well. He was, for example, a strong advocate of an anti-dueling statute–a provision he would also try to insert into the Constitution of

56

1829-30–identifying the practice as a besetting sin of the eastern elite.[45] In 1823, Doddridge opposed a bill to reduce the pay of members of the legislature on grounds that clearly related to sectional issues. He argued that such a reduction would have no effect on the aristocratic representatives from the Tidewater but would place a terrible burden on the "middle class" representatives from the West.[46] An avowed and bitter opponent of what he saw as aristocratic privilege, Doddridge would be the most vituperative proponent of democratic reform in the Convention of 1829-30.

Doddridge, despite his role in the convention, never received more than local prominence in Virginia politics. He was, by all accounts, an intelligent and eloquent man. He learned Latin well enough in the local school to do translations and to converse: the story was told that in some early travels he greatly impressed the Spanish governor in Natchez with his conversational Latin.[47] Later, Daniel Webster was said to have considered Doddridge the only man he really feared in a debate.[48] But eastern leaders would not pay him even a grudging respect, and his role in Virginia politics would always be circumscribed by his lack of the kind of background Virginia's leaders demanded of those who would achieve high position.

The convention's leadership represented the constituencies of delegates to the body. The differences among them indicate the sources upon which political divisions were based in the state. In part, and on the surface, the divisions were simply regional, but regional differences were reinforced by those of society and culture which, taken together, provided the framework within which debate and negotiation would take place while the convention was in session.

Here was the situation, then, out of which the conservative strategy had to be created. There was enough similarity between staunch conservatives and moderates for conservatives to believe that connections could be maintained between the two groups. There was no reason for them to try

57

Philip Doddridge

to persuade western democrats to foresake any part of reform, because these men were unalterably opposed to
conservatives, culturally as well as politically, and wanted a
complete reform of the Virginia system. If, however,
conservatives could persuade such reform-minded planters
as, for instance, Thomas Massie, Jr., or William F. Gordon to
work with them rather than with the more democratic reformers, then they could limit constitutional change even if
they felt they could not stop it altogether. John Scott, a
Piedmonter but a consistent conservative, rather self-
servingly described what he hoped his moderate colleagues
would feel as a result of the convention's deliberations:

> Mr. Chairman, the people whom I in part represent,
> have not been in the habit of singing hosannas to the
> present Constitution. They think it has defects and that
> they have suffered evils under its operation. I have
> participated in these sentiments. To remedy these evils
> we have united with our brethren of the West to bring
> about this Convention. But I fear they will prove Roman
> allies, and we shall only have the privilege of changing
> our masters.[49]

Ties of interest and background could make such an appeal
work.

In what ways, then, would conservative efforts to maintain
ties with moderate delegates take shape as the events of the
convention unfolded, and how would such ties influence the
outcome of the convention's proceedings? When the delegates arrived in Richmond, it was unclear to anyone what the
convention might produce; no one could know, in the tense,
divisive atmosphere in which the convention opened, what
the final outcome of debate and negotiation might be. By the
time the primary issue, that of representation, was settled, it
was obvious that the basic connections between moderates
and conservatives would mean that whatever change did
occur would fall well short of what western reformers had
desired. How did this come about?

Following Monroe's election as president of the convention, most of the body's early days were taken up with procedural matters, including the organization of four committees, composed of one delegate from each of the twenty-four senatorial districts, which were to discuss the legislative, executive, and judicial provisions of the 1776 Constitution, along with the Declaration of Rights. Each committee was asked to consider and report what, if any, amendments ought to be made in that part of the constitution committed to it.[50] To the legislative committee would go the controversial issues of suffrage and apportionment.

The committee which was asked to discuss the two issues at the center of the conflict over reform was a distinguished one, for it included some of the most prominent members of the convention, among them Leigh, Randolph, and Doddridge, along with Madison, C.F. Mercer, John R. Cooke, and Chapman Johnson. Four members of the committee were from the West, nine from the East; six were from the Piedmont and five from the Valley. Not surprisingly, the committee had great difficulty agreeing on anything to report back to the convention as a whole. The proposals offered before it were in sharp conflict with one another, and the reform and conservative forces were so evenly divided that neither side had any well-founded hope of carrying the day on either question.

Representation was clearly, however, the main issue on the committee's agenda, as it was on the convention's as a whole. Although the legislative committee was not the first of the four to report its findings back to the convention—the committee on the Declaration of Rights would be—everyone acknowledged that the question of representation had to be settled before anything else and that report became the highest priority in the order of business.[51] The committee had, in fact, considered several plans for apportionment during its deliberations. Doddridge, at the beginning, for example, had presented the demand reformers had made for so many years that legislative apportionment be based on white population alone. Leigh, recognizing that change had to occur, suggested that it be based on white population and taxation combined—an idea that looked back to St. George Tucker.[52] The deciding voice on the issue would be that of James Madison. When Doddridge proposed two resolutions—one to put the House on the white basis, the other to do the same for the Senate—Madison supported the one, allowing it to pass by a vote of 13 to 11, and opposed the latter, producing a 12 to 12 tie. Accordingly, the committee would recommend that the House be apportioned on the white basis while saying nothing about the Senate.[53]

Madison himself presented the committee's recommendation to the convention, on October 26. The committee's proposal did not, however, meet with smooth sailing when it reached the floor of the convention, now constituted as a committee of the whole. Almost as soon as Madison had reported, conservative John W. Green, of Culpeper, rose to amend the recommendation by proposing that the House be put on the compound basis of population and taxation combined, as Leigh had suggested in the legislative committee. This proposal would clearly show the divisions among convention delegates.

The debate on the Green proposal was hot. Moderate John R. Cooke and westerner Alexander Campbell both spoke against it, Campbell in particular asserting that the proposal recognized no principles of republican government, and Cooke harking back to the principles of the American Revolution. The conservatives looked to Abel P. Upshur to state their case, and he responded with one of the most famous speeches of the convention, in which he contended that government could not be based on principles—abstractions—but had to be founded on practicality and experience. And he advanced, too, the idea that those who had the greatest stake in a government should have the greatest share in its administration. This, for him, meant the land-owning, slaveholding men of the eastern regions. It was a powerful speech, and one which advanced notions to which conservatives would appeal throughout the convention. It was also a speech to which re-

61

formers would have to reply in trying to defend the white basis for legislative apportionment, and they would do so mainly in the way Leigh's old friend Chapman Johnson did, by declaring government to be more than a matter of "expediency" and by holding up, again and again, the legacy of the principles propounded, as they said, by Virginia's founding fathers.[54]

The debate continued in this vein for several weeks until, on November 14, Green's proposal was defeated, with Monroe, as president, casting the deciding vote.[55] The convention was then presented with several alternatives. Leigh proposed to base representation on the "federal numbers," that is, on the white population plus three-fifths of the slaves, the practice of the United States Constitution, but this measure was defeated 47 to 49. Other compromise plans were offered. Upshur proposed to base representation on an average of three ratios: the white population, the so-called compound basis which combined population and taxation, and federal numbers. Leigh would have averaged white population and federal numbers, as would have John Marshall. But the convention's attention would ultimately focus on two plans originated by moderate delegates. One, offered by James Pleasants, a delegate from Goochland on the Fall Line, proposed to base the House of Delegates on white population; the Senate, on federal numbers. The other, offered by William F. Gordon, simply divided the state into four sections, giving an equitable number of senators and representatives to each. Deciding between the two led to some of the most bitter politicking in the convention, as eastern and western delegates were completely divided, and delegates from the Piedmont and the Valley sought to settle on a plan.[56] For over two weeks both plans would lie on the table as, amid threats from both sides to bolt the convention and even to dismember the state, conservatives and reformers caucused, negotiated, and worked to gather votes.

Those who favored reforms in apportionment, including many moderates, preferred Pleasants' plan from the beginning. John R. Cooke, in particular, tried to cement moderate support in its favor since this would carry the plan despite eastern opposition. On November 30, Cooke offered the Pleasants' plan to the convention. The West fully supported Pleasants because, though a compromise, it would have based at least one house of the legislature on the white basis, and Doddridge became its principal champion.[57] The West, however, could not gain sufficient support to carry the convention. Even as reformers had tried to marshal support for the Pleasants' plan, easterners had been busy both in negotiations and in debate, and, after days of wrangling, the Gordon plan had become, for all practical purposes, almost identical to the "mixed basis" for apportionment which had earlier been proposed by Upshur. Indeed, Upshur had given his support to Gordon, having recognized that some measure of compromise on apportionment was inevitable. Conservatives and moderates rallied behind Upshur, and such men as Cooke, seeing that Gordon's plan was the best reform possible under the circumstances, also withdrew their support from Pleasants. Thus, the issue was decided.[58] On December 5, the delegates met as a committee of the whole and voted down Pleasants while approving Gordon. A roll-call vote would later ratify the decision by a count of 55 to 41.[59] The new provision would give the lower house 134 members. The 26 counties west of the Alleghenies received 31 representatives, the 14 Valley counties, 25, the Piedmont's 29 counties, 42, and the 36 Tidewater counties, 36 representatives. For purposes of apportioning the 32-member senate, the state was divided in half, with the West receiving 13 senators and the East 19. The legislature was to reapportion representation according to districts every 10 years.[60]

The West simply did not get what its leaders had wanted out of the Gordon plan, and western delegates voted unanimously against it. They had to take its adoption as a defeat because, not only would westerners remain a minority to the plantation-dominated eastern and Piedmont representatives in the legislature, but the democratic principles which

63

informed plans for apportionment on the white basis were unacknowledged. Hence, after the convention, Doddridge would issue a virulent attack on those moderates–especially on Cooke who had helped to resolve the issue by supporting the Gordon plan.[61]

But moderate delegates had been lobbied hard to throw their support to the East and to Gordon. Some, especially from the Piedmont, had received petitions from their constituents urging such support, based largely on a fear that a shift of power to the farming West would be as deleterious to the plantation economy of the Piedmont as it would be to the East. Additionally, according to Claude H. Hall, there was a measure of propaganda directed at the Piedmont citizenry, as when a dozen horsemen rode through Madison's Orange County "explaining to Piedmont residents that the white basis meant that Westerners would take their property to 'level the mountains.' "[62] Playing on what they saw as a basic similarity of conservative and moderate interests, and acting both within and outside the confines of the convention, opponents of reform had put in much effort to bring moderate leaders to the conservative side. And on this main issue before the convention, they achieved a compromise which effectively limited the scope of reform.

On the issue of suffrage, too, the convention reached a compromise with which conservatives could live. The resolution of the suffrage question took place during the impasse over representation, and, though a compromise, was reached without the complex maneuvering that had occurred on that more volatile issue. Suffrage, too, had first been referred to the legislative committee, and, again, the committee had been presented with several proposals to consider. Doddridge, on the first day, October 12, had proposed suffrage for all taxpayers, restricting it, at the same time, to one's county of residence. A day later, however, John R. Cooke made the most significant proposal. Like Doddridge, he proposed residency and tax paying as requirements, but he made explicit what was by then a permanent part of the reform case by tacking on the first sentence of Virginia's Declaration of Rights, asserting that because "all men are by nature equally free and independent," there could be no justification for a suffrage restricted only to freeholders.[63] Robert B. Taylor, the renegade easterner, had tried a similar tactic in reporting for the committee on the Bill of Rights, by adding suffrage guarantees to the Declaration.[64] Neither effort was successful, but each shows clearly how reformers would argue their case, even as conservatives, consistent with their position on representation, would assert the continuing practical wisdom of maintaining the freehold.

The legislative committee reported a compromise to the convention, proposing to break the freehold principle as such, but extending suffrage only to leaseholders and housekeepers, an extension which fell far short of the "universal" suffrage which reformers desired. Almost immediately, on November 17, western delegate Eugenius Wilson, from Monongalia County, reintroduced Doddridge's proposal to grant suffrage to all taxpayers, and the debate was joined. Reformers would not only continue to quote from the Declaration of Rights, but would point out that twenty-two of the twenty-four states in the union were ahead of Virginia in granting such extended rights to vote. Conservatives, in response, would charge reformers with radicalism and would assert the necessity of maintaining a suffrage qualification which demanded the stake in society that property holding gave. The two sides remained, then, completely divided, and it looked to many that the kind of impasse which had developed over representation would develop over suffrage, as well.

The divisions on the suffrage issue were of a different sort from those which divided delegates on representation and, above all, sectional tensions were not as high. Some of those moderates who came to the convention hoping for changes in representation had long been ambivalent about if not downright opposed to any significant extension of the right to vote. At the same time, there were eastern delegates, notably those from the Eastern Shore, who favored a weakening of the freehold requirement. In such a setting, a compromise was somewhat easier to reach than it would be on representation, and finally, on November 23, the convention, already frustrated over the failure at that point to resolve the representation issue, simply approved Charles Fenton Mercer's motion to admit housekeepers to suffrage. The next day, the body voted to admit leaseholders, as well. Although the freehold principle was broken to some extent, ties to property did remain important, and the final provision was hardly the universal suffrage, or even taxpayer suffrage, for which reformers had fought.[65] The revised constitution would extend the vote to freeholders, holders of leases with terms of not less than five years, or taxpayers in town; and it included a residency requirement.[66] Again, conservatives had given a little, but they had been able to stand with moderates against the West and had successfully prevented any victory for either the principles or goals of reform.

The effects of such extension as did take place have been variously estimated. Julian A.C. Chandler, in his 1901 study, believed that the Constitution of 1830 raised the proportion of enfranchised white men to about one-half. Merrill Peterson, more recently, has written that the new constitution meant the enfranchisement of about two-thirds of the white adult males. Either way, the convention led to a gain for Virginia's nonfreeholders, but no basic change in the way Virginia government did its business.[67]

In regard to other areas of Virginia's system of government, there was little change made by the convention, although reforms were discussed after the resolution of the question of representation in early December. The executive branch remained much as it had been under the Constitution of 1776. There was heated discussion of a proposal by Doddridge for a popularly-elected governor, but the proposal was defeated by one vote. The Council of State remained in place, also to be elected by the General Assembly. Despite some sentiment for judicial reform, including the

popular election of judges, specific plans made little head-
way, and even the traditional county court system, long a bul-
wark of Virginia's political tradition, survived all efforts at
reform. The Declaration of Rights was left unchanged.
Although conservatives had compromised on representation
and suffrage, they had not compromised too much, and the
convention adopted a basically conservative constitution.

Reformers recognized this. If they had gained, practically,
from the new constitution, they had not gained as much as
they had sought. An apportionment plan geared solely to
white population and regularly brought up to date would
have given the West a much larger influence in the Assembly
than the plan for apportionment which was finally approved
would ever produce. More than that, the westerners came to
the convention waving the banner of principle, and on that
score they were horribly defeated. The basic reform principle
put person over property as the locus for citizenship, and
neither the plan for apportionment nor that for suffrage
unambiguously incorporated such a view into the new
constitution.

Their perception of defeat was evidenced during the final
days of the convention, when it was time to vote on the new
constitution. The vote to adopt the convention's document
and to submit it to the people for ratification was clearly
based on sectional lines. John R. Cooke was the only delegate
from west of the Blue Ridge to support the document, and,
on a 55 to 40 vote, the East and Piedmont went solidly for it.
This vote was taken on January 14, 1830, and the convention,
having put down a last-ditch effort by hard-line conservative
John Randolph to allow only those qualified to vote under
the old constitution to vote on the new one, adjourned on the
following day.

In the popular vote which followed, the dissatisfaction of
western delegates was echoed by their constituents. The new
constitution was approved with about 63 percent of the vote
statewide, winning 26,055 to 15,563, but there were important sectional differences in this voting. No county in what

would become West Virginia reported for ratification, and in some there was virtual unanimity against the new constitution.[68] In Logan County, for instance, the vote was 2 in favor and 255 opposed; in Ohio, the new constitution was rejected 643 to 3. Doddridge's Brooke County polled no votes for ratification. The East, by contrast, must have seen the new constitution as a victory. Leigh's home county of Chesterfield approved it 461 to 15; Amelia County, which had sent Governor Giles, polled a vote of 250 for ratification to 3 against. What was important, however, was the report of counties which had sent moderates to the convention. In some, including John R. Cooke's Frederick County where it was 451 to 438 in favor, the vote was a close, but in others the new constitution won easily. Albermarle, Gordon's home, approved the document 626 to 7; Loudon, less spectacularly, voted for ratification 505 to 128.[69]

The character of the vote emphasizes the bitterness and sense of defeat with which western reformers looked upon the new constitution. Doddridge wrote a blistering public letter in which he attacked the East, but more especially those delegates from middle Virginia for their "treachery" in supporting compromise.[70] The *Staunton Spectator* while urging moderation and continuing work for further revisions, declared that many westerners felt the new constitution to be an eastern insult to western people, and represented the document as onerous for putting expediency over fundamental principles. The *Spectator* seems to have gauged western opinion accurately. A man from Ohio County excoriated the "aristocratical" character of the new constitution, exclaiming "I cast the unclean thing from me!"[71] Clearly, he was not one of the three from that county who voted in favor of ratification.

So conservatives were, in some sense, triumphant. If they had not succeeded in fully blocking reform, they had at least contained it and had preserved the main lines of the traditional political system. They had done so by holding together and by gaining sufficient support from moderate ranks to de-

68

feat the reformers on critical issues. The sense of similarity between themselves and the moderates on whom they had to depend was there when they needed it.

Key = conservatives' successful appeal to the moderates

NOTES – CHAPTER TWO

1. John Rogers Cooke, Diary, November 8, 1829, Virginia Historical Society, Richmond.

2. Benjamin Watkins Leigh to William Branch Giles, September 10, 1829, Virginia Historical Society.

3. Claude H. Hall, *Abel Parker Upshur: Conservative Virginian, 1790-1844* (Madison: State Historical Society of Wisconsin, 1964), pp. 47-49.

4. Hugh Blair Grigsby, Diary, May 3-October 3, 1829, entry for September 30, 1829, Hugh Blair Grigsby papers, Virginia Historical Society.

5. Charles Henry Ambler, *Sectionalism in Virginia from 1776 to 1861* (1910; reprint ed., New York: Russell and Russell, 1964), p. 145.

6. Grigsby, Diary, October 6, 1829; Gordon to David Cloyd, October 6, 1829, Cloyd family papers, Virginia Historical Society.

7. Hugh Blair Grigsby, *The Virginia Convention of 1829-30* (Richmond: MacFarlane and Fergusson, 1854), p. 48.

8. Irving Brant, *James Madison*, 6 vols. (Indianapolis: Bobbs-Merrill, 1941-1961), 6: 465.

9. *Richmond Enquirer*, April 7, 1829.

10. Littleton W. Tazewell to John Tazewell, October 20, 1829, Tazewell family papers, Personal Papers collection, Archives Branch, Virginia State Library, Richmond; *Richmond Daily Whig*, November 12, 1829.

11. Armistead C. Gordon, *William Fitzhugh Gordon, A Virginian of the Old School: His Life, Times and Contemporaries (1787-1858)* (New York: Neale, 1909), p. 168; *Richmond Daily Whig*, January 12, 1830; James Madison, *Letters and Other Writings of James Madison, Fourth President of the United States. In Four Volumes. Published by Order of Congress* (Philadelphia: Lippincott, 1867), 4: 60.

12. See, for example, Gordon Cloyd to David Cloyd, October 25, 1829, Cloyd family papers.

13. Hugh Blair Grigsby, Diary, Novmber 1, 1829, to May 1, 1830, entry for November 3, 1829, p. 9, Hugh Blair Grigsby papers; *Proceedings and Debates of the Virginia State Convention of 1829-30. To Which Are Subjoined, The New Constitution of Virginia, and the Votes of the People* (Richmond: Ritchie and Cook, 1830), pp. 234-35.

14. Grigsby, *Virginia Convention of 1829-30*, pp. 4-5.

15. The discussion in this paragraph and the information presented in Table 1 are based on a cluster analysis of the voting of all 96 delegates on 46 selected issues coming before the convention, including nineteen relating to apportionment, and thirteen related to suffrage, along with ten on the executive (having to do with the direct election of the governor and the preservation of the Council), one on the county courts, and three regarding final action on the newly-revised constitution. This analysis was done by a computer, locating pairs of delegates and measuring the frequency with which members of those pairs voted together. The result was the identification of blocs of delegates grouped at specified degrees of cohesion. Cluster analyses were also performed on the voting of all 96 delegates on issues relating to apportionment alone and issues relating to suffrage alone.

70

16. Thomas Massie, Jr., to Thomas Massie, February 12, 1810, Massie family papers, Virginia Historical Society.

17. Most of the biographical data on which Tables 3-6 are based are drawn from Robert Paul Sutton, *The Virginia Constitutional Convention of 1829-30: A Profile Analysis of Late-Jeffersonian Virginia* (Ph.D. dissertation, Univ. of Virginia, 1967), pp. 265-90, in which Sutton provides brief biographical sketches of most of the convention's delegates. A major reason why the correlations between cultural variables and voting were so strong is probably that citizens from Virginia's major regions were given to electing certain kinds of men to office: eastern and Piedmont voters elected the kinds of men who had traditionally led the state; voters in the west and Valley, men of different sorts. Thus, statistically significant correlations obtain between region and occupation (chi-square = 27.789, p = .01); between region and religion (chi-square = 39.766, p = .001); between region and education (chi-square = 10.894, p = .01); and between region and political past (chi-square = 10.96, p = .02). Here was, then, yet another way in which regional, cultural differences gave shape to political ones, as discussed in chapter one.

18. *Richmond Virginia Gazette and General Advertiser,* July 16, 1799.

19. William H. Macfarland, esq., "Eulogy on Benjamin Watkins Leigh, Delivered before the Virginia Historical Society," *Southern Literary Messenger* 17 (1851): 123.

20. Ibid., 125.

21. Hugh R. Pleasants, "Sketches of the Virginia Convention of 1829-30," *Southern Literary Messenger* 17 (1851): 148.

22. For a good sketch of Leigh's life, see Edwin James Smith, "Benjamin Watkins Leigh," *John P. Branch Historical Papers* 1 (1904): 286-98.

23. Hugh Blair Grigsby, Commonplace book, 1829-30, Hugh Blair Grigsby papers, section 63, p. 7.

24. Macfarland, "Eulogy," p. 123.

25. Pleasants, "Sketches," p. 149.

26. *Richmond Daily Whig,* November 16, 1829.

27. Pleasants, "Sketches," p. 148.

28. See the sketch of Randolph's life in *Dictionary of American Biography,* 10 vols. (New York: Scribner's, 1926-1937), 8: 363-67.

29. William Cabell Bruce, *John Randolph of Roanoke, 1773-1833,* 2 vols., 1922, reprint ed. (New York: Octagon, 1970), 2: 73, 92-93.

30. Hall, *Abel Parker Upshur,* 5.

31. See ibid. for the details of Upshur's life.

32. Ibid., p. 15.

33. Sutton, *Virginia Constitutional Convention,* 96.

34. Gordon, *William Fitzhugh Gordon,* 162.

35. See ibid. for details of Gordon's life.

36. Ibid., p. 346.

37. For a convenient sketch of Campbell's life, see the *Dictionary of American Biography,* 2, 446-48.

38. A.S. Hayden, *Early History of the Disciples in the Western Reserve, Ohio; with Biographical Sketches of the Principal Agents in Their Religious Movement*

(1875; reprint ed., New York: Arno Press, 1972), p. 52.

39. Ibid., p. 34; William E. Tucker, *J.H. Garrison and the Disciples of Christ* (St. Louis: Bethany Press, 1964), p. 17.

40. *Christian Baptist* 7 (1829), p. 640.

41. Ibid., p. 569.

42. See W.S. Laidley, "Hon. Philip Doddridge, of Brooke County, Virginia," *West Virginia Historical Magazine Quarterly* 2 (1902): 54-68.

43. W.T. Willey, *A Sketch of the Life of Philip Doddridge* (Morgantown, West Va.: Morgan and Hoffman, 1875), p. 16.

44. Laidley, "Hon. Philip Doddridge," p. 60-61.

45. Willey, *Sketch,* p. 33.

46. Ibid., pp. 27-28.

47. Ibid., pp. 11-12.

48. Laidley, "Hon. Philip Doddridge," p. 67.

49. *Proceedings, 1829-30,* p. 124.

50. Ambler, *Sectionalism,* p. 147.

51. Merrill D. Peterson, *Democracy, Liberty, and Property: The State Constitutional Conventions of the 1820s* (Indianapolis: Bobbs-Merrill, 1966), p. 275.

52. "Committees of the Virginia Convention of 1829-30" (N.p.: n.d., in Virginia State Library), p. 7.

53. Ambler, *Sectionalism,* p. 147; Sutton, *Virginia Constitutional Convention,* p. 80.

54. *Proceedings, 1829-30,* pp. 54, 70, 117.

55. Peterson, *Democracy, Liberty, and Property,* p. 277.

56. Ibid., p. 278.

57. Ibid.

58. Hall, *Abel Parker Upshur,* p. 59.

59. Peterson, *Democracy, Liberty, and Property,* p. 279.

60. Fletcher M. Green, *Constitutional Development in the South Atlantic States, 1776-1860: A Study in the Evolution of Democracy* (1930; reprint ed, New York: DaCapo Press, 1971), pp. 221-22.

61. Philip Doddridge, printed letter, March 1, 1830, Virginia Historical Society.

62. Hall, *Abel Parker Upshur,* p. 57.

63. "Committees of the Virginia Convention," pp. 7, 13-15.

64. *Proceedings, 1829-30,* p. 39; see Peterson, *Democracy, Liberty, Property,* pp. 274-75.

65. Peterson, *Democracy, Liberty, and Property,* pp. 280-81.

66. *Proceedings, 1829-30,* p. 900 (Art. III, sect. 14).

67. Chandler, *History of Suffrage,* p. 40; Peterson, *Democracy, Liberty, Property,* p. 281.

68. Hall, *Abel Parker Upshur,* p. 62.

69. *Proceedings, 1829-30,* p. 903.

70. Doddridge, printed letter, March 1, 1830.

71. *Richmond Daily Whig,* January 28, 1830; February 13, 1830.

CHAPTER THREE

Of Human Nature
and History:
the Conservative Case
Against Reform

Conservatives had faced the Convention of 1829-30 with a strong sense of urgency about the safety of Virginia's political order. They had fought against the convention movement for years and, justifiably, they could not be sanguine about their hopes for preventing significant reform gains. Conservative Hugh Blair Grigsby had anticipated the convention by declaring that, "The very day, that the people of Virginia resolved to call a convention, told our doom"[1] and if the prophesy were not fully borne out, it nonetheless correctly conveyed conservative attitudes toward the business of constitutional revision. Thus, conservatives, in the convention, would try to convey this sense of urgency about constitutional revision to others, particularly to those moderates who, however much they wanted change, shared so much with the conservatives themselves. They did this by asserting, in very general terms, that security and social order were always exceedingly difficult to maintain. According to conservatives, human nature tended to move in ways contrary to the welfare of society, and human beings were poorly equipped either to create or to maintain a comfortable, stable social or political order. Hence, when a government seemed to be functioning fairly well—as conservatives would claim Virginia's to be—it was better to leave matters alone than to provide opportunities for men, acting in the fluid setting of a changing order, to make things worse or even to destroy all that was good. Their argument depended, therefore, on strong conceptions of human nature and historical possibilities.

Conservatives presented a thoroughgoing picture of human weakness, even perversity, in portraying their fears for the state. John Scott put the matter as starkly as one could when, having acknowledged the many examples of "self-sacrifice on the altars of patriotism and virtue" that were a part of history, he asserted that however many there seemed to be, they were "few when compared with the sacrifices of patriotism and virtue on the altars of ambition and avarice; and serve by their splendour to render more visible, the dark shades of the human character." He went on to emphasize that here, for those interested in principle, "we have a great principle founded in human nature" (125).[2] The purpose of government, Scott and other conservatives would claim, was simply to protect men from each other's avariciousness and ambition, and neither basic human nature nor this basic need for government had changed in recorded history (157).

The key factor in human nature according to which conservatives made such negative assessments was passion, a concept which played a prominent role in the Convention of 1829-30. As the words of Scott show, for example, conservative Virginians drew a picture of man as a creature who was, by nature, passionate, motivated by such things as "ambition" and "avarice." If left to himself, he would naturally act according to the dictates of passion, because self-aggrandizement was a more powerful motive force than was the good of the community. Those who were most likely to act with excessive passion, it was argued, were least fit to govern. Conservatives saw danger chiefly in the avariciousness and licentiousness of the mass of mankind and, hence, they argued for the necessity of government to hold the danger in check.

Reformers, even such moderate reformers as John R. Cooke, would often take conservatives to task for ignoring the heritage of the American Revolution and its ideals, for

74

refusing to honor the memory of those "sages and patriots, who had just involved their country in all the horrors of war, in all the dangers of an unequal contest with the most powerful nation on earth, for the sake of the noble and elevated principles" of the Virginia Declaration of Rights (54). But, in fact, the rhetoric of those sages and patriots often made reference to problems of virtue and passion, and in much the same way that conservatives would use such language in 1829-30. Thus, for example, Richard Henry Lee had written in a 1787 letter that, "If all men were wise and good there would be no necessity for government or law—but the folly and the vice of human nature renders government and laws necessary for the Many, and restraints indispensable to prevent oppression from those who are entrusted with the administration of one and the dispensation of the other."[3] Lee's words looked back to much of classical political theory, in which political thinkers had been concerned with the problem of achieving secure government in a world of passionate mortals. If, following Machiavelli, many thinkers had found the answer to this problem in the connection of force with authority, others had found a more satisfying answer in something that would also be acknowledged by Virginia conservatives. The answer was property.[4] It was this answer that served as the basis for conservative arguments in favor of retaining the freehold suffrage requirement.

Why, according to conservative Virginians, should property give stability to a political community formed out of passionate men? One answer had to do with independence, and Virginians had offered it for some time. Revolutionary Virginians, for instance, had idealized independence in an individual, and felt that property-ownership was a prerequisite to personal autonomy.[5] In a world filled with passionate men, those without such independence could be easily manipulated by ambitious men who had the means to influence others. Dependent men could exercise no liberty, but they could be used to destroy the liberty of others. This was a belief that Virginia conservatives would continue to pro-

75

pound up through the 1829-30 convention. The "dependent poor man," as Abel P. Upshur declared, could never go "against the will of his creditor," nor exert "any thing like independence, either in conduct or opinion" (73). Philip N. Nicholas, of Richmond, made much the same point, but in more ominous terms: "As long as political power is placed as it now is in Virginia, in the hands of the middling classes, who, though not rich, are yet sufficiently so, to secure their independence, you have nothing to fear from wealth. But place power in the hands of those who have none, or a very trivial stake in the community, and you expose the poor and dependent to the influence and seductions of wealth. The extreme rich, and the extreme poor, if not natural allies, will become so in fact. The rich will relieve the necessities of the poor, and the latter will become subservient to the ambitions of the rich" (367).

But property meant more than independence. It also meant permanence, growing out of the demands that property made on its owner, fixing him to a place and requiring that his interests be harmonious with the public good. It was the best evidence of permanent attachment and public interest that political participation required. Considered this way, the virtue assigned to property also had a long tradition in Virginia of supporting freehold suffrage. Edmund Randolph had referred to the fixing power of property in defending the 1776 Constitution's provision for freehold suffrage, and he, like later Virginians, was strongly assured that land was the most desirable sort since it "fixes a man to his country more than a merely personal or moveable right, which travels with him at any distance and in any direction."[6]

It was for this reason, for example, that Virginia philosopher-planter John Taylor of Caroline, anticipating later conservatives, had turned much of his own polemical wrath on those "paper aristocrats," the capitalists of the North. In an essay on parties, Taylor wrote, "Political property is distinguishable from natural property. Land cannot be increased by law—paper-money may. Land, being incapable of an artifi-

76

cial multiplication, cannot by increasing its quantity, strengthen its influence—with paper the case is different. Land cannot be at enmity with the public good—paper money is often so."[7] Taylor had many reasons for arguing as he did, but his words were acceptable to later Virginians. Land, as one conservative would argue in 1829, might change hands, but it "still remained in the country."[8] Thus, property, by its permanence, made a good foundation for a political system.

But property also lent permanence to government because it forced men to identify their interests with the community and, by implication at least, with the status quo. The argument here was closely connected to conservative views of human nature and history. Conservatives stressed man's passionate nature and his selfishness, but in property they claimed to find the one thing that tempered selfishness by turning it toward community needs. As one declared, "What is it that makes agriculture flourish? What is it that builds your cities, and makes commerce spread her wings? What inspire the poet and nerves the soldier's arm? It is love of wealth, fame, and distinction. In a word, it is self-love" (125). Men were selfish, to be sure, but when their selfishness focused on the interests of their own property—the permanent foundation of society—then self-interest was also the interest of society as a whole, and could be trusted not to behave in ways that would harm the community. They had, to use the cant phrase, a "stake in society" that was too great to permit them to act contrary to the public good. And they alone had such a stake. Property, then, placed a check on the tendencies of human nature, and the check it provided was real and tangible, a point William Branch Giles made when he declared in convention that, "Land is the best and only solid, indestructible foundation for Government, unless we re-assert the divine right of Kings, which is nothing more than a mere human invention, founded in fraud and falsehood" (240). Land was the one tangible force which could keep society and government in order.[9]

The role conservatives assigned to property was important

because it allowed them to take the high ground against two key arguments for reform. One, significantly, was like conservatism in holding that men were by nature passionate and that such was the chief failing of humanity. The evangelist Alexander Campbell was particularly effective in asserting that the problem of human passion applied to everyone—and he included in that the current leaders of Virginia. As Campbell said, "Men love power, and in proportion as they possess it, does that love increase" (122). Here, too, was an evocation of human depravity hallowed by time. Self-aggrandizement seems, indeed, to be mainly a danger posed by the rich and powerful who are, after all, in the best position to fulfill their desires.[10] During the American Revolution, for example, this had been the main way passion had been used polemically by Americans in their attacks on the British government and, especially, the Crown, and they were not original in so using it.

Virginia conservatives—following, to some extent, the lead of American conservatives, including Federalists, from the early national period—turned this concern about passion around.[11] Asserting that property could place a check on the passions of freeholders, they identified the real dangers to political society with the passions of the many. Reformers were forced to respond to the assertion that the one requirement for any political order was that it be constructed so that "the many may be restrained from plundering the few" (107). "In Republics," James Madison told the convention, "the great danger is that the majority may not sufficiently respect the rights of the minority...man is known to be a selfish, as well as a social being.... The only safe-guard to the rights of the minority, must be laid in such a basis and structure of the Government itself, as may afford...a defensive authority in behalf of a minority having right on its side" (538).

It was from this assignment of the most dangerous passions to the masses, rather than to the few, that conservatives could attack another reform argument, for it was on this basis that

78

they could counter the assertions of natural rights upon which democratic reform rested its case. They did so in terms of a fairly clear position on the purpose of government, and the implications of that purpose for the form of government. Countering reform demands for liberty and political equality, Benjamin Watkins Leigh asserted, "*Liberty* is only a *mean*: the *end* is *happiness*" (173), and, although no one, including Leigh, bothered to define what such "happiness" involved, it was clear from the tenor of his argument that security, not the realization of natural rights, was at the heart of his concerns. And security, as he understood, was not easy to maintain.

Thomas R. Dew, in a lecture delivered at William and Mary in 1829, put the problem in terms that Virginia conservatives would have appreciated. Noting that men preferred comfort over labor, Dew argued the need for government. Without it, men would be without restraint, and "the strong man would lie under a constant temptation to rob the weaker; the industrious would fall prey to the idle: anarchy, disorder, and a want of energy would be seen throughout the world."[12] Dew's Hobbesian defense of government as a creature of necessity, born out of human perversity, was clearly consistent with the conservative point of view.

Such a view of the necessity of government was implicit in the view of human nature which both sides in the convention accepted. If, to reformers, it argued for the need to create a government in which the powerful would be held in check, for conservatives it meant something else. Expressing their fear of anarchy and disorder as primary, conservatives saw from this theory of government a good case for protecting the weak from the strong, the minority from the majority.

Abel Upshur, countering reform assertions of rights, made a strong statement that powerfully summarized the conservative position:

> If there be any thing in the law of nature which confers the right now contended for, in what part of her code, I would ask, is it to be found? For my own part, I incline

79

strongly to think, that, closely examined, the law of nature will be found to confer no other right than this: the right of every creature to use the powers derived from nature, in such mode as will best promote its own happiness. If this be not the law of nature, she is certainly but little obeyed in any of the living departments of her *empire*. Throughout her boundless domain, the law of force gives the only rule of right. The lion devours the ox; the ox drives the lamb from the green pasture; the lamb exerts the same law of power over the animal that is weaker and more timid than itself; and thus the rule runs, throughout all the gradations of life, until at last, the worm devours us all. But if there be another law independent of force, which gives to a greater number a right to control a smaller number, to what consequence does it lead? (66-67)

One way of arguing against a position based on notions of natural rights was to assert, as conservatives did, that human nature itself demanded that government protect a minority from the power of a majority. Law had to restrain nature if there were to be security.

The problem, at the simplest level, was a need, as James Madison saw it prior to the convention, to protect the property-holding minority "against the will of a majority having little or no direct interest in the rights of property."[13] There was a fear, frequently voiced by conservatives, that if non-property holders were given a voice in the government, they would use their power to take property from its present holders. History, Leigh asserted, proved that (157). John Randolph was no less certain. To him, a majoritarian system meant only one thing: " 'We are numbers, you have property.' I am not so obtuse as to require any further explanation on this head. 'We are numbers, you have property.' Sir, I understand it perfectly" (316).

Such an argument would, naturally, have been appropriate to the Convention of 1829-30, given that all of the members had to be property holders—freehold requirements had remained in force for the election of delegates—and given that the moderate delegates represented regions as dominated by plantation agriculture as did conservatives. Some reformers tried to counter, as would John R. Cooke, by describing the conservative view as "a doctrine monstrous, hateful and incredible!" and declaring that "it is founded on the assumption, that men are by nature, *robbers*, and are restrained from incessant invasions of the rights of each other, only by fear or coercion" (60).[14] Cooke asserted that there was a social instinct in human beings that overcame their predatory drives, but the idea of passion remained too important in Virginia thought—and too useful to men on both sides of the issue—for Cooke's views to have much effect. Other reformers, at any rate, did not pick up on his argument, and the convention did not, in essence, represent a contest between optimistic democrats and pessimistic conservatives. For purposes of debate human depravity remained a working assumption, and conservatives played a strong hand when they reminded property holders of where their greatest vulnerability seemed to lie.

Human nature, was, then, one good reason for worrying about the security of society, and it could be used as a good reason for maintaining freehold suffrage requirements, given the positive influence of property on human behavior. But concerns about human nature and even concerns about property were not the only matters conservatives raised as they sought to make others feel uneasy about reform. Other things also contributed to an image of man as not only depraved, but also weak, as a creature who should approach the business of changing society and government with great trepidation. In particular, conservatives argued that, given human nature, one could safely predict only the worst possible outcome for any process of social and political change.

One sees something of this in the hyperbole with which they described the possible consequences of abolishing the freehold suffrage, particularly when, like Benjamin Watkins Leigh, they did so by placing Virginia's peculiar situation in

81

the context provided by history. Drawing on a use of history, familiar in the colonial and early national periods, which emphasized universal patterns of process and behavior,[15] Leigh would declare that, "there has been no change in the natural feelings, passions, and appetites of men, any more than their outward form, from the days of Solon to those of George Washington," and would assert that, "like political or moral causes put in action, have ever produced, and most ever produce, every where, like effects—in Athens, in Rome, in France, in America." All of these republics, he would argue, had tried to divorce power from property, leading to "an end to free government," and, he would add, "all the Republics in the world have died this death" (157). It was not simply that one could learn an object lesson from earlier republics, moreover. Rather, because Virginians were essentially no different from Athenians or Romans, the success of reform goals would have to lead inexorably to disaster for Virginia; the state could not be immune from history's universals.

The point that conservatives sought to make here was important. They were not so captivated by any myth of American uniqueness as to exempt even their own society from a process that was almost biological in its inevitability. Thus, conservatives in the 1829 convention argued in ways quite consistent with a point that had been made by James Monroe four decades before, during the debate over the Federal constitution, when he declared that, "Political institutions, we are taught by melancholy experience, have their commencement, maturity and decline." The best anyone could hope for was not eternal life, but only to take "precautions that are calculated to prolong our days."[16] The temporality of any political system was a notion that was basic to the conservative understanding of republican history.[17]

Such a lesson was clearly consistent with the underlying ideas about human nature upon which much conservative rhetoric was based. As Leigh's words show, the problem which had led to difficulties in every historical republic had been that of human passion, and as long as human nature

82

remained constant, no republic could escape that problem. Again, property was important, because even if it could not prevent passionate men from acting in politics, it could hold the passions themselves in check. Restricting political participation to freeholders, in other words, was one precaution which might prolong the days of republican Virginia, and it was a better precaution than any others which might be proposed. The point for Leigh and other conservatives was that all the republics he had named, excepting the American, had disappeared for want of just such a precaution.

Implicit in such a reference as Leigh's however, was the more general concern for human weakness. If, as he said, all republics had died for want of a proper safeguard against human passion, it implied that, given human nature, the republican form of government was itself an extremely fragile one. Reformers could attempt to deny such a view by asserting the distinctive character of Virginia's population. Thus, for example, Alfred H. Powell, of Frederick, would assert that "a Representative Republic, founded upon elementary principles, essentially belonging to such a form of Government, is the best and happiest system for obtaining the end of all Government that can be devised, when the people have the essential qualities to suit them to such a form of Government" (104), but Powell's efforts to make the Virginian a different kind of person went against all that history had shown about the fundamental qualities of human nature, always and everywhere. Republics would inevitably be unstable, conservatives asserted, precisely because of those fundamental qualities and, hence, the real effort in any republican society had to be directed toward its defense and not toward changes in it.

But conservatives were not content merely to argue from history that change was dangerous. In addition, they asserted that there was a problem of control whenever change occurred, particularly the sort of change proposed by reformers. Human beings, according to conservatives, simply did not have the mental power to be sure that any proposed

83

change would improve a social order. This was particularly the case when change was to be based upon a set of fundamental principles, as reformers said it should be.

Since the early nineteenth century, reformers had based much of their case for reform on deductions from a major premise provided by the Virginia Declaration of Rights. If, as the Declaration of Rights stated, "all men are by nature free and independent," and, as reformers said, all white adult males are men, then, they could conclude, all deserve equal political rights. This meant, simply, "universal" suffrage and legislative apportionment based on white population. Principle, they asserted, should be embodied in policy, and such argumentation was to be a reform staple in the Convention of 1829-30. The Tidewater reformer Robert Taylor began his remarks to the body by referring to "truths, so simple and self-evident, that their most perfect demonstration is furnished by the terms of the proposition itself," and here, he announced, was to be the cornerstone of his argument for major changes in the state's constitution (46). Alexander Campbell would similarly argue that "in the science of politics, there are, as in all other sciences, certain fundamental principles, as true and unchangeable as any of the fundamental principles of physics or morals" (117). Such principles, reformers said, implied equality in representation and in suffrage.

Conservatives answered the reform position in two ways. One was to deny the usefulness of arguments from principle for arriving at truth. John Randolph of Roanoke made this point with typical flair by means of a little story:

> I saw one of the best and worthiest of men on a visit at some distance from home, urging his lady to make preparation to ride, "for the Sun was down"—his lady said, "The Sun was not down." Her lord gravely replied, "the Sun sets at half past six: it is now past that time." (Every man's watch is right and his was in his hand.) The company looked out of the window and saw the Sun in all his blaze of glory—but the Sun ought to have been down,

84

and fleas are not lobsters: whether it be because they have not souls, I leave to St. Jerome and the Bishops to settle (533).

Making the point that experience and evidence had more to do with truth than did conclusions based on reason alone, Randolph buttressed his story by pointedly referring to Jefferson's famous, theoretically elegant, and practically ineffective plough of least resistance (533). Rhetorically, however, conservatives went beyond simply denying the relevance of reform arguments, asserting the impropriety of allowing fundamental principles to serve as a basis for any political action.

Abel P. Upshur virtually summarized this position in his famous comment in convention that *"there are no original principles of Government at all . . . .* Principles do not *precede*, but spring out of Government" (69). If, to such a reformer as Alexander Campbell, this was like arguing that "we must build the house and then lay the foundation" (117), conservatives made much of opposing experience to principle as the proper foundation for a political system. John Randolph would carry this notion to its conclusion: "As long as I have had any fixed opinion," he declared, "I have been in the habit of considering the Constitution of Virginia, under which I have lived for more than half a century, with all its faults and failings . . . as the very best Constitution; not for Japan; not for China; not for New England; or Old England; but for this, our ancient Commonwealth of Virginia" (313). "The African," suggested Abel P. Upshur, "paints the devil white" (69), and the point was appropriate. Government, they were arguing, grew out of the distinctions and interests which existed in a particular society. It was meant to maintain the order that society had naturally developed and to protect existing interests, not to reorder society according to fundamental principles, however good those principles might seem in the abstract.

The rejection of fundamental principles should not be taken as evidence of conservative anti-intellectualism because this point of view allowed conservatives to make an argument that, intellectually, was quite contemporary, as they proclaimed that truth had to do with accuracy rather than with consistency, and accuracy meant the fit of an idea with empirical evidence.[18] Truth, they consistently argued, was based on experience. At the same time, however, their rejection of fundamental principles allowed them to respond to reformers in a way that was consistent with the key theme of conservative rhetoric, the innate weakness of man.

Conservatives took the position that, because human reason was itself limited, people ought to be willing to settle for a system of government that worked, even if that system appeared imperfect when held up to the light of fundamental principles. Indeed, they would assert, it was pretentious to search for perfection in anything based on human devising, given what Leigh would call "the wretched finite wisdom of man" (158). As one conservative, signing himself "A Backwoodsman," wrote to the *Richmond Enquirer* in 1825, if governments "are to be altered, changed or abolished, for speculative and abstract objections, no government will be retained: The works of the creator themselves may have sentence of condemnation passed upon them; the Sun may be rejected for the spots on its disk; and the spirit of reformation may aspire to amend the system of the Universe."[19] Another made the same point emphasizing that the ideal always looked better than the actual because experience had never revealed "the inconveniencies and evils of the former."[20] To measure reality against "fundamental principles" was inevitably to condemn reality; it was to do so, however, against a false standard.

No one on the conservative side argued that the Virginia system was perfect. Certainly, as John Randolph had stated, it could not be perfect for all time and everywhere since it had developed out of Virginia society and to suit Virginia conditions. Beyond that, however, no one advanced even the case that the constitution was perfect for Virginia. The point for conservatives was that the constitution worked well enough that Upshur could feel confident in demanding that western men cease arguing from principle and begin pointing out specific abuses caused by the government (78). Given human weakness, conservatives were willing to concede, no constitution could be perfect. Nevertheless, because the leaders of 1776 had chosen not to tear down the foundations of the past in the name of principle, Virginians had inherited a fine document.

It was because of human weakness, in fact, that recourse to principles—to speculative schemes—could be so dangerous. One sees something of this in the conservative condemnation of reason alone as a guide to truth, since it lacked a grounding in experience. But, as conservatives asserted in convention, speculation was more than faulty. Put into practice, it was dangerous.

To make this point, conservatives would again turn to the worst-case scenario, drawing most effectively on an event which had had a powerful impact in the recent history of western civilization, the French Revolution. Here, they would assert, was a good example of what would happen when one tried to use fundamental principles as a guide for the creation of a state, especially when those principles were oriented toward democracy. The rights reformers were proclaiming were those which had guided French revolutionaries, a point Benjamin Watkins Leigh made when he asked of Virginia, "how large a dose of French rights of man it can bear, without fever, frenzy, madness and death" (151). He used strong language to equate Virginia reform with French Jacobinism. John Randolph used even stronger language when he echoed Scott's point that moderates might have more to fear from reform principles than they suffered under the existing order. He did so by drawing reference to the Duke of Orleans, an aristocrat who nevertheless tried to cooperate with the radical leaders of the revolution. According to Randolph, "he lent himself to the *mountain* party in the Convention, in the vain and weak hope of grasping political power, perhaps of mounting the throne, still slippery with

87

the blood of the incumbent" (316), and he warned moderates to examine their own motives as well as the possibilities should they decide to work too closely with the leaders of reform.

The excesses of France were, of course, tailor-made for conservative argument, and attention had been drawn to the French example from the earliest days of reform agitation. The revolution in France, as one Virginia legislator declared in 1817, had roused the fondest hopes, only to blast those hopes in the "the wildest excesses," culminating in the reign of a Bonaparte.[21] As an example, it brought together much that conservatives asserted as part of their case. The behavior of the leaders of the revolution and, more especially, of the masses, provided a confirmation of what would happen should political participation be broadened extensively. It showed, in a horrifying way, the dangers of letting oneself be guided by principles rather than trying to maintain a government that had evolved naturally and in a way coherent with the peculiar conditions of the society. And, above all, it was a testimony to human weakness. Those who sought to order society according to principles were not necessarily evil men (although some, like the ill-fated duke, might use principle as pretext for satisfying selfish ambitions). Rather, the problem was that they sought to order a world, of which they could have only imperfect knowledge, according to principles based on the calculations of that "wretched finite human wisdom" which Leigh had mentioned. Any sort of artificial ordering for society, whether it were fundamental principles or, as Giles had mentioned, a doctrine like the divine right of Kings—"a mere human invention"—could never be adequate to capture society's complexities. Such a reformer as Alfred Powell might assert that there was something peculiar about the French that made them, like Turks or Russians, unfit to live under a republican form of government (104), but to conservatives the issue was different. It was a fundamental fact of human history that when passion guided human weakness, the result would be presumption and, finally,

88

disaster. The lesson of France was universal in its significance.

But there was another aspect of this attack on principle that was no less important, and it powerfully synthesized the kinds of points conservatives made when they referred to France or when they referred to the importance of matching government with existing conditions. In early 1829, debating on the convention bill, a member of the House of Delegates had raised a pointed question on the "fundamental principle" of political equality. Such a principle, he argued, was absurd: "This is an elementary principle: follow it in its full extent, and to what monstrous conclusion are we brought? Are not slaves men?"[22] The argument, needless to say, would be repeated incessantly by conservatives during the convention itself. To men of the East and the Piedmont, the force of the argument would have been especially strong, given their stake in the institution.

Here, again, one sees an argument that worked in more than one way. First, it served to arouse a general distrust of speculation by showing how following speculation could lead to a *reductio ad absurdum*—to votes for slaves or, as some would claim, even for women or children. And, of course, this forced reformers to acknowledge that they, too, accepted limits on political participation. The reference to slaves, in addition, augmented distrust with fear. Speculation leads to excess, and this can be dangerous, in a slave society when the excess is one of liberty. Conservatives had their favorite example of revolutionary France to show what speculative principles could produce. But, they also had a related example from closer to home that they could use with even greater power—Santo Domingo. Thus, answering reform references to the famous first clause in the Declaration of Rights, Philip Barbour argued for a relativistic interpretation. The words, he said, had reference "to the time when, and . . . to the people on whom they were intended to operate." He then declared, "And if you were to give to such a declaration its full operation, without the modifications which I have stated, you

89

might as a natural consequence, soon expect to see realized here, the frightful and appalling scenes of horror and desolation, which were produced in St. Domingo by a declaration of much the same tenor, issued by the famous National Assembly of France" (91). Here, boldly presented, was an episode at once historic and emotionally powerful, calculated to arouse the most ardent fears of a slaveholding people against the potential dangers of change for the sake of principle.

One should not underestimate the importance of the specific fear conservatives sought to arouse. Slavery was certainly an issue in the convention, although it occupied only a small part of the debates, and, indeed, some conservatives saw the need to protect slavery as an important reason for defeating reform. Abel P. Upshur, for instance, noted the "peculiar" nature of eastern property (75). Even James Madison strongly urged the need to protect slavery and to provide protection for the slaveholding part of the state in any constitution that was approved (538). Here, in great measure, was the hidden issue behind much that occurred on the question of reform, and it was a significant factor on which moderates and conservatives were united in distinction from the western delegates. Because moderate and conservative delegates alike represented plantation districts, where citizens had a stake in a slave society, too much talk of fundamental principles and political equality was incompatible with the stability of their world.

The Virginia Convention of 1829-30 was held over two years before the climactic debates in the state's legislature on emancipation and about two years, as well, before Nat Turner's spectacular rebellion would produce its profound effect on the Virginia mind. To conservatives, and even moderate reformers, however, slavery had become an established institution, one which they were committed to protecting. No one apologized for it, even as an unfortunate necessity, in 1829-30, although such apologies had been offered frequently during the Revolutionary years and even during much of the early national period. While no "positive good" arguments

90

emerged from the Convention of 1829-30, conservatives clearly took it for granted that slavery was, had been, and would continue to be a part of Virginia's way of life.

At the same time, conservatives presented fears for the institution that would anticipate Southern views up to the time of the Civil War. Slavery, they saw, was an inherently unstable institution. On the one hand, it had to be protected from outside threats, and they were prepared to find such threats in any action that challenged the established order. On the other, the slaves themselves were always a danger. There had been enough rebellions in the world, including the spectacular success of Santo Domingo, that Virginians would not need Nat Turner to have some idea of the danger, and most moderates, like conservatives, lived in areas where slaves were numerous. By tying such concerns for slavery to the very structure of the reform argument, conservatives had a powerful emotional weapon to turn against the entire enterprise of constitutional revision, especially on the crucial questions of suffrage and representation. They made a strong attack on the central theme of reform.

In talking of conservative strategy in this regard, one should not suggest that the arguments conservatives used were wholly selfserving or offered cynically. There is no doubt that conservatives shared in the fears for slavery which they tried to arouse in other delegates. The events of Santo Domingo had made a grave impression on the South of the early nineteenth century, and, indeed, a general distrust of speculation, shown by the horrors of France, seems to have been genuinely shared. When, for example, William Halyburton wrote to William Branch Giles in 1824 of his own democratic past, he was probably sincere: "Inflated with the spirit of French liberty," Halyburton confessed, "many of us about the year 1789 predicated our principles upon the metaphysics of Locke, the sophistry of Raynal, the madness of Rousseau, & Sir Thomas More," only to learn, as he said, "that every innovation or change was not an improvement." And he went on to deprecate abstractions not only in politics, but in every other area, including religion, where it "converts a christian into a savage, a moralist into a cold blooded calculator."[23] Given the reception of the French Revolution by Virginians in the late eighteenth century, many had probably gone through an experience like Halyburton's, particularly when faced by democratic demands in their own state. In any case, they had reason to feel the fears they expressed.

But the importance of the slavery question to the convention should not obscure the extent to which Virginia conservatism, as an ideology, was more generally antidemocratic in its thrust. Conservatives sought to deny the very basis for the apportionment and suffrage reforms against which they argued, and this meant that they had to go beyond treating those reforms only as bad alternatives for the Virginia political system. Their arguments had to show the basis of those reforms in democratic ideas to be false, and they did this by equating democracy itself with disorder. Such an equation was at the heart of their references to the French Revolution, and it was equally important to their evocations of Santo Domingo. Rampant democracy and not abolition was the target of attack in this setting.

What, then, did conservatives themselves offer as a proper alternative for a political system? Given their accounts of human nature, and particularly their acknowledgment of human weakness, it is not surprising that they professed to place great reliance on clearly established rules and procedures for governing what political men could do. Just as property provided a tangible check on greed and ambition by making men responsible, so too did an adherence to well-formulated rules provide a check on the way men could act in governing a society. Thus, from this point of view, conservatives could make a strong case against not only the goals of reform but the means by which reformers hoped to achieve those goals. Writing in 1825, for example, one "Mason of '76" (probably Leigh) declared that the reformers' "intemperate zeal for the attainment of their ends . . . blinded

92

them to the dangerous and anarchical tendency of their means," and on this basis would "condemn the principle" of the Staunton Convention held that year because people had gone outside normal channels in their drive for constitutional reform.[24] William Brockenbrough, refusing an appointment to that same Staunton Convention, made a similar point. For the people to take initiative in political affairs that takes them outside "regular" channels for action invites disorder; to maintain such channels is the only way to insure political security.[25]

It was from this perspective, too, that conservatives talked about the nature and meaning of constitutions. Jefferson, in a famous letter to Samuel Kercheval, had ridiculed men who "look at constitutions with sanctimoniousness and reverence,"[26] but this was a fairly accurate assessment of conservative arguments. To reform assertions that constitutional change was necessary in order to reflect changing conditions, conservatives replied that constitutions were too important, and the Virginia constitution too hallowed by tradition, to be revised. One politician, arguing against revision in 1817, made the argument in a way that was a virtual paradigm for years to come:

> Can I . . . without pangs unutterable, give up this Constitution, the instructor of my youth, from which I formed my first political opinions, this more than gift from Heaven, this temple of liberty, erected by the wisdom and cemented by the best blood of our fathers, in which I have devoutly worshipped for more than 40 years . . . Save, for God's sake, save the Constitution—"Don't give up the ship."[27]

Mixed metaphors notwithstanding, in citing the familiarity of the constitution, this speaker aroused feelings for the "old ship" that later conservatives would also declare. Giles drew on a structural metaphor himself when, in convention, he declared his faith in the 1776 Constitution. To criticize that document was to attack the fathers of the country. "Instead of tearing down the splendid structure they have raised," he said, "let us call them from their tombs, and award them the highest posthumous honors" (256).

But here as well, conservatives sought above all to arouse their audience's fear of change. The existing system had been devised by great men; subsequent generations had prospered under it. It was a fixed system of laws and rules, hallowed by time, with which everyone was familiar. Hugh Grigsby, in a letter to young John Tazewell, had asked, rhetorically, if men were "prepared to say that they will part with solid good to realise an Utopian scheme?"[28] John Coalter, of King George, said something similar in convention. Stressing that Virginia's Constitution was "the *first written instrument* of the kind," Coalter prophesied that should it be "expunged . . . and if our people shall be as happy during the next fifty years, we will have made a lucky escape" (518-519). It was not the reform argument alone about which conservatives sought to arouse fears. It was, again, the whole question of change.

And this, too, could be tied to conservative concepts of human nature and to the defense of the freehold. As "Mason of '76" wrote in one of his 1825 newspaper pieces, "It is an essential quality in the definition of republican government, that it is a government of *fixed and certain laws*, not a government of mere *will*, whether exercised by one or many."[29] Here was a position that justified conservatism as it answered reform arguments. Deprecatory toward human nature, conservatives could easily assert the importance of rules for maintaining a political order, because rules were designed to prevent any individual from acting selfishly. Like property, rules offered a tangible check against human greed and ambition and helped to insure that action would be for the public good. When rules became uncertain, however, as they would if they were too easily subject to change, then anyone with sufficient strength of will would be encouraged to exercise it for his own benefit. Human will was inevitably at odds

94

with social order; change, because it gave opportunity to willful men, could only place any order in grave danger.

To be sure, in arguing the dangers of change, conservatives were in a difficult position. First, they also liked to suggest that government ought to be suited to a particular time and place. Secondly, they claimed that change was undesirable and dangerous. What, then, if society changes so much as to require a different form of government? As Jefferson had written to Kercheval, "as new discoveries are made, new truths disclosed, and manners and opinions change, institutions must advance also, and keep pace with the times. We might as well require a man to wear still the coat which fitted him when a boy, as civilized society to remain even under the regime of their barbarous ancestors."[30] Real changes in society, reformers could argue, required corresponding changes in institutions.

The conservative response was simply to deny that changes had occurred, at least to a degree that would justify major alterations in the form of government. According to Philip Barbour, the convention was trying to form "a Constitution which is to last for ages, and we should be careful not to mistake temporary and fluctuating varieties of interests, for those of a permanent and irreconcileable nature" (102). Along these lines, Barbour and other conservatives would dismiss Jefferson's view, also asserted by later reformers, that evolving differences of "situation and circumstances" among Virginia's regions should mandate constitutional changes, as well. The nature of constitutions and the inability of men to understand the complexities of the world made adjustments to a plan of government ill-advised and dangerous, just as the reasons proposed for reform were themselves insufficiently justified. Change might have to occur in history, but it should occur only when historical conditions forced it, not in response to transient fluctuations in demography or interest.

There was one other way in which conservatives sought to evoke among delegates a fear of change. This was through

95

their use of metaphor. Conservatives used metaphorical language sparingly in their speeches. They did use it some, however, and in ways that were remarkably revealing of their attitudes toward the state of the political system.

By far the greatest amount of imagery in conservative speeches was related, in one way or another, to human biology. The body, its characteristics and needs, provided speakers with apt metaphors for conveying their thoughts and feelings. It summarized much that they believed about human nature and society. In particular, conservatives tended to draw on images of pain and disease in order to present ideas about political events. Such metaphors clearly cohered with much they wanted to say about politics. The human body, they often noted, was both strong and fragile, composed of bone and sinew, but subject to fatal disease. Pessimistic and mistrustful of human nature, conservatives most liked to evoke that human vulnerability, through metaphors of infection, weakening, and healing.

Littleton W. Tazewell made a fairly typical use of figures taken from biology when, warning the convention to treat the constitution with prudence, he asked, "Will you dissect, will you dissever the body said to be gangrenous, before you know where the gangrene is? Will you at once cut into the vitals and separate it limb from limb, under pretence of searching for the unsound part?" (17). In this, Tazewell evoked the fragility of the system as, at the same time, he argued for limits on the degree of "liberty" that society could allow. John Randolph made a similar case against reform demands, especially those based on principles, when he likened reform efforts to trying to "at once prescribe all the medicines in the Pharmacopoeia, not only for the disease I now have, but for all the diseases of every kind I might ever have in future" (313). Characterizing reform demands as excessive and based on a lack of awareness of the specific conditions of society, Tazewell and Randolph also emphasized the dangers which reform—like careless medicine or reckless Pharmacopoeia—could pose to a stable social order.

96

This bodily imagery, focusing as it did on disease, conveyed important feelings about the mortality and fragility of the political system. It is perhaps no accident that John Randolph, who used such metaphors to powerful effect, was also a confessed hypochondriac.[31] Disease struck often in that time, and it was, moreover, something against which people were relatively helpless in those days of poor sanitation and hit-and-miss remedies. This is not to advance a "disease theory" of Virginia politics. It is to say that metaphors of disease were particularly useful for talking about the fragile quality of the temporal order and about the relative weakness of men to preserve that order against the ravages of evil forces, because one could readily see the ravages of disease.

Something similar may be said about another important group of images in Virginia rhetoric, those having to do with nature. Nature was invoked by conservatives in several ways, one of which was to express orderliness and permanence. Men exposed to Enlightenment views, they acknowledged order to be the law of the universe and referred, as did Piedmont conservative Philip Barbour, to "the light of the sun, bright, constant, and uniform," which, he said, was like experience, something to be relied upon (96). It was in this same spirit that "Backwoodsman," in his letter to the *Richmond Enquirer,* had argued that one does not reject the sun "for the spots on its disk" and suggested that "the spirit of reformation may aspire to amend the system of the Universe."[32]

However, as "Backwoodsman's" remarks suggest, the real problem was that if nature were an orderly system it was, nevertheless, not entirely accessible to human understanding or prediction. There were the eternal verities, as Barbour said, but the same nature which had created the sun had also produced the meteor, "transient in its splendor, and uncertain and irregular in all its movements," and if experience could be likened to the sun, the meteor was an apt metaphor for human experiment, for efforts at innovation. It might look spectacular, but its course was far from regular (96). This point of view was caught not only in cosmic metaphor,

97

but in those metaphors of nature which were closer to experience, those of weather. Reform, conservatives would claim, was a tempest, a storm, a flood which had to be withstood. Like the meteor, weather indicated an aspect of nature to which all were subject, but over which no one had the slightest control. That such a view was compelling in an agricultural society where men's fortunes were subject to the weather is beyond doubt.

Indeed, the frailty of man's works in the face of nature was a point that conservatives made frequently in their remarks. Surely the most hackneyed metaphor in the Virginia repertoire was that of the ship—of state, of the nation, the constitution—launched out onto troubled waters. Men of every political persuasion used it to cover a multitude of matters, and had done so for years. Madison, writing to Jefferson on the problems facing the United States in 1785, advised "Congress have kept the Vessel from sinking, but it has been by standing constantly at the pump, not by stopping the leaks which have endangered her."[33] Patrick Henry, taking the antifederalist position in the convention of 1788, would declare, " 'Tis the fortune of a republic to be able to withstand the stormy ocean of human vicissitudes," later denying that "the worms have taken possession of the wood, that our strong vessel—our political vessel, has sprung a leak."[34] He did not share Madison's fears, nor those of George Washington that the nation was headed toward "a political shipwreck."[35]

Maritime metaphors would continue through the years, and with about the same usage. In 1829-30 John Coalter would use one to describe the convention itself and the 1776 Constitution, declaring, "we are thrown on rather a tempestuous ocean; and not being accustomed to such voyages, I am getting somewhat sea-sick. I wish, it possible, to see land; to see my family, and to see my friends and constituents, who are looking out for the *good old ship*, the Constitution with no little anxiety" (516). His words evoked a general misgiving many Virginians would express toward human efforts. This may have been a period in which intellectuals throughout

98

western civilization were becoming increasingly optimistic about man's ability to know and to control nature,[36] but such optimism would have been inconsistent with the general thrust of the conservative case. These men tended to use metaphor in a way that supported their assertion of man's lack of control over his world, whether they spoke of his knowledge of nature, or disease, or his ability to build ships. Their images tended to stress, instead, the weakness of human achievements and the vulnerability of man to time and nature. In this, they metaphorically expressed their own pessimism by pointing out human pretence in claiming to create anything in a world where nature, including human nature, was finally in command.

That they should have used metaphor in making this point is revealing. Robert Shalhope, in an important essay on Jefferson, has pointed out that the technical vocabulary of the day was inadequate to describe many of the social changes occurring in America during the early nineteenth century. Hence, Shalhope suggests, Jefferson had to speak and write metaphorically in order to talk about those things.[37] Something similar may be said in regard to Virginia conservatives. They, too, faced a changing ideological and social reality, which was presented to them quite graphically by the reform movement as it gained strength after 1800. Such new challenges, it may have been, caused them to turn to metaphor, even if to traditional metaphors, in order to put those challenges in a clearer perspective. It is a measure of this that there was an increase in the use of metaphor by conservatives as the debate escalated during the century.

The metaphors conservatives used in 1829-30 performed, in other words, a vital cognitive function. Figurative language serves in rhetoric primarily to identify the unknown or the abstract by reference to something familiar.[38] By linking difficult political notions analogically or emotionally with the world around them, orators or writers are able to make political situations appear more tangible and more intelligible to their audiences and, thus, to persuade people that they are

99

receiving a valid characterization of events. Metaphor makes any position seem understandable and real. Conservatives' metaphors thus gave a graphic account of the fear of reformers and of reform proposals which they hoped to convey to moderate delegates. At the same time, one should not ignore the importance of the fact that they relied, by and large, on traditional metaphors in getting the message across. Putting the reform challenge in terms of a figurative language that had been used for years to characterize political discussion on a range of issues, they found a way of making reform familiar and of evoking a response which had also been evoked successfully in the past. Conservatives thus sought to force moderate delegates to see western reform as a movement like others which, as allies of the East, they had confronted in the past. Poetic metaphors allow us to see old things in new, vivid ways; those of political speaking make the new appear old and call forth familiar modes of action and it was in this way that conservatives used them in 1829-30.

The same may be said of the more general conservative predictions of the catastrophes likely to follow any major change. In oratory or debate, speakers draw heavily on their culture for what they say, explaining events in terms of the kinds of causes and elements most people in the society agree to be possible. They create "hypothetical patterns of reality" according to which events may be understood and predictions made.[39] The conservatives' awful predictions represent such projections. Given what we know about human nature, they would argue, disaster will occur if we approve of reform. Having created a hypothetical reality based on human nature and history, they could make their dire predictions from it. At the same time, however, when they put these projections into the language of disorder—of rapine, of violence, even of disease or storms—they were attempting to involve their audience emotionally in their predictions. They wanted to create strong doubts and fears in those who had made commitments to moderate change.

Much of the thrust of Virginia conservatism, then, lay in

100

conveying a fear of change. Conservative Virginians some-how had to convey such a fear not only to each other but also to those moderates with whom they had to work if the impact of reform were to be limited. Ideas alone would not have been enough, nor would simple appeals to interest, since there were conflicts there. They had to address the emotions, to create fear about western demands, and they sought to do this cognitively and affectively in their accounts of human nature and history, and in their presentations of human weakness and vulnerability.

At the same time, one should note, the attack upon reform was not the conservative argument's only focus. Conservatives also portrayed some positive characteristics of the existing system. In his valuable study of the Federalist party, David Hackett Fischer has shown the skill with which members of that party were able to employ republican rhetoric to justify their pursuit of decidedly elitist policies.[40] Virginia conservatives, who shared many Federalist views, also expressed great respect for republican government, but, on questions of government and policy, they did not try to hide their "real" interests. What their rhetoric shows is something more complex. By the time of the Convention of 1829-30, they had come to identify their interests fairly completely with slaves and land and to understand that those interests were threatened by western reformers. Again, they wanted to convince moderates to act on the same kind of understand-ing. Adopting an interest view did not, however, mean that they felt compelled also to adopt the liberal acceptance of a society composed of competing interests. To the contrary, they tended to retain the main emphases of classical politics, stretching them to cover what was a seemingly new state of affairs—a society in which the governing hegemony was fac-ing a strong challenge from men whose interests really were quite different from their own.

Despite their recognition of the necessity of interest poli-tics, Virginia conservatives claimed to see no virtue in com-petition, whether social, political, or economic, and they

101

tended to ascribe conflicting interests to passion. They valued stability and order, and for reasons that were quite consistent with their general views. Most conservatives would have agreed with a letter writer of 1825 who declared, "Order, the first law of the Universe, is the basis and foundation of human happiness."[41] In general, moreover, Virginia conservatives were in agreement as to what a proper social and political order should be like.

Virginia conservatives, almost from the opening of the reform effort, had to face strong charges from reformers of desiring aristocracy. Addressing conservatives in the convention, and responding to their anti-majoritarian arguments, Alexander Campbell declared, "if this does not squint towards aristocracy, if it does not lead us towards the principles assumed by the monarchists of the old world, I am not a judge of such matters" (118). Conservatives, of course, often professed their devotion to republican government, but they did not, at the same time, acknowledge human equality. For them, the basis of order was hierarchy, and they clung to the rightness of inequality tenaciously. According to them, hierarchy was a product of the diversity of mankind. Some men were simply more gifted than others, just as some were of different colors, and abstractions could not make them equal in fact.

Virginians' notions of inequality were related, in part, to contractarian views of government. Governments, they said, were compacts in which each party surrendered some of his sovereignty in exchange for order and security. But conservatives did not separate the necessity of contracting from their negative assessments of human nature. Hobbesians in so many ways, conservatives approved Philip Barbour's contention that governments "are founded in jealousy and guarded by caution" (97). Such caution was best expressed by George C. Dromgoole, who would be a delegate from Brunswick, in an earlier speech to the legislature opposing the convention. "When society emerges from the chaos of nature," he declared, "when government is instituted, when the actions of man are subjected to the salutary restraints of municipal law, and when for the common good some are invested with powers which others do not possess, the natural equality of man is then necessarily destroyed."[42]

The way Dromgoole put his ideas was important. The issues were suffrage and representation, and conservatives like Dromgoole made it clear that they were denying neither natural rights nor natural equality—not denying, that is, the first sentence of the Virginia Declaration of Rights. They were arguing, however, that political rights were distinct from natural rights and that political rights were the product of conditions, not of nature. Barbour put the view succinctly in convention, asserting, "it is the very nature of the social compact, that all who enter into it, surrender a portion of their natural rights, in exchange for which they acquire other rights, derived from that compact and dependent on it, both in character and extent." (91). Here was simply an active version of the assertion that principles of government were derived from practice: significant rights, too, grew out of the reality of a particular society, and what this meant, above all, was that some men more than others had the right to as well as the need for political participation.

Here, clearly, was the import of Dromgoole's remarks before the legislature. The common good requires that some should have "powers which others do not possess," and, again, for conservative Virginians, this view could be most clearly stated in terms of property. Those who had the independence and community-interest property conferred were those most fit to decide political questions. They were also the ones who had the greatest need for the security that government provides. But there was a corollary to this argument, since Virginia conservatives admitted only one kind of property as conferring both privilege and need—land. In this, conservatives were describing a society in which only a single criterion was to determine social position, in which relative control over a single resource was to rank everyone. Hierarchy, as a result, was necessary to their version of soci-

103

ety, just as the validity of competing systems for ranking was dismissed. Hierarchical contractarian assumptions, then, reinforced ideas of the moral influence of property on its holders to justify limited participation in Virginia politics. It was not, however, simply an assumption that hierarchy was somehow natural and, hence, correct, because such an assumption could not have been comfortably maintained in the face of their more relativistic assertions about political principles. Instead, and with more sophistication, conservatives acknowledged the relative character of distinctions while asserting their necessity, and they argued for a consistent criterion, *in Virginia,* upon which distinctions should be based.

J.G.A. Pocock has rightly pointed out that in classical politics there was a general inability to devise a satisfactory theory of party,[43] largely because of the dichotomy between passion and interest. Conservative Virginians decried party, or faction, often enough, and, committed to a view that rejected the possibility of competing interests with equal claims, they could not present party in other than negative terms. History showed that men could and would combine to conspire against the public good, and it was to such combinations that conservatives meant to refer when they spoke of party or faction. But, in 1829, they were not really concerned to devise a satisfactory theory. The point was to denigrate reform, not to come to terms with it, and this their views of hierarchy allowed them to do.

The men of the West were offering a competing status system, based on age, on sex, on natural rights, and on color. Virginia's conservatives could address their colleagues and the moderates on two grounds. One was, consistent with the general fears they evoked, the instability that would result when the proper harmony of society was disturbed through the acceptance of a social arrangement in which status could be interpreted in terms of competing criteria. Secondly, moderate delegates were united with conservatives in the East by their own position in the single system conservatives would accept, one based on property-holding and slave owning. On that ground, conservative status was moderate status, too.

NOTES – CHAPTER THREE

1. Hugh Blair Grigsby to John Tazewell, February 3, 1829, Tazewell family papers, Personal Papers collection, Archives Branch, Virginia State Library, Richmond.

2. *Proceedings and Debates of the Virginia State Convention of 1829-30. To Which Are Subjoined, the New Constitution of Virginia, and the Votes of the People* (Richmond: Ritchie and Cook, 1830), p. 125. In this chapter, subsequent citations to the *Proceedings* will, like this one, be by page numbers, in parentheses, in the text.

3. Richard Henry Lee, *The Letters of Richard Henry Lee*, ed. James Curtis Ballagh, 2 vols. (New York: Macmillan, 1911-1914), 2: 441-42. See, on this general issue, Bernard Bailyn, *Ideological Origins of the American Revolution* (Cambridge: Harvard Univ. Press, 1967), p. 59; J.G.A. Pocock, *The Machiavellian Moment: Florentine Political Thought and the Atlantic Republican Tradition* (Princeton: Princeton Univ. Press, 1975), pp. 522-27.

4. Pocock, ibid., pp. 333, 463.

5. Edmund S. Morgan, "Slavery and Freedom: The American Paradox," *Journal of American History* 59 (1972): 5-29.

6. Edmund Randolph, *History of Virginia*, ed. Arthur H. Shaffer (Charlottesville: Univ. Press of Virginia, 1970), p. 257.

7. John Taylor, *A Definition of Parties; or the Political Effects of the Paper System Considered* (Philadelphia: Francis Bailey, 1794), p. 9.

8. *Richmond Daily Whig*, January 28, 1829.

9. See, on this, Albert O. Hirschman, *The Passions and the Interests: Political Arguments for Capitalism Before Its Triumph* (Princeton: Princeton Univ. Press, 1977), pp. 40-41, 63-64.

10. This, too, was a familiar opinion. See ibid., p. 70.

11. Gordon S. Wood, *The Creation of the American Republic, 1776-1787* (1969; New York: Norton, 1972), p. 405.

12. Thomas R. Dew, *Lectures on the Restrictive System, Delivered to the Senior Political Class of William and Mary College* (Richmond: Samuel Shepherd, 1829), p. 12.

13. James Madison, *Letters and Other Writings of James Madison, Fourth President of the United States. In Four Volumes. Published by Order of Congress* (Philadelphia: Lippincott, 1867), 4: 3.

14. Cooke's words reproduced, almost verbatim, part of an earlier pamphlet, "The Constitution of '76." By a Member of the Staunton Convention (Richmond?: 1825? pamphlet in the Virginia Historical Society), pp. 44-45.

15. Douglass G. Adair, " 'Experience Must Be Our Only Guide': History, Democratic Theory, and the United States Constitution," in *The Reinterpretation of Early American History: Essays in Honor of John Edwin Pomfret*, ed. Ray Allen Billington (San Marino: The Huntington Library, 1966), p. 132.

16. James Monroe, *The Writings of James Monroe, Including a Collection of His Public and Private Papers and Correspondence Now for the First Time Printed*, ed. Stanislaus Murray Hamilton, 7 vols. (New York: Putnam's, 1898-1903), 1: 341.

17. See, on the ancestry of this view, W. Paul Adams, "Republicanism in Political Rhetoric Before 1776," *Political Science Quarterly* 85 (1970): 412-16.

18. Donald H. Meyer, *The Democratic Enlightenment* (New York: Putnam's, 1976), pp. 98-100.

19. *Richmond Enquirer*, August 13, 1825.

20. William Halyburton to William Branch Giles, May 25, 1824. Virginia Historical Society, Richmond.

21. *Richmond Enquirer*, January 30, 1817.

22. *Richmond Daily Whig*, January 15, 1829.

23. Halyburton to Giles.

24. *Richmond Enquirer*, June 28, 1825.

25. Ibid., June 3, 1825.

26. Thomas Jefferson, *The Writings of Thomas Jefferson*, ed. Paul Leicester Ford, 10 vols. (New York: Putnam's 1892-99), 10: 42.

27. *Richmond Enquirer*, February 1, 1817.

28. Hugh Blair Grigsby to John Tazewell, January 17, 1829, Tazewell family papers.

29. *Richmond Enquirer*, June 28, 1825.

30. Jefferson, *Writings*, ed. Ford, 10: 43.

31. John Randolph, *Letters of John Randolph, to a Young Relative: Embracing a Series of Years, from Early Youth, to Mature Manhood* (Philadelphia: Carey, Lea and Blanchard, 1834), p. 204. This collection shows Randolph to have been frequently in ill health.

32. *Richmond Enquirer*, August 13, 1825.

33. James Madison, *The Writings of James Madison, Comprising His Public Papers and Private Correspondence*, ed. Gaillard Hunt, 9 vols. (New York: Putnam's, 1900-1910), 2: 178.

34. *Debates and other Proceedings of the Convention of Virginia, Convened at Richmond, on Monday the 2d day of June, 1788, for the purpose of deliberating on the Constitution recommended by the Grand Federal Convention* (2d ed. Richmond: Ritchie and Worsley and Augustine Davis, 1805), p. 107.

35. George Washington, *The Writings of George Washington from the Original Manuscript Sources, 1745-1799*, ed. John C. Fitzpatrick, 39 vols., (Washington: Government Printing Office, 1931-1944), 30: 41.

36. Carl Becker, *The Heavenly City of the Eighteenth-Century Philosophers* (New Haven: Yale Univ. Press, 1932), p. 65.

37. Robert E. Shalhope, "Thomas Jefferson's Republicanism and Antebellum Southern Thought," *Journal of Southern History* 42 (1976): 538.

38. Philip Wheelwright, *Metaphor and Reality* (Bloomington: Indiana Univ. Press, 1968), pp. 72-73.

39. Doris A. Graber, *Verbal Behavior and Politics* (Urbana: Univ. of Illinois Press, 1976), p. 48.

40. David Hackett Fischer, *The Revolution of American Conservatism: The Federalist Party in the Era of Jeffersonian Democracy* (New York: Harper, 1965), p. 49.

41. *Richmond Enquirer,* August 13, 1825.

42. *Richmond Daily Whig,* March 11, 1829.

43. Pocock, *Machivellian Moment,* p. 483.

CHAPTER FOUR

A Gathering of Gentlemen: Political Culture and Conservative Strategy in the Convention of 1829-30

Why did conservatives argue as they did in the Convention of 1829-30? Given all the possible grounds on which they could have stressed an identity of status and interest between themselves and moderate delegates, conservatives still chose to make a case that was heavily ideological in putting forth a theory of government and in looking to conceptions of human nature and history in order to justify that theory. Moreover, they chose to use a certain kind of political language in making their case: a limited but consistent stock of metaphors, a rejection of dependence upon fundamental principles, a continuing use of references to France and Santo Domingo. That they should have presented the case as they did was no less important to the conservative strategy of allying with moderates than was the substance of the arguments as such. Conservatives made the kinds of arguments they did because they and their moderate audience had rather strong expectations about how political deliberation should take place, expectations which were themselves relevant to the meaning to be derived from those arguments. Such expectations provided an important link between what conservatives said and the experiences of those whom they addressed.

To understand the expectations regarding political process that united conservative and moderate convention delegates, one must examine, first, the political culture that had been accepted and used by Virginia leaders, especially those in the traditional, eastern-based elite, since at least the late colonial period. "Political culture" may be defined, following Sidney Verba, as "the system of empirical beliefs, expressive symbols, and values which defines the situation in which political action takes place." As such, it would include the political style, the cognitive predispositions, and the operative ideals which are accepted in a political community,[1] and one may see it most clearly by examining the ideas members of a group profess about how political process does take place and, perhaps more importantly, their ideas about how it should take place. The political culture traditional in Virginia, and the one professed by conservatives in 1829-30, might best be summarized by drawing analogy to the atmosphere of a social occasion. According to this view, political decisions ought to be made by means of an open, candid deliberation involving men of similar status and similar interests. The best political leaders would act, as Judith Randolph wrote to her husband John, with a "disinterested integrity," and all proceedings would be characterized by what George Tucker called that "cool and sober discussion of a subject, which is alone favourable to the elucidation of truth."[2] Gentlemanliness, amiability, candor, and disinterestedness were to mark the discussions of issues.

To be sure, this view of politics was an ideal. One need not look very hard to find situations in which conservatives themselves strayed far from the standard, but, as an ideal, it was still important to moderates and conservatives alike in the early nineteenth century. One sees it expressed, for example, in an 1825 letter written to the *Richmond Enquirer* by a moderate, in which he charged one of his more conservative colleagues with "a violation of public decorum" and, he added, "The public are interested in this as it has an interest in the preservation of propriety in the *discussions* of political and moral questions, as well as in the conduct of those whose talents or confidence enable them to take a part in them."[3] As

110

an ideal, even if often breached, it provided an important standard for Virginians who sought to present themselves and their arguments in the most effective way during the Convention of 1829-30.

The major role of this political ideal was to underlie many of the crucial points Virginians sought to make in the convention, because of the ways it implied the necessity of maintaining the existing system against the kinds of changes sought by democratic reformers. For one thing, it was a model that virtually demanded homogeneity among those who took part in political discussions. Just as conservatives sought to reject the possibility of permanent, competing divisions along lines of interest in the political system, so too would such a rejection inform their understanding of the deliberative process as such. To a great extent, it was a matter of the inability of men, in such a situation, to take part in the kind of honest, open discussion that ought to characterize the decision-making process. Permanent divisions meant that the deliberative body would be composed of factions rather than individuals coming together as equals, and when men were part of factions, their sole interest tended to be, as Henry St. George Tucker wrote in 1808, to "follow their file leader with all the scrupulous exactness of a prussian recruit."[4] Here, there was no give-and-take, only a lining up of votes.

Virginians, in fact, embodied this point of view in speeches they made in the Convention of 1829-30. Abel P. Upshur, who was not solidly in the conservative camp though he tended to speak on the conservative side, made an appeal in which he combined this rejection of factionalism with an ideal for political decision-making that involved compromise and candor. Beginning a strongly conservative speech in opposition to basing apportionment on white population alone–and referring to reform as "the other side"–Upshur nevertheless professed to be "without any feelings of local partiality or local prejudice," adding, "it is my duty to consider myself the representative of the whole State, and not of

111

any peculiar part of it." Then he would assert his own willingness to seek a middle ground on the question of apportionment:

> In a community like our own, no Government can gain undivided affection, nor secure the undivided support of the people, unless it spring from a fair and equitable compromise of interests. It was therefore my earnest hope, that there would be no necessity for a formal array of parties upon this point ... I was, and still am ready, to advance quite, nay, *more* than half way; for I feel entirely assured, that the great interests committed to our charge, require this temper in every one of us.

It was not a "temper," he added, easily found on the reform side.[5] Upshur's comments are revealing, and not only because they represented what moderates had to hope for in the convention. In an attack leveled mainly at reform leaders, Upshur's words themselves referred back to political norms that were important in Virginia, providing the context within which arguments were to be made. No one could enter a debate stating that his mind was made up on any issue, because, in that event, he would be unlikely to participate openly and disinterestedly in the discussion which took place.

However, homogeneity meant more than simply the absence of permanent divisions. It meant, too, the kinds of similarities which enabled men to talk to each other easily, and this implied that there had to be some control over who was allowed to take part in political discussions. Indeed, this view provided one excellent justification for opposing "universal" suffrage. Nathaniel Beverly Tucker made precisely this point when he described the democratic state of Missouri, then on the frontier, as a place inhabited by "disconnected individuals," asserting that men "likely to be elected by universal suffrage" were themselves unlikely to be familiar with each other. "Where all are new to each other," he wrote, intelligence and virtue were simply "too apt to be discountenanced by intrigue and sophistry and the flattery of demagogues." Here was a major point underlying Virginia

112

arguments against extending political participation. If men knew each other, they were more likely to talk to each other honestly because it would be far more difficult for them to engage in deceit or dissimulation. In such a situation, one could not easily get away with an insincere performance.[6]

Tucker's point indicates yet another way in which Virginia normative politics underlay conservative concerns. As opponents of democracy, conservatives professed to have little faith in the mass of the people, pointing often to what they had characterized as the noxious influence of the people on political life: in their arguments, conservatives had characterized the people as the chief source for disruptive passions in society. In the narrower confines of the political process as such, conservatives would predict with great frequency that any extension of the right of suffrage "would produce tumultous and corrupt elections,"[7] and beyond that, as Tucker's words suggested, it would cause politicians to be concerned less with talking to each other than with talking to their constituents, merely using the deliberative assembly as a rostrum.

As Virginians understood the matter, addressing oneself to "the people out of doors" would have the same effect on deliberation as would faction. Political leaders would be less interested in listening to each other than in maintaining popularity with their constituents. As St. George Tucker once noted, on a related matter, the administration of the law often meant doing the unpopular thing, and this could be extremely difficult if the lawmakers' ears were tuned primarily to the wishes of the electorate. The deliberative body itself, relatively homogenous in composition, was to be the focus of a legislator's attention.

In the convention, then, when conservatives asserted the necessity of order and hierarchy in a political system, when they condemned faction, and when they spoke of the licentiousness of the masses, their words referred back to key components of their political culture: to a value on homogeneity and sociability and to a belief, stressed by their

113

rejection of appeals directed "out of doors" that a community of leaders ought somehow to stand apart from the rest of society. The main connotation which this view of politics gave to the conservative argument lay in its implication that, as the state was governed, such a community of leaders did exist in Virginia, its integrity guaranteed by its foundation in property-holding and its continuing control over channels to political power in the state. Thus, underlying the specific content of the arguments offered in the convention was a belief, reinforced by the standards of their more broadly-based political culture, that there was a community to be preserved and that the challenge of reform was in great measure a challenge to the survival of a proper way of conducting the state's affairs. The threat was not simply to the system, but to the moral foundations of that system as well.

One sees how conservatives treated reform as such a threat, for example, in their use of the charge of demagoguery against reform efforts. Demagoguery, one should note, virtually apotheosized aspects of political life that were antithetical to Virginia political culture. For one thing, demagoguery depended upon appealing to people "out of doors," and it depended, as well upon having an audience whose passions were not restrained by the salutary force of property. In addition, the demagogue himself was the very opposite of what a political leader should be, not only because he addressed the wrong audience but also because he placed little importance upon honesty and candor in himself. "Like the *Hyena*," St. George Tucker once wrote, "he whines and counterfeits gentleness, disinterestedness, and *patriotism*, amongst those whom he wishes to cajole, & enlist in his party." But, having succeeded in winning them, "he finally throws off the mask, and becomes a *Tyrant*."[8] In the charge of demagoguery Virginians were able to bring together and use some major aspects of their political culture.

Not surprisingly, given this, conservatives made frequent use of the charge as they sought to counter reform. Thus, for example, in 1817, William Branch Giles would write a news-

114

paper piece describing reform arguments as offering little more than the doctrine that, "the people can do no wrong," and, he added, it was merely a part of "the business of hunting popularity. . . by cajoling and flattering the people, under various ingenious disguises."[9] Reform was, in other words, dangerous demagoguery, a flattering of the people for the reformers' own destructive, selfish ends. Thus considered, one could condemn both reform goals and reform leaders in an effort to win moderate support, by bringing main themes of the political culture to bear on issues of constitutional reform.

To be sure, the political culture of nineteenth-century conservative Virginians was not new to them. Virginia leaders in earlier times had also professed similar views on political life, and for much the same reasons. In 1787, for example, George Mason had anticipated the Philadelphia convention which would later produce the Federal Constitution with the hope that "a proper Degree of Coolness, Liberality, & Candour" would mark the proceedings.[10] One "Decius," writing in 1789, presented a virtual catalog of sins when he wrote that politics had come to be dominated by "designing" men: "Some perhaps may wish to create differences and distinctions which may endanger our dearest rights; and others may intend *to smile in our faces* and *fawn at our feet*, to throw us off our guard, and stab us to the heart."[11] Thus, when the Chair of the Convention of 1829-30 had to rule that it was "not in order to attribute a want of sincerity to members of the House,"[12] he was referring to an application of political norms that had been known for some time. It was an important background conservatives could draw on in the face of movements for political reform.

But the relevance of this political culture to the conservative argument went deeper than simply to provide a basis for charges of demagoguery. Again, one element of conservatism was founded on the implication that as Virginia's leadership was constituted, the state's political life was ordered in terms of the main components of the political culture, or, at

115

least, that the culture was more likely to survive under conservative leadership than under that of the West. This implication depended, first, upon the basic similarity of moderate and conservative delegates, a similarity which grew out of common cultural and political characteristics that distinguished these men from those of the West. At the same time however, if conservatives' identification of themselves with the values and norms of the political culture were to make sense and if such a charge as that of demagoguery were not to be empty, then there had to be certain rather specific areas of political behavior to which conservatives could point as they distinguished themselves from reformers. Such specifics would give weight to what conservatives said about themselves and their opponents and, as Upshur's words show for example, would provide a framework within which conservatives could make their own words and actions appear to approach their political ideals. That is to say, conservative political culture greatly influenced its defenders' sense of how to make an appropriate argument in the convention setting.

In keeping with the emphasis on deliberation in Virginia political culture, a major focus for its application by conservatives was on political language, its use and abuse. Language-use was valuable in this regard, because it was the most tangible aspect of political behavior to which Virginians could refer as they sought to apply the norms of their political culture. The specific issues of language-use made concrete the main themes of political culture, allowing Virginians to judge each other's behavior and guiding them as they sought to behave in the most acceptable and, hence, the most effective way.

To see why this was so, one should note, first, that conservative Virginians did assign great importance to political language as such. In political deliberations, language could move others to act and this meant that conservatives had to have the best speaking if they wanted to win in the Convention of 1829-30. Some evidence for this is found in the prep-

116

arations Virginia's leaders made prior to the convention's opening. Men on both sides of the reform issue thought enough of the debates to do a good deal of homework in advance of the convention, corresponding with each other as they outlined the arguments they would make when the body met. Moreover, each side had its spokesmen, and, again, such an observer as Hugh Blair Grigsby was able to identify them with some accuracy well in advance of the convention. Their importance may be emphasized by pointing out that in the convention, only thirty-nine of the ninety-six delegates made major addresses, and of those, only four took the floor to make such an address as many as five times. The three men who accounted for almost half of the major conservative speeches, Randolph, Leigh, and Upshur, were widely known in Virginia as powerful orators. One did not have to be a great or even a good orator to achieve political success in early national Virginia, but good orators occupied an important place in the political process.

Virginians' practices in this regard merely manifested views of political language which they often professed. When, for example, William Halyburton suggested to William Branch Giles that, "words are weapons, by which cunning men govern the world,"[13] he presented his own rather pessimistic view of the power of language in the political arena. Educated Virginians, moreover, had learned to make a similar assessment of the power of language when, as all educated people had, they enrolled in college rhetoric classes. Thus, a William and Mary student in the early national period would note, in a class based on George Campbell's popular rhetoric textbook, that, "No one can be eloquent without producing the desired effect," and that, "If an orator fails to produce the desired effect the fault is in himself."[14] Language was, to them, a powerful resource in any political situation.

Indeed, because language was powerful its abuse could seriously endanger the deliberative process. Virginians reserved special condemnation for the eloquent man who was

117

less than candid in taking a position, who, like the demagogue for instance, used his eloquence to further selfish but hidden ends. Philip C. Pendleton, who had been a delegate to the convention, had this in mind when, in an 1856 letter about his distinguished ancestor Edmund Pendleton, he spoke of the qualities of eloquence as being "potent for good or evil—for *good*, when combined with sound judgement and purity of purpose—for *evil*, when devoted—as they too often are—to the accomplishment of selfish, wild and sinister ends."[15] In addition, since propriety in an open discussion meant being candid and not hiding behind words, one also had to avoid any possible aspersions on one's own honesty. Conservative Littleton W. Tazewell was, in fact, dogged by such a charge, which had first surfaced when he led the fight against calling a constitutional convention in 1816-17. According to Tazewell, reformers had spread the opinion "that he can make as good an argument on one side of a question as on the other," and he reported that even after several years had passed one man had refused to argue with him, "for he knew that he could first convince him that he was wrong, and then convince him that he was right."[16]

The practical issue, was, then, how to use political language in ways consistent with the main themes of political culture. What specific ways of making an argument were consistent with tradition and culture, and where could one learn them? One obvious source for such information was rhetorical theory. As educated men, many Virginia conservatives and moderates would have been familiar with the teachings of the major rhetoricians of the period. At William and Mary, for example, students were exposed to the works of such dominant British rhetoricians as George Campbell and Hugh Blair. In addition, Virginians' libraries and personal papers suggest their familiarity with such other figures as Thomas Sheridan and Edmund Burke, and even with the New Englander John Quincy Adams. Moreover, Virginians themselves were occasionally moved to write brief essays on rhetoric, although these essays lacked the breadth

118

and systematic quality of formal texts. From these sources, they could have learned valuable techniques for using political language in ways that accorded with their own political culture. For one thing, because questions of propriety in political discourse were addressed by rhetoricians, and because many conservatives and moderates were aware of what the rhetoricians had said, the discipline of rhetoric could provide useful rules for remaining within the bounds of respectability when using political language. But, in addition, because rhetoricians were concerned with teaching people how to be persuasive, and because much of their teaching was consistent with the main themes of Virginia conservative political culture (perhaps even contributing to it), they would have provided a useful guide for getting the most out of the political process. As a result, much that the rhetoricians had to say contributes valuably to the framework for understanding conservative ideas.

One good example of the ways in which theories of rhetoric reinforced Virginia conservatism may be seen in the attacks conservatives made on reform arguments that depended on fundamental principles. As conservatives represented their own position, to base any government on principles rather than experience was to court disaster, because one was engaging only in speculation. But conservatives could get quite technical in their objections. Littleton W. Tazewell, for one, asserted in the convention that he could never give his support to any plan that was "a clear syllogistic deduction from any supposed general truth,"[17] stressing in this way that the process reformers used to arrive at their proposals was itself objectionable and productive only of false conclusions. No less illuminating, along these lines, was a conversation which took place between conservative delegate Philip Barbour and the moderate William F. Gordon. Gordon was roundly denouncing logic, declaring there to be no distinction between true and false logic, when the conversation turned to the properties of the syllogism. The problem was clear to both men. "Grant me

119

my premises," said Barbour, "and I can prove anything." And what one achieved through syllogistic argumentation was not truth, but a conclusion that depended solely on the ingenuity of the "syllogist." One might even prove, according to Barbour, "that a dog is man"—indeed, he had seen it done.[18] And, by implication, here was precisely the sort of case reformers were trying to foist on Virginians in the debates.

Rhetoric, as such, reinforced conservatives' objections to reform principles, and even gave them a way of talking about those principles in argument, and in very concrete terms. In rhetoric, it was a matter of method, and the key focus of Virginians' training in this regard had been on the nature of "syllogistic reasoning," a question which had been of great interest to eighteenth-century rhetoricians. George Campbell, in particular, had attacked the syllogism, urging that induction be the usual method by which speakers should construct their arguments, and students of his work at William and Mary had been made aware of his opinions on, as one recorded, "Why will not syllogisms enable us to discover truth."[19] It was because of such considerations as these that conservatives had a very clear way of pointing to the excessive use of abstraction in political argumentation. They could identify the use of "syllogisms" in reform presentation.

But far more important than questions of logic, and mainly because it tied together conservative political culture with substantive arguments, was the matter of passion. Conservatives were of two minds about the role of passion in a political setting. On the one hand, they recognized that, just as excessive passion could destroy a stable political system, as they had argued in the convention, so too, in a smaller realm, could it destroy the correct atmosphere for political deliberation by foreclosing any possibility for a proper discussion of the issues. As William Branch Giles declared in 1827, speaking of the advocates of a convention bill,

> I hope I may be permitted to say that I see, or I think I see, a zeal so ardent for the consumation of this measure, that I cannot hope to obtain even a listening ear,

120

much less an impartial kindly one, to any thing I may
have to offer upon this subject. No, Sir, the passions are
up; they seem to be on tiptoe; and human passions have
no ears.

Once the passions had been aroused too strongly, people
stopped listening to each other. On the other hand,
conservatives did acknowledge man's passionate nature, and,
thus, they did not prize an oratory from which the passions
were wholly absent. The reason for this, also consistent with
conservative political culture, was that some measure of passion was a significant mark of honesty and candor in any
political discussion. Virginians recognized that human passion was an inevitable part of any activity; their main defense
of property as a basis for rights, after all, had been that it tied
selfish concerns to social needs, not that it did away with such
concerns altogether. In political deliberations, men were also
moved, unavoidably, by passion, but the honest man openly
acknowledged his own passions, even if he inhibited them
from overpowering his willingness to discuss matters with
others. Virginians distrusted the speaker who, "with cold
composure," as one writer observed, gave no sign of his own
passions, for such a man seemed also to lack a sincere conviction of the truth of what he was saying. To speak without passion gave every indication of attempting to conceal one's real
motives, and this, clearly, was contrary to conservative political ideals. Passion was, then, both necessary and dangerous,
and conservative Virginians had to find some way of coming
to terms with it properly in political debate.[20]

On the issue of passion Virginians would have learned
much from the rhetoricians. This period was one of the great
ferment in the discipline of rhetoric, a period in which rhetoricians themselves were increasingly turning away from seeing rhetoric as an aspect of the communication of forms of
information and knowledge and toward an emphasis on
problems of elocution and persuasion.[21] It was, too, a period
in which rhetoric's intellectual reputation was in serious decline.[22] But, as a discipline devoted to setting forth the most

121

effective modes of performance and persuasion, rhetoric was peculiarly the discipline to devote attention to what most men of the eighteenth century believed the seat of human action to be, the passions. In a very real sense, rhetoricians became the "scientists" of the passions, advising speakers and writers how to use the passions most effectively. To be sure, rhetoricians were not alone. Moral philosophers, political thinkers, and economists were all urging upon their readers the significance of the passions. Rhetoricians did, however, put passion in an eminently practical form.

Given the relationship Virginia conservatives perceived between rousing the passions and the requirements of political deliberation, rhetoric would, therefore, be a discipline of some importance to them. The lessons available from rhetoric were most prominently stated in the highly influential work of the British writer Hugh Blair, much of whose noted *Lectures on Rhetoric and Belles Lettres*, first published in 1783, would be devoted to dealing with the problem of passion in oratory and deliberation. Recognizing the danger of the passions to any discussion, Blair nevertheless considered the passions to be "the great springs of human action," and taught that no one could hope to be persuasive without addressing himself "to the passions more or less." Giving advice on such diverse aspects of oratory as gesture, manner, and the use of language, Blair would show orators how to use passion in order to "kindle the mind, without throwing it out of the possession of itself."[23]

Blair was, certainly, the preeminent figure in rhetoric in Virginia throughout the early national period, just as he exerted some influence on much of American letters at the time.[24] His *Lectures* guided William and Mary students at least from the time that Hugh T.W. Mercer took notes on them in 1794 until Warner Jones did the same in 1836. There is little evidence that Virginians were uncomfortable with the use of Blair; and they should not have been, because his ideas were quite compatible with their needs. The conservative Littleton W. Tazewell acknowledged as much in writing to his son, in 1824, of his wish that the young man "read Blair very carefully and attentively."[25] Blair was taken in Virginia as a source for good rhetorical practice.

And Blair assigned to passion a role which was quite compatible with Virginia political ideals. He wrote, "The most virtuous man, in treating of the most virtuous subject, seeks to touch the heart of him to whom he speaks; and makes no scruple to raise his indignation at injustice, or his pity to the distressed, though pity and indignation be passions."[26] For Blair, too, passionate discourse and sincerity were inextricably tied and, as he noted, one had to be in earnest in order to persuade.[27] Passion, whatever its dangers, was inseparable from honesty and candor in discussion and, therefore, was not simply out of place in the sort of discussions conservatives claimed to find proper. Blair taught, then, how to deliver a speech such that it did not violate the kinds of norms conservatives professed in regard to political debate.

The comments Virginia conservatives made about their own best orators show how compatible such teachings about passion were with their ideals. Thus, Benjamin Watkins Leigh would be commended for an eloquence "that awakened every mind and produced its influence on every heart." If he was "clear in his reasonings," as Grigsby wrote, he was also a speaker who "responded with marked effect to the passions that frequently agitated him." His manner, according to Grigsby, was "admirably adapted to display his passions." Moderate William F. Gordon made a similar assessment of Leigh, describing him as having a "natural and ardent" manner, and noting that "he seems to feel sensibly himself everything he utters."[28]

Leigh was said to have done the trick largely through his manner, and judging by most accounts, a careful use of invective. In addition, there appears also to have been an appearance of suppressed anger in Leigh's performances. Leigh himself acknowledged almost as much in a letter to Littleton Tazewell in direct regard, not to oratory, but to an anti-Jef-

123

ferson essay he thought of publishing in 1824. "I know the warmth of my temper as well as anybody," he wrote, "and that my pen is apt to run away, as well as my tongue–but I am bridle-wise, I hope, and can run over the ground without stumbling or bolting."[29] The metaphor was apt, because nothing could have conveyed more clearly the conservative ideal for political oratory: it was to be a performance in which passion informed without overpowering the man who had great issues to be discussed.

There can be little doubt that conservatives themselves attached great political importance to such views of what constituted proper political language. One sees something of this in the way it became a commonplace among elite Virginians to say that, since the American Revolution, true eloquence had become hard to find, largely because the quality of political life, itself, had changed. St. George Tucker, in a manuscript essay, declared his own doubts "whether there exist in all America as many Eloquent men, as the number of righteous who might have saved Sodom from Destruction," and he criticized, particularly, the excessive use of those devices designed to display agitation. But the cause he identified for this was completely consistent with conservative political culture, and he showed this by his comparison of contemporary speakers with the leaders of the American Revolution, men who "listened long, and attentively, before they presum'd to speak: and when they spoke, it was with the deference and respect of one asking for information, and not with the obtrusive arrogance of one dictating to others, better inform'd, wiser than himself."[30]

In such remarks as these the role of rhetoric itself in the creation and maintenance of a proper political community was stressed in a significant way. When writers like St. George Tucker idealized the oratory of earlier times and decried that of "the present age," they were, above all, talking about the changes that had come in Virginia's political life. No longer could politics be fully dominated by gentlemen who conformed in every way to the colonial, aristocratic ideal–and to

124

the main lines of conservative political culture. Such men as Philip Doddridge and Alexander Campbell also had a part to play in Virginia's social and political life, even though they were not of the stuff of which traditional leaders were supposed to have been made. Campbell himself recognized this, and he could only have confirmed the worst conservative fears when he remarked, in the convention, on the differences separating western and eastern spokesmen: "But a Pennsylvania, a New-York, an Ohio, or a western Virginia Statesman, though far inferior in logic, metaphysics, and rhetoric, to an old Virginia Statesman, has this advantage, that when he returns home, he takes off his coat, and takes hold of the plough. This gives him bone and muscle, Sir, and preserves his Republican principles pure and uncontaminated."[31] Be that as it may, it did not make him a gentleman. As Robert Shalhope has argued, from the late eighteenth century on, the old social forms of deference appeared to be under increasing challenge to conservative Virginians,[32] and these remarks on the decline of rhetoric were one way of expressing their anxiety over the situation.

Hence, it is not surprising that conservatives would use rhetorical standards related to passion not only to commend each other but also to condemn their opponents. In 1828, for example, Thomas Miller dismissed the arguments of reform leader Philip Doddridge as "barking & threatening," and described Doddridge himself as "a finished Demogogue." A year later, when the convention was in full swing, Grigsby would dismiss reformer C.F. Mercer on the quite relevant ground that, "When his cup of passion is full, he is *voiceless*."[33] Focusing on how a speaker performed not only gave conservatives a tangible way of accusing someone of dealing more in passion than in reason, but, at the same time, it allowed them to dismiss reform arguments by dismissing the reformers themselves for an inability to contribute properly to political discussion.

Thus, their use of concepts about passion and their relating those concepts to matters of appearance and manner

125

shows not only the extent to which conservatives were familiar with issues raised in theories of rhetoric but also shows their ability to apply those issues in a way that fit in with both their own political culture and with the demands posed by the debate over constitutional reform. It is, of course, difficult to know how accurate conservative descriptions of other orators were, however great the differences in the printed remarks of conservative and reform speeches. But conservatives were not especially concerned to give an accurate account, for posterity, of their opponents' performances. Rather, they were concerned to express to each other reasons for resisting reform demands, and one way to do this was by holding reformers themselves up to the standards of Virginia political culture, much as they had done when accusing reform spokesmen of demagoguery. What they knew about rhetoric gave them still another way of making that evaluation, and of doing so in terms of rather clear patterns of behavior.

Above all, as they made such evaluations, conservatives drew important connections between the substance of their arguments and the experiences of their audience. Passion was, clearly, a broad concept in Virginia political thinking. At one level as used in the conservative arguments in the convention, it referred to zeal for a cause or to a desire for power or for wealth that, carried to excess, made passionate men unmindful of the public weal. At another level, as used in rhetoric, it referred to excessive stubbornness in holding to a position or, even more, to a display of emotion that could easily pass beyond the expression of those felt convictions that signalled honesty and candor on the part of a speaker. Because the concept was so broad, conservative and reform speaking, as conservatives described each, virtually dramatized the reasons why constitutional revision had to be avoided in Virginia. Like characters in some play, reform orators became representative of the kinds of men who would dominate a democratic society, men incapable of ruling wisely because of an inability to keep their own passions in

126

check. Conservatives, by contrast, represented men who, through the discipline of rhetoric, were able to control themselves even in the heat of battle and, no matter how vehement they might become, would never lose sight of the need to deliberate issues fully and well. In their rhetorical concerns, in other words, conservatives gave life and meaning to the more apparently abstract notions of passion and restraint so prominent in their arguments, as they implied their own fitness, and the reformers' unfitness, to lead the state.

In what ways, then, did such ideas about rhetoric influence the actual substance of the arguments conservatives would make in the convention? For one thing, such ideas help to explain why conservatives should have made their arguments so heavily ideological. To see this, one must recall, first, the extent to which, in their arguments, conservatives rejected the idea of constructing a political system based on the existence of factions. Permanent divisions in either the body politic or the body of leaders was contrary to the main tenets of their argument as it was to their political culture. The main reason for this may be found in their understanding of factions as such to consist of knots of men whose unbridled passions led them to pursue narrow, selfish goals rather than the good of the whole society.[34] That they were at great pains to deny their own devotion to faction is illustrated by an exordium such as Upshur's, in which he claimed to have no regional attachments despite his obvious involvements in a regionally-based dispute.

Such a connection of passions with faction virtually compelled an ideological argument in the Convention of 1829-30. Any overt, narrowly focused appeal to immediate regional interests could not have provided the frame for conservative argumentation, and such appeals had to remain subordinate to more general, ideological concerns. To be sure, conservatives would assert regional differences in the convention, particularly in terms of the need to protect slave property from a western population for which slavery was a minor interest, but the central thrust of their argument was

127

ideological and general. The ideal was, again, to give the impression of "disinterested integrity," and this meant that one could not appear obsessed with the kinds of narrow, selfish passions that direct appeals to self-interest would have implied. Instead, one had to appear attentive mainly to the well-being of the state as a whole, and one's concerns had to appear to be based on larger concepts of government and society.

Now, this does not mean that, cunning men themselves, conservatives created an ideology mainly out of a search for "code words" by means of which to talk about slavery or sectionalism while seeming to talk more generally about the nature of government or the characteristics of principles. The record would never allow one to make such a judgement: some may have been so cynical, but virtually all spoke and wrote ideologically on constitutional questions even in private correspondence among themselves. It was simply a matter of how one was expected to talk about politics, of the kind of discourse one could use to justify any actions in political affairs and, hence, could offer to others in an effort to get them to act in particular ways. Political ideals, again, determined the limits on acceptable political discussion as well as the characteristics of political discourse which were most likely to be persuasive. In Virginia, this meant that one had to take an ideological approach to constitutional debate. It is doubtful that spokesmen for either side would have turned too frequently to an argument whose central thrust was based on immediate material interests.

It was for this reason, too, that conservatives had to draw on a political vocabulary that extended beyond the narrow issues separating Virginians on constitutional questions, one that came from the American political tradition and that had been applied to a range of issues for many years. Here, above all, was a language which allowed them to deal with social and political questions in terms of the kind of rhetorical expectations which they had to meet. It gave them a way of talking about themselves and their society and about the need to op-

128

pose democracy and change in an intellectually respectable way and also in a familiar way. It was a language with which most educated men would have been familiar and whose meaning they would have understood even as they appreciated its propriety for political deliberation.

From this, one can draw some conclusions about the role of ideology as such in influencing the outcome of the convention. To be sure, one can never know for certain the extent to which Virginians actually voted as they did on constitutional questions for ideological reasons. Most likely, some did support conservatism or reform on grounds that were mainly ideological, just as some voted on purely economic or social grounds. However, given the makeup of the convention and, in particular, given the background of those moderates who provided the margin on any vote, no one could have voted as he did in the absence of a strong, ideologically-based argument to support his position. This does not mean that ideology determined a vote, but it does mean that an acceptable ideology had to be available in support of whatever position one took in the convention. Ideology was, thus, a major factor in the outcome of the convention, making possible, if nothing more, the kind of support conservatives needed to stem the movement for democratic reform.

The rejection of excessive passion helped, then, to give the convention its ideological cast. Still, if Virginia conservatives were forced to deny excessive passion, they could not eschew appeals to the passions altogether. Again, they had learned that the passions had to be mobilized to some degree if an appeal were to work. In performing, for instance, they sought to appeal to the passions through such devices as a proper vehemence of manner or a careful use of sarcasm and invective, but what, in language as such, would also do the trick for them, and what sorts of emotions would they hope to arouse by their words? The clearest place to look for this is in the conservative effort to evoke the dangers of change, something they would attempt to do both intellectually and emotionally. One can appreciate the emotional content of this

129

aspect of their argument, however, only if, in recognizing it as an effort to bring passion to their cause, one appreciates that conservatives did so by means of at least one rather well recognized rhetorical technique.

Conservatives appealed to the passions in arguing against change by drawing on that area of language which the rhetoricians themselves had most closely tied to the passions, the use of metaphor. "Figurative language," as the rhetoricians termed it, was preeminently the language of the passions. Thus, for example, Blair had emphasized that such language had to be used very carefully. Of personification, as one form, he wrote, "The first rule is, never to attempt it, unless when prompted by strong passion, and never to continue it when the passion begins to flag. It is one of those ornaments which can only find place in the most warm and spirited parts of composition; and there, too, must be employed with moderation."[35] "Figures" and passion were closely tied, Blair taught, as had other authors, and this point can deepen our appreciation of conservative language in debate.

Nineteenth-century Virginia conservatives, with the exception of John Randolph, tended to be fairly sparing in their use of figures. Their use of metaphors in convention was quite limited and tended to take place in ways that homed in on their own worst fears about constitutional change. Drawing mainly on biology and on nature, conservatives found in figures a useful way of evoking a sense of human weakness and vulnerability as well as the potential for disaster in any change in conditions. The point was not merely to say that such things were dangerous; it was to express one's feelings about the dangers involved, and to try to evoke those feelings in others. Given the oratorical self-consciousness of Virginia's most eloquent men, one should not expect that they relied on figurative language with a lack of awareness of what its impact was supposed to be.

One form of figurative language which worked to the same end and which conservatives did use with some frequency was, however, the language of the sublime. The idea of the

130

sublime was important in the aesthetic theory of the late eighteenth century, and Virginians could have learned of it easily from Blair, although the theory owed mainly to Edmund Burke, as Blair himself acknowledged.[36] Young Hugh Mercer, at William and Mary, took copious notes from Blair on the nature and use of the sublime. He learned, chiefly, that the sublime had most to do with the evocation of grandeur, and that, "Disorder is very compatible with Grandeur; nay, frequently heightens it." Hence, he could appreciate Blair's recommendation to look, in trying to evoke the sublime, to "all Ideas of the solemn & awful Kind, & even bordering on the terrible," and, indeed, evocations of terrible power, even fear, came immediately to mind–natural disasters, war, or "the deep Sound of a great Bell, or the striking of a great Clock," especially when "heard in the Night." The importance of these examples is great, for young Mercer would learn, three lectures later, that the very emotions associated with the sublime were those most basic to human life, those most natural: "In the Infancy of all Societies," he noted, "Fear & Surprise, Wonder & Astonishment are the most frequent Passions of Mankind." To call up the sublime was to address the most primitive of human passions.[37]

Another young William and Mary student, Armistead T. Mason, delivered a Fourth-of-July address to the college in 1807 on the subject of suffrage. Mason, who would later achieve some prominence and who would die in a duel, followed Blair's instruction on rhetoric almost as if that text had been a cookbook. He began his oration by literally telling his audience how they ought to feel. Evoking that "dark and dreary age, when a Gothic gloom o'er spread the world," Mason called on his audience to look forward to a scene which would alleviate the "pain" his evocation brought to the mind. He continued,

> That scene, the sublime events of later times ushers [*sic*] in; the mind feels a conscious elevation, when those energies of soul, those manifestations of genius, which first dawned upon a benighted world, are passing in review

131

before it. The magnanimity and heroism of some great spirits animated by a celestial fire of virtue, evincing a contempt of difficulties, of dangers and of death, diffuse a placid benignity, an awful grandeur over the mind.

Turning the American Revolution into a sublime event through metaphor and through the evocation of heroism and death, Mason hoped to arouse his audience while he educated them in political thought.[38]

Such an appreciation of the sublime and of its power to synthesize feeling and ideas was not confined to student speeches. Whether inspired by Blair or not, Virginians expressed their understanding of many kinds of things in sublime terms. Thus, John Henry Strobia, visiting a gallery in 1817, came upon Ward's painting of the Anaconda and was quite taken by it. It was a picture of a "tremendous serpent" wrapping itself around "a beautiful white horse, and a native Indian, his rider." Strobia's description from there was an illustration of the sublime. The rider, he recorded, "in vain struggling for relief, exhibiting in every muscle the torture he endures, and his countenance betraying every symtom [*sic*] of horror and despair. The other victim, the noble horse, seems almost yielding to his fate,—writhing in torment, and making an agonized gnash at the head of the enormous reptile, whose horrific brilliancy, and high and masterly finish, produces a most singular effect."[39] Garry Wills has recently discussed the importance of the sublime aesthetic—which he attributes mainly to Edmund Burke—in the thought and expression of late eighteenth-century America, especially in Jefferson.[40] Sublimity was an idea that had great influence on the organization of expression during the period.

In learning rhetorical theory, Virginians learned to put sublimity to practical effect, evoking the awesome and the terrible as they sought to convince others of the rightness of their views. In the Convention of 1829-30, conservatives would rely quite heavily on the sublime in their effort to undermine arguments for reform, and an appreciation for

132

the power of the sublime had much to do with the characterizations of history and society that dominated conservative presentations in the convention.

There was, in fact, something of the sublime in the metaphors of illness and nature that conservatives used. In particular, the "tempests" of conservative rhetoric were straight out of Blair, however hackneyed they might otherwise have been in Virginia oratory during the period. But, looking at ideas of the sublime, there was something else that tied them all together. Blair himself directly connected disorder with the sublime, and his examples of natural disasters or even a loud noise, especially when heard "in the night," show that one key to the sublime was that it represented that what was unexpected and unpredictable in nature, as well as what was disastrous. The sublime was, with particular power, the language of human weakness and vulnerability and, as such, the language of fear. Edmund Burke made a similar point when he equated the sublime with passions of pain and, ultimately, with feeling the need for self-preservation.[41] To a great degree, then, fear, expressed in the language of the sublime, brought together and synthesized the main concerns in the conservative argument against reform.

Indeed, one sees this especially well in conservative efforts to evoke fears by reference to historical rather than natural disasters, none of which was more powerful in this regard than the French Revolution. Whatever the usefulness of Revolutionary France as an antidemocratic cautionary tale, its power was enhanced by the way conservatives could describe it in a language of horror and terror. When Leigh asked of Virginia, "how large a dose of French rights of man it can bear, without fever, frenzy, madness and death,"[42] he sought not only to condemn reform arguments but to do so in a way that evoked the fears aroused by what Burke and Blair had called the language of the sublime. One sees an even more clearly sublime characterization of the French Revolution in a description offered by Philip N. Nicholas. Using a source of terror Blair had noted as a part of his

133

description, Nicholas would place his attention on the revolution's early leaders. Most of them were, he thought, "virtuous and enlightened men. But they were more of philosophers and theorists, than practical statesmen":

> They raised a storm, which they had not the power to direct, and of which they became the victims. They devised schemes of Government, which were either not adapted to the state of the times, or which the people were incapable of living under. They did not know how free Governments would work: meanwhile, there arose factions, to which revolutions not unfrequently give birth, consisting of men who had nothing to lose and every thing to gain—men dissolute and depraved—who, under the mask of patriotism, were bent on the acquisition of wealth and power. Those persons collecting round them all the men of desperate fortunes, aided by the mobs of Paris, began pushing revolutionary principles to an extreme, which those who commenced the work of reformation never contemplated.

"Every man must reflect with horror," Nicholas added, "the bloody scenes, which took place in France."[43] Evoking terror, vulnerability, and, above all, the uncontrollable nature of change, however apparently noble, such language went straight to the heart of the conservative case against reform.

This way of evoking fear, with it roots in the power that disorder could exercise over human thought and feeling, summarized many of the points on which conservatives rested their case, particularly those relating to human weakness and vulnerability and to the inadequacy of human reason for comprehending—let alone manipulating—natural and historical forces. But, it also looked back in important ways to the political culture to which conservatives tried, in several ways, to demonstrate their commitment. The kind of fear conservatives sought to evoke emphasized the importance of that commitment. Using a language of vulnerability and disorder, conservatives also used a language of fragility, intended to show the ease and suddenness with which a

134

peaceful setting could become a nightmare of chaos and violence. Political communities, as France had shown, were themselves very fragile, and this would apply as much to Virginia as to any other polity. Conservatives used language in a way that, they had learned, could make this point, stressing that the convention was itself a very threatening situation, one which could, like a dormant volcano or a calm sea, erupt at any moment. The standards of Virginia political culture would, implicitly, serve to forestall such an eruption by enforcing proper behavior among those who acted in the political arena. The homogeneity of the leadership would, similarly, work to prevent the triumph of disorder. But let any of this be eroded, conservatives said, and no one could know what the effects on Virginia life would be.

Figurative language was, then, an important aspect of that plea for unity which conservatives had to make in the convention. Just as such positive assertions of political culture as the ideological orientation of argument or the claims of sociability made in regard to manner or in exordiums urged conservatives and moderates to recognize similarities of outlook, so did conservatives' use of figurative language express a sense that conservatives and moderates were in a similar predicament in the face of any possible change that might occur, given the threat of change to the maintenance of political ideals. In this, it gave emotional reinforcement to the conservative assertion that, in the absence of significant problems, the political system should be left alone.

It was because of this effort that one should emphasize the rhetorical role of, for instance, the French Revolution and not its specific history in order to understand its importance to the conservative argument. Conservatives were not simply equating Virginia nonfreeholders with the Paris mobs, as reformers sometimes asserted, nor were they predicting a Virginia bloodbath should suffrage be broadened. For reformers to characterize the arguments that way, as, for example, Alfred H. Powell had, was irrelevant to the discussion, because the conservative use of references to France had much deeper connotations. As a rhetorical event, the French Revolution conservatives described was a comment on the nature of life in the world, a dramatization of the weakness of man, the fragility of his institutions, and the vanity of his hopes. In the convention, references to France were part of an effort to situate delegates in such a world, forcing them to interpret the issues of constitutional reform within the atmosphere conservatives' language created, a language of potential and unpredictable disaster.

The political culture of many Virginians, especially conservatives and moderates, operated in two ways on the convention. First, because it was composed of certain norms and values for political behavior, it provided a set of guide-lines according to which conservatives constructed their arguments, creating limits on what could prudently be said and grounds for choosing to stress certain themes and images in making a case against reform. Secondly, that political culture itself provided a point of reference for the conservative cause, serving as a ground for unity over against reformers and as the background to a rationale for unity in the face of strong efforts to make changes in Virginians' usual ways of conducting political business.

Here, then, was a second level at which conservatives sought to make a case against reform in the Convention of 1829-30. At one level had been the specific arguments offered on the convention floor. But those arguments were themselves given deeper meaning by the connotations pro-vided by the political culture in terms of which the ar-guments were framed, for here were questions of human nature and potential considered not at the level of ideas—as was the case with the arguments as such—but rather at the level of experience. By using rhetoric which referred back to the political culture, conservatives could force themselves and moderates to recognize what a weak and passionate humanity looked like and to appreciate, too, the kind of self-control and discipline it took to keep passion in line. And it was designed to force moderates not merely to recognize that

136

republics were unstable systems, but to appreciate, first hand, that fragility itself. Political culture, supported by rhetorical devices, provided an important link between what conservatives said and the kind of experience which would make their words seem valid.

NOTES—CHAPTER FOUR

1. See Robert D. Putnam, *The Beliefs of Politicians: Ideology, Conflict, and Democracy in Britain and Italy* (New Haven: Yale Univ. Press, 1973), pp. 3-4. I am grateful to Professor William Schonfeld for making me aware of this useful book.

2. Judith to John Randolph, January 18, 1808, Tucker-Coleman collection, Earl G. Swem Library, William and Mary College, Williamsburg, Virginia; George Tucker, *Essays on Various Subjects of Taste, Morals, and National Policy, By a Citizen of Virginia* (Georgetown, D.C.: Joseph Milligan, 1822), p. 277.

3. *Richmond Enquirer,* August 9, 1825.

4. Henry St. George Tucker to St. George Tucker, March 3, 1808, Tucker-Coleman collection.

5. *Proceedings and Debates of the Virginia State Convention of 1829-30. To Which Are Subjoined, the New Constitution of Virginia, and the Votes of the People* (Richmond: Ritchie and Cook, 1830), pp. 65-66.

6. Nathaniel Beverly Tucker to St. George Tucker, March 10, 1822, Tucker-Coleman collection.

7. *Richmond Enquirer,* January 14, 1817.

8. St. George Tucker, "For the Old Batchellor," #9, ms. writings of St. George Tucker, Tucker-Coleman collection.

9. *Richmond Enquirer,* March 14, 1817.

10. George Mason, *The Papers of George Mason, 1725-1792,* ed. Robert A. Rutland, 3 vols. (Chapel Hill: Univ. of North Carolina Press, 1970), 3: 880. On the importance of "self-control" and "disinterest" in colonial Virginia, see Jack P. Greene, " 'Virtus et Libertas': Political Culture, Social Change, and the Origins of the American Revolution in Virginia, 1763-1766," in *The Southern Experience in the American Revolution,* ed. Jeffrey J. Crow and Larry E. Tise (Chapel Hill: Univ. of North Carolina Press, 1978), p. 82.

11. *Decius's Letters on the Opposition to the New Constitution in Virginia, 1789* (Richmond: Augustine Davis, 1789), p. 11.

12. *Proceedings, 1829-30,* p. 724.

13. William Halyburton to William Branch Giles, May 25, 1824, Virginia Historical Society, Richmond.

14. Campbel's [*sic*] Rhetoric, unidentified student's ms. notebook, William and Mary College Archives.

15. Philip C. Pendleton to Hugh Blair Grigsby, June 10, 1856, copy in Hugh Blair Grigsby letterbook, Grigsby papers, Virginia Historical Society.

16. Hugh Blair Grigsby, Diary, October 16, 1829 (p. 76), Grigsby papers.

17. Grigsby, Diary, October 12, 1829, p. 45.

18. Grigsby, Diary, October 8, 1829, pp. 18-20.

19. Campbel's Rhetoric.

20. William Branch Giles, "Speech (in the House of Delegates, January 26, 1827)," (Richmond: T.W. White, [1827]), p. 4; *The Old Bachelor* (Richmond: Printed at the Enquirer Press, for Thomas Ritchie and Fielding Lucas, 1814), p. 211.

21. Wilbur Samuel Howell, *Eighteenth-Century British Logic and Rhetoric* (Princeton: Princeton Univ. Press, 1971), pp. 5, 153, 181, 261-67.

22. Walter J. Ong, S. J., *Rhetoric, Romance, and Technology: Studies in the Interaction of Expression and Culture* (Ithaca: Cornell Univ. Press, 1971), p. 8; Hayden White, *Metahistory: The Historical Imagination in Nineteenth-Century Europe* (Baltimore: The Johns Hopkins Univ. Press, 1973), p. 53.

23. Hugh Blair, *Lectures on Rhetoric and Belles Lettres*, 2 vols. (London: W. Strahan, 1783), 2: 6, 189.

24. On Blair's influence in the United States, see Perry Miller, *The Life of the Mind in America* (New York: Harcourt, 1965), pp. 64-65; see, also F. O. Matthiessen, *American Renaissance: Art and Expression in the Age of Emerson and Whitman* (New York: Oxford Univ. Press, 1941), p. 18.

25. Littleton W. Tazewell to John N. Tazewell, March 7, 1824, Tazewell family papers, Personal Papers collection, Archives Branch, Virginia State Library, Richmond. One might note, however, that John Randolph of Roanoke was a good deal less favorable toward Blair, preferring Burke in this, as he would in everything. See Mason Gerald Daly, "The Political Oratory of John Randolph of Roanoke" (Ph.D. diss., Northwestern Univ., 1951), p. 239.

26. Blair, *Lectures*, 2:189.

27. Ibid., 2: 7.

28. Grigsby, "Sketches," p. 320-21; Armistead C. Gordon, *William Fitzhugh Gordon, A Virginian of the Old School: His Life, Times and Contemporaries (1787-1858)* (New York: Neale, 1909), p. 168.

29. B.W. Leigh to Littleton W. Tazewell, May 23, 1824, Tazewell family papers.

30. St. George Tucker, "For the Old Batchellor," #23.

31. *Proceedings, 1829-30*, p. 119.

32. Robert E. Shalhope, *John Taylor of Caroline: Pastoral Republican* (Columbia: Univ. of South Carolina Press, 1980), p. 58.

33. Thomas Miller to Littleton W. Tazewell, December 22, 1828, Tazewell family papers; Grigsby, Commonplace book, p. 13.

34. See, on this, John Zvesper, *Political Philosophy and Rhetoric: A Study of the Origins of American Party Politics* (Cambridge: Cambridge Univ. Press, 1977), pp. 33-36.

35. Blair, *Lectures*, I: 334.

36. Blair discussed both his debt to and disagreements with Burke, in ibid., I: 70-71.

37. Hugh T. W. Mercer, "Notes on Blair's Lectures on Rhetoric and Belles Lettres," Lectures III, VI, ms. notebook, dated January 11, 1794, in William and Mary College Archives.

38. Armistead Thomson Mason, *An Oration, Upon the Restriction of Suffrage; Delivered on the Fourth of July, 1807, from the Rostrum of William and Mary College* (Richmond: S. Grantland, 1807).

39. John Henry Strobia, Diary, July 13-September 17, 1817, entry for September 4, 1817 (p. 147), Virginia Historical Society.

40. Garry Wills, *Inventing America: Jefferson's Declaration of Independence* (Garden City, N.Y.: Doubleday, 1978), pp. 265-72.

41. Edmund Burke, *A Philosophical Enquiry into the Origin of Our Ideas of the Sublime and Beautiful* (2nd ed., 1759; reprint ed., New York: Garland, 1971), pp. 57-58. See, on this, Samuel Monk, *The Sublime: A Study of Critical Theories in XVIII-Century England* (1935. Ann Arbor: Univ. of Michigan Press, 1960), p. 87.

42. *Proceedings, 1829-30,* p. 151.

43. Ibid., p. 367-68.

CHAPTER FIVE

Manners, Morals, Habits:
the Foundations of
Conservative Political Culture

Conservative and moderate Virginians in 1829-30 could appreciate the connections traditional political culture provided between ideas and experience because of the background of assumptions and values they brought to political affairs. They could accept the notion that human weakness was an important political fact because they believed that, in general, human beings were weak and subject to passion—that political man was, after all, man nonetheless. They could understand why change was to be feared because they knew that, generally, no society was very strong, that it took a great deal of effort to keep any society in order, and that no change was likely to be an improvement. These were assumptions and values, in other words, that went well beyond the realm of politics and that informed delegates' views of their experiences in almost every area of life; as such, they comprised the foundations of Virginia conservatism in the early national period.

Notions of social fragility and human weakness were significant and widespread among those Virginians who had strong ties to the traditional elite. From a variety of sources, such people learned that almost any social system, any level of social interaction, was inherently unstable and liable to disruption, even from the most trivial causes. Moreover, they also learned that human beings were inevitably weak, passionate, and incapable of achieving perfection—at least in this life. Such views were inculcated by education, religion, even ties of friendship and family life—all experiences in which moderates and conservatives were more like each other than they were like western reformers—and, taken together, they comprised that body of "fundamental truths" which gave validity to the conservative case.

What form, then, did such assumptions of social fragility and human imperfection take, and how were Virginians likely to have learned them? The most important of them were part of the "equipment for living" that every Virginia gentleman was expected to acquire as a member of a polite, elite society, growing out of the great importance members of Virginia's elite attached to social life and social ties themselves. Anyone familiar with the history of Virginia—indeed, of the antebellum South—is aware of the traditions of hospitality and "visiting" that marked the lives of the great plantation families. People expected to entertain and socialize as a matter of course and, too, they expected others to return their hospitality when the occasion arose. But being hospitable was more than just a pleasure; it was also a major duty in the lives of Virginians from the colonial period until well into the nineteenth century. It was a duty simply because it was the only proof Virginians had that society and social ties were in a state of good health.[1]

Those who shared in the background of Virginia's traditional elite learned of the importance of this duty early, as part of the family experience. For elite Virginians, the ideal family was one built on ties of affection and mutual dependence. Thus, for example, Henry St. George Tucker wrote to his father, the noted St. George Tucker, of his own gratitude "for the tender manner in which you always speak of me in your letters," exclaiming, "God forbid! indeed, that, like the bird, I should forget not only the feelings of nature, but the dictates of gratitude, by becoming independent."[2] A decade and a half later, Maria Gooch in a letter to her husband spoke of the deep feelings his absence created in her and concluded, "I find that my happiness is entirely interwoven with yours."[3] Here, in two expressions, was the

142

Virginia elite's family ideal, an ideal of dependence and strong feeling, shared and reciprocated among all the members.

The problem was, if their letters and diaries be any guide, Virginians needed a good deal of reassurance that ties of affection were being maintained and reciprocated among all the members of the family. St. George Tucker, surely as moderate and composed a man as lived in Virginia, was constantly nagging his sons for their failure to demonstrate sufficiently strong attachment to him, and constantly receiving their reassurances of their love. Beverly, for example, had to deny, in 1802, the accusation that he "had forgotten that I had a father," assuring his father that, "did you know all, you would find that you alone & my dear Mama were remembered when every one else was neglected."[4] Such words formed a leit-motiv in letters from the sons to their father, and the concern went the other way, too. Hence, in 1808, Beverly would write to John Randolph of his chagrin at his father's "neglect": "From him, since I saw him, I have received two letters only, if that name can be properly applied to one page of paper containing a register of deaths &c. & one other apologizing for not writing." He went on to say, "I have not yet learnt to be insensible to this, and painful as my feelings are, I can hardly wish to become so."[5] Family relations, from this point of view, were important, but one could never be sure of how strong, or permanent, those relationships were.

This sort of concern about family relations seems to have existed among Virginians from at least the late colonial period up to the time of the Civil War, and with very little change.[6] The growth of sentimentalism—as opposed to sentiment—and the increasing value on individualism which marked American family history during the late eighteenth and early nineteenth centuries,[7] seems, by and large, to have passed elite Virginians by. This is not to say that many Virginians, especially the young men, did not often lead lives corresponding to that rugged "gentry style" with its hyperindividualism that Rhys Isaac has delineated so well.[8] It

143

is to say that their elders interpreted that life-style in terms of a view in which such individualism was strongly disapproved, in favor of that professed rejection of "independence" with which Henry St. George Tucker attempted to soothe his own father.

What one sees in this sense that the family was both important and insecure is yet another expression, at a more mundane level, of basic tenets in the conservative argument and of the central concerns that informed conservative political culture. Elite Virginians were worried about what they saw as man's antisocial tendencies, tendencies which grew out of the weaknesses of human nature. Left to themselves, people were far more likely to indulge themselves and their desires rather than to cultivate ties on which family life depended. Thus, one could depend no more on people's good will for a satisfactory family life than for stability and security in politics and government. Both, after all, had to be created out of the weak material of humanity.

The concerns Virginians expressed about the family, moreover, were not exclusively fears for family relations. What was occurring in Virginia was not so much an historical crisis of the family growing out of a re-evaluation of dependency, as Edwin Burrows and Michael Wallace have described for the North.[9] It was, instead, one expression of a larger concern for the security of all human relationships, based primarily on notions about human nature and society. One sees this, as well as the endurance of these concerns, by looking at two Virginians, separated by over a generation, who were notably articulate in what they had to say about family and social relations: Landon Carter from the colonial period, and John Randolph who was active during the early part of the nineteenth century.

Landon Carter, a Virginia leader during colonial times, shared with most men of his day a conviction of human weakness and of antisocial tendencies in himself and others. Carter was also a man convinced of the difficulty of finding

144

decency in this world. Everywhere he looked, as Jack P. Greene has said, he found evidence of human wickedness as men sacrificed truth to self-aggrandizement. And, as Greene has also said, the problem was ever the same: weak and corruptible, men could not be trusted to act properly in the face of selfish temptations.[10]

Carter's sense of human weakness was almost overwhelming, for he saw evidence of human imperfections wherever people had to deal with each other. The corruptions of political institutions, Carter could easily assign to a fallible human nature and, in words anticipating those of the conservatives in 1829-30—though without their apparent complacency—he would see injustice and oppression as inevitable products of any "earthly Supremacy." Even at the level of social life, Carter's sense of human weakness was strong enough to make him assert, at one point, the impossibility of genuine friendship. To be sure, Carter, like others, placed great importance on social ties and understood such ties to occupy a central place in human existence. Nevertheless, since human nature was always and everywhere the same—weak and corruptible—life with other people, at any level, was always likely to be difficult and unsatisfying.[11]

It was in terms of these broadly cast social views that Carter understood his own family life as yet another situation in which human imperfection corrupted human relationships. He was encouraged in this, no doubt, by his rebellious and apparently hopeless son, Robert Wormeley, and by a daughter-in-law whom Landon Carter described as a "mean spirited creature and sordid without remission." The son, according to his father, was a man who had no ability to withstand the world's idle pleasures, especially gambling and drinking. As if that were not enough, Robert Wormeley Carter was abusive, rarely if ever showing the kind of respect and affection a father deserved. In Landon Carter's opinion, his son's character could be described simply: "An impudent rascal. But so it is, a scoundrel determined to abuse his father

145

will be contradictory and as Confident about what he does not know." Robert Wormeley Carter was neither gentleman nor son, as Landon Carter understood those words.[12]

So, Landon Carter's son failed to measure up in terms of those virtues which were crucial to all levels of human society. In his apparent devotion to vice and abusiveness, Robert Wormeley was guilty of letting fleeting impulse destroy himself and those relations which should exist not just between father and son, but among all people. The younger Carter seems to have been unusually remiss on these grounds, but the source for his misbehavior was that commonly alluded to for explaining similar situations. When, for example, Beverly Tucker once offended his father, Beverly apologized, pleading "the heedless wayward impetuosity of my temper, increased by the pressure of distressing circumstances has, I fear made me sometimes appear indifferent to an affection which it would be my pride to merit, and my joy to possess."[13] Beverly Tucker was no Robert Wormeley Carter, but the point was the same in both cases. If ambition and a lust for power were men's chief political sins, self-indulgence in one's habits and relations were his social ones, and Robert Wormeley Carter stood guilty. Unable to discipline his habits or his temper, Robert Wormeley Carter bore the mark of a sinful man, destroying his family as he made no place for himself in society at large.

Landon Carter died in 1778, but his ideas about practical morality did not die with him. They were widely shared in the culture, and persisted well beyond his lifetime. John Randolph of Roanoke, born just five years before Landon Carter's death, was one who, for all his noted eccentricities and flamboyance, differed little from a man like Carter in his moral ideas. In a series of fascinating letters written to Theodore Bland Dudley over a fifteen year period beginning in 1806—and published in 1834—Randolph showed the extent to which fears of willfulness and self-indulgence remained important in the practical morality of a thoughtful, conservative Virginian.

146

Randolph took great interest in Dudley as the young man went through training for and then embarked on a career in medicine. Claiming to feel toward Dudley "as a father" and hoping the feeling would be reciprocated, Randolph took it upon himself to make sure that Dudley would "turn out a respectable man, in every point of view." He took the responsibility quite seriously. Randolph replied at length to the young man's letters, and not only helped Dudley with various of the problems involved in growing to manhood, but also offered critiques of the letters themselves in matters of style, spelling, and grammar. Finally, Randolph was not unsparing in apparently unsolicited advice to guide Dudley through life.[14]

Like Carter, Randolph believed that men were less evil than weak for, as he said, "To form good habits is almost as easy as to fall into *bad*,"[15] but, also like Carter, Randolph saw more people with bad habits than with good. Much of what he saw to be wrong with society was, in fact, strikingly similar to what had troubled Carter. One passage in his letters might, in its thrust, have been written by Landon Carter, too:

> A petulant arrogance, or supine, listless indifference, marks the character of too many of our young men. They early assume the airs of manhood; and these premature men remain children for the rest of their lives. Upon the credit of a smattering of Latin, drinking grog, and chewing tobacco, these striplings set up for legislators and statesmen; and seem to deem it derogatory from their manhood to treat age and experience with any degree of deference. They are loud, boisterous, overbearing, and dictatorian: profane in speech, low and obscene in their pleasures. In the tavern, the stable, or the gaming-house, they are at home; but, placed in the society of real *gentlemen*, and men of letters, they are awkward and uneasy: in all situations, they are contemptible.[16]

Succumbing to the temptations of frivolity and showing no respect for what another observer would call "the sober wisdom of age"[17] were no less wrong to Randolph in 1807 than they had been to Landon Carter over three decades before.

The sins of youth troubled Randolph. He saw too many young men of "fashionable manners" around him, and what he liked least was their arrogance and self-indulgence. Their uncultivated pleasures were signs of an attitude that precluded those relationships which were marked by a proper affection that the proper nature of such relationships was a matter of great importance to Randolph is clearly indicated in his correspondence with Dudley. Randolph summarized the ideal when he wrote, "It is the office of friendship to accomodate itself to mutual and incurable infirmities." As the statement implies, the office was not always easy to fill, and Randolph feared that he and Dudley might not reach the ideal. The matter was, essentially, one of feelings and sentiments, and Randolph's were hurt with remarkable ease. Once, when Dudley had visited Randolph, but had spent only a short time in his company, having felt a need to help someone else on business, Randolph scolded, "I assure you that nothing . . . has given me so much pain, (growing out of it,) as that you should have offered the request, or even the *importunity*, of any person in the world, as a reason for departing from the pointed injunctions of him, who flattered himself he had more weight with you than the whole world besides." This was not the first time Randolph had been upset. Three years earlier, in 1807, Randolph had been receiving short letters from Dudley, but had been satisfied until he learned that someone else had received a long one. Then, Randolph wrote, "I was *hurt*. I know that the only way to deserve the confidence of another, is to give your own," which, he added, he had done. And he declared his desire, always, for "a frank communication of your opinions and feelings generally." Randolph's letter was, itself, frank and full of feeling, based on a strong desire to strengthen the bond of affection between the two men.[18]

The letter's tone, however, and Randolph's scolding of Dudley, emphasize the extent to which Randolph both valued

148

and felt insecure about human ties. And Randolph himself is an important figure to look at in this regard. Flamboyant, eccentric, and as spectacular an orator as Virginia produced, Randolph was, nevertheless, a man who frowned on excess, one who had, as Henry Adams accurately described him, a "consuming rage for noteriety, contemptible even in his own eyes."[19] He shared fully in his culture, and all his flamboyance did not mean that he had developed an egotistical ease in human society. Social relations and self-indulgence, as far as Randolph was concerned, were incompatible, but maintaining the one and restraining the latter were difficult tasks, tasks at which all too many men were failures.

Popular ideas about social life were, then, as bleak as those which conservatives advanced in the convention, portraying little or nothing in human nature, as such, that would offer hope for stability and security in life. Even doctrines of natural sympathy—cited by John R. Cooke, for instance, as he sought to counter conservative portrayals of human nature and society—had little adherence among conservatives. John Randolph made this point when he noted, in his commonplace book, "*Natural* affection nothing: affection from principle & duty very strong."[20] As his words imply, and other Virginians agreed, only the conscious cultivation of virtue and the exercise of self-discipline could preserve social harmony. But as much that Randolph and others wrote also makes manifest, one could not be too secure about social relationships in any situation.

The words of such men as Carter and Randolph were typical for members of Virginia's eastern-oriented elite. The perspective on society they betray—a perspective emphasizing both the importance and the fragility of social life—was professed with remarkable consistency by elite Virginians, almost as if there were a kind of code to which a good Virginia aristocrat had to give open assent. Conservative political culture, which also stressed the importance of sociability and the fragility of community, was one manifestation of that code.

Indeed, the belief expressed by Randolph and others that

149

society had to be based on cultivated and not natural affection helps to explain why ties of kinship and friendship, even of "aristocracy," would be so important to conservative political culture. One sees something of this in an interesting letter Thomas Massie, Jr., once wrote from Ohio to his father in Virginia. Henry Massie, Thomas's brother, had made plans to marry a Kentucky girl, a rather strange step, some thought, for a young, elite Virginian to take:

> his relations here [in Ohio] are very solicitous she should be a girl of *family*—It is really laughable that this little village should be divided into circles some of whom think themselves far better than others on account of the dignity of their blood. It allways reminds me of a farce I have seen of exquisite ridicule called high life below stairs.[21]

At first glance, Massie himself appears to be ridiculing the very idea of aristocracy, but, given Massie's own antidemocratic prejudices, such an interpretation would be off the mark. What was more likely at issue for Massie was the possibility of aristocracy in a little Ohio village, out on the American northwest frontier. In such a spot, all of the necessary supports for an aristocratic community would be absent—not only the material needs for an aristocratic life style, but, more importantly, the cultivated ties of kinship and friendship upon which any community was believed to depend. One could not conduct the high life below stairs.

This was an important point, because it tied any pretensions to "aristocracy" in Virginia to larger concerns of social morality. One sees something of this in a letter Thomas Jefferson, in Paris in 1785, wrote containing thoughts with which conservatives could have easily agreed—if they agreed with little else Jefferson ever said or did. He had observed American students in Europe, and was worried about what he had described as their degeneration in knowledge, morals, health, habits, and happiness, especially about their succumbing to the sexual temptations Europe offered. "Cast your eye over America," he wrote: "who are the men of most

150

learning, of most eloquence, most beloved by their country men and most trusted and promoted by them? They are those who have been educated among them, and whose manners, morals, and habits are perfectly homogeneous with those of the country."[22] One may recall, along these lines, Nathaniel Beverly Tucker's assigning of political corruption in Missouri to the diversity of its population, to the fact that those who led were unfamiliar with each other and, hence, irresponsible toward each other. And he would see this as a besetting sin in Missouri society as a whole.[23] Homogeneity, which made an aristocracy possible, also made social morality easier to achieve.

The virtues and sins of political life had their foundations, then, in the far more general social concerns which elite Virginians would profess. But where did such social concerns come from? In the main, conservatives and moderates in 1829-30 would have learned them simply as a part of growing up in their society. As family letters make clear, these concerns were a major part of what their elders—those, at any rate, who hoped their sons would become gentlemen—had been trying to teach young Virginians for at least a generation. In addition, one may think of how, for example, a young Abel P. Upshur, under the legal tutelage of William Wirt, was to learn not only to be a fine lawyer but also a cultivated gentleman. The virtue a contemporary found in Upshur as "one of the most amiable" companions he had met was wholly consistent with the kinds of concerns that informed Virginians' views of social relations. And, indeed, "amiability" was a primary virtue as conservative Virginians conceived of social life.

But it would be a mistake to look solely, or even mainly to Virginia for the roots of such an understanding of social virtues and sins. As Richard Sennett has shown so well, one may find similar expressions of social views among European conservatives of the same period.[24] Indeed, if anything, what one finds among elite Virginians represents a carrying-over of a set of social values and attitudes which had been promi-

151

nent among the elite of western civilization during the eighteenth century. No doubt, although this would also have been true for Europeans, the fragility Virginians perceived in society was made to appear especially threatening by the challenges of new people and new styles of leadership emerging in their society, but the attitudes themselves were products of a way of looking at the world which referred to more than the local character of Virginia society.

Thus, conservatives would find one source of support for their social views in much that they were familiar with from European, and particularly British letters. Elite Virginians have long been known for the wealth of their library holdings and for their literary attainments. The conservatives and moderates who were active in the Convention of 1829-30 were no exceptions to this image. Peppering their speeches with snippets, some in Latin, from the major works, they also sought the authority of the great writers in support of their positions. The breadth of their citations indicated the diversity of their reading. At various points in the debates, Leigh alone would refer to such writers as Swift, Burke, Defoe, Locke, Pope, and Cervantes. Other conservatives would add, in addition to these, such figures as Shakespeare, Milton, Hobbes, and Addison, along with the American, and fellow-delegate, James Madison. And this is not to mention those whose works they attacked, particularly Rousseau and, of course, Thomas Jefferson.

Of all the figures they quoted, and of all the works they read, however, conservative Virginia readers did have a few clear favorites. John Randolph, discussing his own reading habits, cited, in particular, Jonathan Swift, Alexander Pope, the historian Lord Bolingbroke, Samuel Johnson, and Edmund Burke, along with Shakespeare, Milton, and even the romantic Byron—although he confessed Burke to be his favorite. More to the point, these were also his key sources for quotation. Hugh Blair Grigsby once tried to draw a "parallelism" between Randolph and Byron, but had to confess he had never heard Randolph actually "mention the writing of

Byron," nor that of any of the other great Romantic figures, such as Shelley, Wordsworth, or Keats. Shakespeare, Milton, Pope, and Johnson, along with the somewhat less-compatible Oliver Goldsmith and William Cowper, appeared to be Randolph's more usual sources. The best Grigsby could do with his "parallelism," incidentally, was to note that, "both Lord Byron and Mr. Randolph were very fond of dogs and hares," and that both wore very small hats.[25]

Randolph's list of favorites provides a useful indication of the ties between the social concerns of Virginia's elite and those of Europe, particularly Britain. First, one should note, Randolph was not eccentric in his reading habits. His list of favorites could have been compiled by other well-read Virginians: the authors most prominently quoted in the Convention of 1829-30 were those he enjoyed, as well. But if one were to focus on those writers who did most to reinforce Virginians' social outlook, one would find the greatest insight in the works of the early eighteenth-century English tradition of Augustan humanism. Two of the leading figures of that tradition—Jonathan Swift and Alexander Pope—not only had great popularity as sources for conservative quotations, but had long occupied an important place in the reading habits of elite Virginians. Pope, in particular, had been the most popular poet in colonial Virginia, and his works had continued to do well in the market-place until well into the nineteenth century. Pope's dictum, from the "Essay on Man," that "self-love and social be the same," provided conservatives with a very quotable defense of their view that property-holding made men responsible.

That Virginia conservatives should have found the Augustan writers comfortable companions should not be surprising. Developing and receiving its greatest exposition in the early eighteenth century, the Augustan tradition was itself very much a part of the political conditions in England at the time, particularly of the emergence of an urban capitalist society, displacing a more traditional, aristocratic one. The greatest figures in its development were those Tory writers—

153

especially Swift, Pope, and Bolingbroke—who sought to turn back from the individualistic, optimistic culture they saw growing up around them, and to maintain older, hierarchical social forms. For them, too, society was something very fragile that had to be protected from the passions of unruly men.[26] The line of descent from these writers would include such other important figures as Samuel Johnson and Edmund Burke.

The main tie between the Augustan tradition and elite Virginians' social concerns lay in the Augustan assertion that humanity's sole claim to distinction from the other animals lay in man's social nature.[27] The Augustan tradition was, above all, a moral tradition. Such writers as Swift and Pope accepted the view that the chief function of literature was instruction and that the special property of literature was to provide moral teaching through the medium of pleasure.[28] Although the Augustan writers were convinced of the basically negative properties of human nature,[29] none set out merely to condemn human failings—not even the Swift whose "Yahoos," in *Gulliver's Travels,* presented mankind at its worst.[30] People might behave terribly, and might even have a tendency to do so, but they could find fulfillment only in social existence and a major purpose for the Augustan writers, even as they deplored human weakness, was to indicate human social possibilities.

Thus, the Augustan writers confirmed the Virginia view that virtue grew mainly out of an awareness of one's own weaknesses and tendencies toward bad behavior.[31] Samuel Johnson, in one of his essays, remarked, "No weakness of the human mind has more frequently incurred animadversion, than the negligence with which men overlook their own faults, however flagrant, and the easiness with which they pardon them, however frequently repeated." Johnson made clear that the frequent animadversion was well justified, and that the blindness or arrogance which made people seek to deny their own weaknesses was a major cause of vice.[32] If, however, one could cultivate a self-awareness, even a self-dis-

154

trust of his own tendencies to misbehave, then he might achieve that virtue toward which all individuals should strive.

The problem was, of course, that of human nature. On the one hand, there was the matter of human pride, and all the Augustans were like Jonathan Swift in being propelled by what Bonamy Dobrée described as a "tremendous urgency of the desire to humble human pride."[33] But, compounding the effects of pride was a human tendency to indulge those independent and selfish passions which made the fulfillment of humanity's social possibilities unlikely. All the Augustans anticipated conservative Virginians in finding man's main moral duty to be the suppression of natural, antisocial impulses while following the dictates of sociability, as did the Whig Joseph Addison, another writer from the Augustan period who was extremely popular with nineteenth-century Virginians.

Although not all of Addison's views were compatible with those of his Augustan contemporaries, he, like them, emphasized man's social nature and the need to cultivate an amiable disposition. His major writings were the essays published in *The Spectator* and *The Tatler*, and both journals were well known to Virginians of the nineteenth century; indeed, Addison's essays were the most important models for Virginians' own efforts at the form.[34] In one of his *Spectator* essays, Addison made a point about the passion of envy that clearly contrasted the problems posed by that vice with the virtues of fulfilling a social nature. "The envious man is in pain upon all occasions which ought to give him pleasure," Addison wrote. "The condition of the envious man is the most emphatically miserable; he is not only incapable of rejoicing in another's merit or success, but lives in a world wherein all mankind are in a plot against his quiet, by studying their own happiness and advantages."[35] The similarity between Addison's view and that of later Virginians is striking. Thus, for example, in a manuscript essay about avarice, "amongst the most unamiable of the human passions," St. George Tucker wrote, "it absorbs and annihilates every noble

155

sentiment, and every tender feeling, of the heart," adding, "An avaricious person in the midst of his family, and friends, is as perfectly alone, as if he were in a desert."[36] Such a man was to be condemned not because he was evil but because, thinking only of himself, he did not cultivate the ties of affection which were necessary to society.

Conservative social morality thus drew on a background which was not purely Virginian. Although the experiences of social and family life provided the most direct source from which Virginians would learn the ideas and values which would guide them through life, they would receive important reinforcement for those ideas and values when they read, even for pleasure, such writers as Addison, Swift, Pope, and Johnson. These writers of the Augustan period kept Virginians in touch with older, European ideas, and because they stated so very well the notions about society which Virginians themselves would profess, they provided valuable confirmation to the rather unsystematic body of values and attitudes of the Virginia elite. These may not have been the only writers with whom Virginia readers were familiar—indeed, they were not—but they occupied an extremely important place in the teaching and maintenance of that outlook which informed the social and political life of Virginia's early national leadership.

If reading provided one major reinforcement for Virginia conservative social values and ideas, another which drew heavily on the British social background but was a more intimate part of Virginia life was religion. Virginia conservatives and moderates were overwhelmingly Episcopalian,[37] and this was a religion which strongly reinforced a view of the world in which human beings were seen as weak and corruptible. More significantly, it was also a religion which, emphasizing social morality, stressed the idea that, however important it was for people to live proper lives, the achievement of moral goodness was a difficult, even unlikely accomplishment in this world.

The role of Anglicanism as such in Virginia culture and

society during the late colonial and early national periods has not been sufficiently understood, even if the conflicts between Virginia Anglicanism and the developing evangelical churches has been thoroughly studied, as has been the profound influence of evangelicalism on Virginia thought and culture.[38] The reason for this neglect is not hard to appreciate. While there were close ties between Anglicanism and leadership in Virginia during this time, they were not comparable to, say, those which existed in Massachusetts. One cannot easily point to obvious influences of religious ideas on Virginia social and political thought. By all accounts, the Virginia Anglican pew was an extremely comfortable place to sit. Preaching an official, established Arminian-based doctrine and focusing on problems of secular morality, the Anglican and, later, Episcopal clergy were by and large an uncontroversial lot. People went to church and supported religion (albeit not with noteworthy largesse) viewing it, primarily, as one more element in a stable social order.

This is not to say, however, that elite Virginians were unfamiliar with religion, or unmoved by it. Most had grown up with the church; many were familiar with the best devotional literature of the day. Moreover, their letters and diaries, as well as such things as keepsake books, were filled with devotional sayings and devotional poetry, all showing a familiarity with religious thinking and religious concerns that should not be lightly dismissed. Elite Virginians, clearly, were not religious enthusiasts, and they strongly rejected religious enthusiasm in others. Nevertheless, they stayed in easy but close company with religion, and it provided significant support for their social ideas.

Moderate Anglicanism was, above all, a religion that taught social morality and good works. When John Randolph, in an open letter to Episcopal Bishop William Meade in 1815, expressed his great devotion to God and his desire for salvation, he also mourned his own sinfulness: "I know that I deserve to suffer for my sins," he wrote; "for time misspent, faculties misemployed; but above all, that I have

157

not loved God and my neighbour as we are commanded to do."[39] For Randolph, salvation was essentially a matter of following the divine commandments, mainly by living right and serving society. He emphasized this point in a different way in the opening inscription to his diary for 1824, where he cited eight verses from the Old Testament book of Proverbs. All dealt with the importance of discipline—for example, Proverbs xxv: 28, "He that hath no rule over his own spirit is like a city that is broken down and without walls"; or, xix: 18, "Chasten thy son while there is hope, and let not thy soul spare for his crying"—and did so in ways that were quite compatible with Virginia ideas generally.[40] Religion, according to Randolph and others, had one major task. As St. George Tucker wrote, the inculcation of morals was "the real fruit of true piety,"[41] and morality, as most men saw it, was very much a matter of discipline.

Virginia Episcopalians received this message from their own ministers, as when John D. Blair, in 1809, warned them against the "impetuosity and bad effects of the passions."[42] They received it even more powerfully, perhaps, from the one figure who had the greatest intellectual impact on the church during the colonial period and after, Archbishop John Tillotson. Tillotson, a seventeenth-century English divine whose life seems to have been devoted to finding the middle way in any religious dispute, was a significant figure in Virginia Anglicanism for all of the eighteenth century. According to Bishop Meade, who remains the historian of Virginia Anglicanism before 1850, Tillotson's were the sermons of the church. At a time when the Anglican clergy was both timid and in short supply, lay readers offered many of the sermons, and those they read were inevitably by Tillotson.[43] Marked, as one writer has said, by a prudential, utilitarian ethic, Tillotson's religion was both reasonable and moral. Even revelation, for him, was essentially a reiteration of moral law.[44] Here was a religion with which conservative Virginians could comfortably live.

Tillotson succeeded, above all, in creating a moderate reli-

158

gion in a time of conflict. His most noted sermon, "Against Evil-Speaking," was a sterling example of his moderate approach to a difficult moral problem. Concerned mainly with "saying things of others which tend to their disparagement and reproach, to the taking away or lessening of their reputation and good name," whether true or false, Tillotson described such speaking as contrary to Christian "charity and goodness." He then continued, however, to point out the "due bounds and limitations" of the prohibition which was his text, "Speak evil of no man" (Titus iii: 2). There were times, he assured his congregation, and generations to come, when "evil-speaking" was not only unavoidable but necessary, when one did good service to God and man in "blasting the reputation" of one's adversaries. Then, he concluded with the evil roots of the practice, which were several and included "ill-nature and cruelty of disposition"—according to Tillotson, "Men do commonly incline to the censorious and uncharitable side—as well as maliciousness, envy, and a desire to meddle. The message in Tillotson was simple and familiar for Virginians: people incline to evil speaking; they even enjoy it. To avoid acting in this way, they needed to accustom themselves to ignore others' faults and, above all, to "set a watch before the door of our lips, and not speak but upon consideration." They needed, that is, to discipline themselves in the sight of God and against their natural dispositions to do ill.[45] Tillotson's was a religion that gave strong support to the main themes of popular morality, especially its emphasis on restraining natural impulses in order to maintain social relations.

Bishop Meade, commenting on Tillotson's influence in Virginia, was not altogether pleased that it had led many to "substitute reasoning, natural religion, and morality for the Gospel."[46] Such was a position generally taken by critics of Anglicanism in the late eighteenth and early nineteenth centuries. Thus, for example, Councilor Robert Carter's conversion to the Baptist church from Anglicanism was based on his sense that the established church was far too greatly concerned with social morality and too little interested in matters of faith.[47] The most powerful critic of Virginia Anglicanism in the early national period was, however, a member of the body with some standing, the Reverend Devereaux Jarratt. Jarratt's critiques of Virginia Anglicanism were important because, focusing on Anglican teaching about the individual's relationships with God, they not only illuminate the social meaning of that religion but also indicate the extent to which Anglicanism, while it stressed the importance of discipline, contributed to Virginia conservatives' insecurities about the possibility of achieving social virtue in this life.

Jarratt himself was the most powerful Anglican preacher, and among the most powerful preachers of any denomination, that Virginia ever produced. He has been best known in the history of Virginia religion for his ties to early Methodism and his rather un-Anglican belief in the necessity of religious experience. But Jarratt's place in the Anglican tradition is no less important. No enthusiast, neither was he open to the "democratic," leveling tendencies of much of evangelical religion.[48] His criticisms of dominant Anglican practices were not, then, those of an outsider motivated by denominational rivalry.

The Devereaux Jarratt who began his career in 1763 was an admirer of the Anglican tradition, but he had no admiration for many of its Virginia practitioners. From their preachers, he recalled, the congregations "heard little else but morality and smooth harangues, in no wise calculated to disturb their carnal repose," and church members were little better, displaying "gross ignorance of divine things, combined with conceited wisdom and moral rectitude."[49] But Jarratt's complaints were aimed at something worse than moral smugness, and his objections were not simply to the preaching of morality. It was the prominence given to morality in preaching to which he took exception. According to Jarratt, Episcopal preaching left out the two prior terms in any religious condemnation of immoral conduct: original sin and the nature of divine grace. Men, according to Jarratt,

160

were by nature "degenerate and corrupt,"[50] but, more importantly, they were unable to "evade the sentence of the law...by their power, merit, or good works."[51] His message was the essence of good evangelicalism, albeit also consistent with the "Articles of Religion" of the Anglican Church, but it was not a message to which Virginia Anglicans were accustomed.

Jarratt did not preach the religion most conservative Virginians accepted, but he reveals, by contrast, what it was like, and in two important respects. First, clearly, theirs was a human-centered religion of works which gave little place to matters of divine sovereignty and grace. Not at all Calvinist nor even quite Arminian in its thrust, the practical religion of Virginia conservatives was one in which the good behavior of the individual was the major concern. It supported, then, a view of humanity and of history in which human endeavor rather than divine providence had the greater influence over the outcome of events. The cosmic implications were no more significant than the social ones. In preaching morality without stressing depravity, Anglican preachers confirmed a belief in human weakness while giving little importance to the power of divine grace to produce a moral change. The possibility of virtue was not denied by the practical theology of Virginia's Anglican preachers; nor, however did they deny the human frailty which led men to misbehave. People were impetuous and passionate, the clergy told their congregations, but those preachers also implied that it was solely up to people to keep the passions under control. There would be no divine intervention on anyone's behalf, nor would virtue reflect a sudden change in one's life.

The importance of this point emerges when one compares this conservative Anglican position with the central concerns of the evangelicals. Edward Baptist put the issue very clearly when, in his diary, he described his father as "a moral, orderly, respectable citizen, though not a Christian, in the evangellic [sic] acceptation of the term." Baptist added, "He was partial to the Episcopal church." The difference between being moral and being Christian, for Edward Baptist and other evangelicals, was large. At the center of evangelicalism was a spectacular experience of conversion, in which the soul, by grace, was converted to Christianity and given assurance of salvation. And attached to that belief in conversion was an equally important belief in the possibility of sanctification. As Baptist recounted his own experience, once he had become determined to "become religious," "I felt a solemn sense of guilt fasten on my conscience, which increased daily and hourly until the blood of Jesus Christ wiped it all away." Baptist was making a statement here that was typical of the evangelicalism of his day. Conversion was a spectacular event, initiated by the divine, that not only boded well for eternity, but that meant a present change in this life, as well.[52] Conservative Anglicanism offered nothing of this. For conservatives, discipline and moral life were the only ways to salvation; at any rate, they were all one could do if he desired to live well. Human effort, not divine power, stood at the center of conservative religious life.

Anglicanism, as practiced in Virginia, thus gave profound support to conservative social views and, therefore, to traditional political culture, as well. Emphasizing human frailty, and ignoring the power of divine providence to overcome that frailty, this religion offered no grounds for optimism about social possibilities. Instead, it was a religion that encouraged believers to recognize the imperfections of life in the world, and to strive continually to make adjustments to those imperfections, rather than to seek perfection in oneself or in one's society. Such a religious perspective on life could only have reinforced that sense of human weakness and social fragility upon which so much of Virginia political conservatism rested.

But there was one other way in which Episcopal practices, focused as they were on social morality, would have contributed to a culture in which conservative ideas could have some power, and this was in the Episcopalian form of worship. In 1745, the British Governor in Virginia, Sir William Gooch, expressed his opposition to the growing evangelical movement in the Virginia colony, accusing its followers of "blaspheming our sacraments, and reviling our excellent liturgy."[53] The point would often be made in accounts of eighteenth-century conflicts between the established church and dissenters. According to Robert Semple in his classic history of the Virginia Baptists, for instance, Anglican leaders often visited dissenter churches, attacking the seeming anarchy of dissenter services.[54] With the formation of the Methodist Episcopal Church in the late eighteenth century, a major issue was what to do with the Anglican liturgy, and the response of the Conference of 1779 was to liberalize the order of worship, at least to a degree.[55]

Conservative Virginians often accused the evangelicals of appealing too much to the passions and of exciting their audiences for a few days while effecting no genuine change in them,[56] but it was not simply a matter of whether passion and feeling should be introduced into religious worship that worried conservative Virginians. Religion without feeling was hardly a thing to be prized. The ideal, for conservatives, was to put feeling within bounds, to guide it and focus it and, above all, to order it. This was probably a major virtue of the tightly-ordered service prescribed by the Anglican and later the Protestant Episcopal *Book of Common Prayer.* Autonomously expressed emotions, immediately inspired, were a distinguishing feature of evangelical religion. These expressions took spectacular form in the exercises and exhortations of the camp meeting in the early nineteenth century, as they had in the Whitefield services of the Great Awakening, and immediate inspiration and expressive autonomy were also important to the less spectacular services of the major evangelical groups. But Angelican liturgy, however emotionally powerful it may be, and however moving is its ceremony and language, allows little if any room for the autonomous expression of emotion. Feeling is channeled into the words and actions which liturgy prescribes, and prescriptions cover almost every moment of the service. In Anglican worship,

163

natural impulses are to be controlled—just as natural impulses must be controlled if one is to achieve social virtue—and the individual's relationship with God is to be mediated through prescribed liturgical forms. The social experience of ritual is stressed more than the direct contact with the divine which could take rather visible, if not spectacular form in evangelical worship. In this, then, Episcopalian religion gave strong, if implicit support to an outlook on society, or politics, which stressed the dangers of independence while finding virtue in the constant maintenance of proper relationships with others.

Virginians of various political leanings were not entirely unaware of the relationships between religion and politics. Democrats, for their part, often cited ties between evangelical religion and democratic politics.[57] In the denominational wars, for instance, the most democratically-organized groups would claim to have special virtue in this regard, as when John Rice declared that, "the more decidedly a man is a presbyterian, the more decidedly is he a republican." And, in fact, most Presbyterian delegates were on the reform side in 1829-30. By contrast, men of old families often looked aghast at the political activism and ideas of the evangelicals. Thomas Massie, Jr., a moderate in 1829-30, practiced medicine in Ohio in 1809, and, while there, decried the influence of "Methodists and Presbyterians" on that state's politics. They brought, he felt, sentiments of "Liberty equality and the omnipotence of the people," much to the detriment of order and efficiency in government.[58] Even some of the language of debate shows religious influences, as reformers sought a "regeneration" of the political order while conservatives looked skeptically at the "millennial" expectations of reform.

The importance of religion was, however, less as a direct influence on political thought than as a powerful support and symbolic expression of a world view that accepted certain possibilities for human life. Emphasizing human imperfection and social needs, it contributed much to that insecurity about society which lay underneath conservative ideas.

In emphasizing the foundations of Virginia conservatism in social morality, one does not, to be sure, mean to minimize the more direct intellectual sources from which that ideology came. Thus, for example, it is not difficult to trace the intellectual origins of Virginia conservatism back with some clarity to that realistic, Machiavellian tradition that J.G.A. Pocock has detailed so magnificently[59] or to American Federalism—indeed, to *The Federalist* itself.[60] However, Virginia conservatives had far more practical ends in mind than the preservation of an ideological tradition, and it is unlikely that Machiavellian notions or those of the Federalists would have appeared in conservative arguments had they not corresponded in some way to the broader views of human nature and society that Virginians had learned from family and social life, and from their conservative Episcopal religion. These ideas were what made the ideology acceptable, and not the reverse.

One may see this clearly, for instance, in the role conservatives assigned to property. Conservatives argued for the freehold suffrage because they claimed that man's passionate nature made such a tangible check on his actions indispensable to political order. Such a need would not have seemed so pressing, however, had conservatives and moderates not shared in a view of the world which stressed the difficulty of avoiding the self-indulgence which led to acting in ways contrary to the preservation of society. Those who accepted the values of Virginia's elite were disposed to be skeptical of any argument which placed much faith in the individual—as reform arguments seemed to do.

The social foundations of Virginia conservatism also help to explain why, history should have been of such importance to conservatives' arguments against reform. When Virginians read history, what they read was proof of their main concerns for human nature and society. Thus, the then-contemporary historian, John Gillies—whose work Littleton W. Tazewell recommended to son John in 1824—wrote an account of ancient Greece in which explained events on the basis of the "certain, because uniform, current of human passions."[61] It was such a view of history that Leigh had drawn on in arguing before the convention that "there has been no change in the natural feelings, passions, and appetites of men" throughout time. Using this point of view to deny American exceptionalism and to assert the fragility of their own society, Virginia conservatives were on familiar ground because, again, of the common view of the dangers of the passions to social life and the common acceptance of human weakness that they and moderate delegates professed for all areas of life.

But, one must note, the social background to Virginia conservatism was also important to the role played by the one thinker whose works did have direct influence on conservatives in the convention, Edmund Burke. This was particularly true of Burke's noted book *Reflections on the Revolution in France* (1790), which Virginia conservatives used eagerly as a model for citing the events of Revolutionary France in arguing against social and political change. For Burke, the French Revolution had meant nothing so much as the triumph of indecency in politics, the end of a political life in which government operated for good and in which leadership lay in the proper hands. Strongly antidemocratic, Burke advanced the view that licentiousness and the growth of faction were inevitable results of doing away with the kind of stability that hierarchy could provide and of letting the masses take a voice in public affairs.[62]

There is no doubt that Virginia conservatives found Burke valuable and that his role in the convention was important. Conservatives referred often to the wisdom of Burke; reformers, just as frequently, felt called upon to attack him. Thus, at one point in the debates, reformer Lucas Thompson said of the conservatives that, "Burke, Filmer, and Hobbes, judging from their arguments, have become the textbooks of our statesmen."[63] Thompson was certainly wrong about Filmer, and conservatives only rarely cited Hobbes, however much his views seem to have informed theirs. But, in men-

166

tioning Burke, Thompson was right on the mark. Burke was
the writer conservatives mentioned most often and most favorably in their public efforts and in their correspondence.
He was, for example, John Randolph's favorite author, and
William Halyburton described his works to William Branch
Giles as the best guide for policy and for public action.[64] His
approach to politics anticipated, in almost every respect, the
Virginia conservative position in 1829-30 and, more significantly, the bases for that position in political culture and social morality.

It is, in fact, possible to show a variety of areas in which
Burke and the Virginia conservatives argued from similar
views. Like them, for example, Burke was not only opposed
to democracy, but saw the chief purpose of government as
the restraint of passion.[65] Burke also urged that the greatest
reliance be placed on custom and tradition in the development of a political system even as he decried a spirit of innovation that seemed to be getting ever stronger. But perhaps
the most significant connection lay in Burke's own rejection
of abstract principles as a guide for political action. Indeed,
much of Burke's *Reflections* really amounted to an attack on
those who would change any government, even in Britain,
for reasons of abstract principle. Referring to them at one
point as "literary caballers, and intriguing philosophers" in
league with "political theologians, and theological politicians," Burke would use the example of France to argue that,
as he said, rights were politically false in proportion with
their metaphysical truth.[66] Experience, not principles, had to
guide political action, a point William Branch Giles would
acknowledge in 1817 when he wrote that, after France, "the
world is at this time awfully admonished of the horrible
effects of political theories."[67]

But what made Burke's views so compelling was the way in
which he connected the reliance on principles, in particular,
with the kind of social concern that stressed the necessity of
moral sentiment in any human organization. For Burke, the
excessive reliance on human reason was destructive of the

167

most important of human social bonds. Thus, he would argue, the downward slide of western civilization into the horrors of France had begun with the Enlightenment, with its exaltation of reason above social ties and social custom. Enlightenment rationalism had brought with it the loss of a decent, chivalrous society, Burke claimed. Its leaders had been men, as he put it, of "cold hearts and muddy understandings," and Burke opposed the political implications of their views, embodied in France, to the gentlemanly spirit of European tradition, to what might be called a politics of decency.[68]

Burke's view in this regard was illustrated and dramatized by his pathetic, striking account of the routing of the French queen, Marie Antoinette, from her chambers by the people of Paris. Falling asleep on the evening of October 6, 1789,

> the Queen was first startled by the voice of the sentinel at her door, who cried out to her, to save herself by flight— that this was the last proof of fidelity he could give—that they were upon him, and he was dead. Instantly he was cut down. A band of cruel ruffians and assassins, reeking with his blood, rushed into the Chamber of the Queen, and pierced with a hundred strokes of bayonets and poniards the bed from whence this persecuted woman had but just time to fly almost naked, and, through ways unknown to the murderers, had escaped to seek refuge at the feet of a King and husband, not secure of his own life for a moment.[69]

Burke's position here was important. Horrified that monarchs, deserving of respect, should be so cruelly treated, Burke was also showing just how indecent a society would become when abstractions triumphed over the social relations which had developed out of centuries of custom and tradition. Thus, it is revealing that while conservatives in the Convention of 1829-30 never made direct reference to this episode in Burke's *Reflections*, reformer Richard Henderson once felt obliged to declare in convention, "Let not the brilliant and ravishing description which Burke gives us of the unfortunate Marie Antoinette, beguile us into the belief that any argument against our principles can be founded on the story of her sorrows, or of those of her country."[70] Perhaps there was a touch of Southern "gyneolotry" involved here, but it does not detract from the important connection Burke made, and Henderson felt, between the quest for theoretical perfection and the loss of decency in political life.

Virginia conservatives were themselves aware of the connections that could be made between the abuse of reason and the loss of decency in human relationships. Thus, for example, conservative William Halyburton would condemn "abstract metaphysical reasoning" as a mode of thought because, he wrote, it "blasts the fairest blossoms of moral sentiment."[71] They could have learned the reasons for rationalism's explosive power from, among others, the Augustans, who taught that the abuse of reason grew out of unfounded human pride even as it put cold principle above human feelings.[72] There were, then, cultural reasons as well as rhetorical ones for the conservative rejection of abstraction. But, above all, Burke, in reacting to France, put the case against democracy and democratic principles in a way that emphasized the importance of society and social relationships and, of course, he did so with unsurpassed eloquence. He had, therefore, direct relevance to the needs of Virginia conservatives in 1829-30.

Still, one cannot see the influence of Burke or of any political theorists as formative in Virginia ideology. Virginia conservatism was, primarily, a cultural conservatism, growing out of values and attitudes developed when Virginia government and politics were controlled by an established elite and when, therefore, governing actually was an extension of social and family life. The application of that conservatism to political controversy was a product of events and not of any internal implications of the conservatism itself. The triumph of conservative ideology in 1829-30 was testimony to the social relevance of its cultural foundations.

NOTES – CHAPTER FIVE

1. See, for example, Thomas Bolling Robertson Diary, July 20, 1818, Skipwith papers, Virginia Historical Society, Richmond, and see, on this, for the colonial period, Michael Zuckerman, "William Byrd's Family," *Perspectives in American History* 12 (1979), p. 306.

2. Henry St. George Tucker to St. George Tucker, October 15, 1802, Tucker-Coleman collection, Earl G. Swem Library, William and Mary College, Williamsburg, Virginia.

3. Maria Gooch to Col. Claiborne W. Gooch, May 11, 1819, Gooch family papers, Virginia Historical Society.

4. Beverly Tucker to St. George Tucker, November 24, 1802, Tucker-Coleman collection.

5. Beverly Tucker to John Randolph, March 20, 1808, Tucker-Coleman collection.

6. See Dickson D. Bruce, Jr., *Violence and Culture in the Antebellum South* (Austin: Univ. of Texas Press, 1979), chap. 2, in this regard, and for the South generally.

7. Philip Greven, *The Protestant Temperament: Patterns of Child-Rearing, Religious Experience, and Self in Early America* (New York: Knopf, 1977).

8. Rhys Isaac, "Evangelical Revolt: The Nature of the Baptists' Challenge to the Traditional Order in Virginia, 1765 to 1775," *William and Mary Quarterly*, 3d ser. 31 (1974), pp. 345-68.

9. Edwin G. Burrows and Michael Wallace, "The American Revolution: The Ideology and Psychology of National Liberation," *Perspectives in American History* 6 (1972), 213.

10. Jack P. Greene, *Landon Carter: An Inquiry into the Personal Values and Social Imperatives of the Eighteenth-Century Virginia Gentry* (Charlottesville: Univ. Press of Virginia, 1967), pp. 11, 12-13, 20-21.

11. Ibid., pp. 15-16.

12. Landon Carter, *The Diary of Colonel Landon Carter of Sabine Hall, 1752-1778*, ed. Jack P. Greene, 2 vols. (Charlottesville: Univ. Press of Virginia, 1965), 1: 485, 436; on the relationship between Landon Carter and his son, see David Hackett Fischer, *Growing Old in America* (New York: Oxford Univ. Press, 1977), p. 76. Michael Zuckerman's research on colonial Virginia suggests that one way in which Carter might have been unusual for his time was in applying what were essentially external, social concerns to family relations, and that it was far more common for men to pay more attention to external than to internal ties. See his "William Byrd's Family," esp. pp. 263-64, 301, 303. Carter may have been "aberrant" in the mid-eighteenth century for bringing social concerns into the home, but by the early nineteenth century, many Virginians were speaking Carter's language.

13. Beverly Tucker to St. George Tucker, June 24, 1808, Tucker-Coleman collection.

14. John Randolph, *Letters of John Randolph, to a Young Relative; Embracing a Series of Years, from Early Youth, to Mature Manhood* (Philadelphia: Carey, Lea and Blanchard, 1834), pp. 146, 25; see, also, 16, 17, 23.

15. Ibid., p. 18.

16. Ibid., pp. 25-26.

17. *The Old Bachelor,* (Richmond: Printed at the Enquirer Press, for Thomas Ritchie and Fielding Lucas, 1814), p. 186.

18. Randolph, *Letters,* pp. 206-207, 71, 77.

19. Henry Adams, *John Randolph* (10th ed. Boston: Houghton, Mifflin, 1887), p. 266.

20. John Randolph, Commonplace Book, under "N," Tucker-Coleman collection.

21. Thomas Massie, Jr., to Thomas Massie, January 29, 1808, Massie family papers, Virginia Historical Society.

22. Thomas Jefferson, *The Writings of Thomas Jefferson,* ed. H.A. Washington, 9 vols. (Washington: Taylor & Maury, 1853-54), 1: 468-69.

23. Robert J. Brugger, *Beverly Tucker: Heart Over Head in the Old South* (Baltimore: The Johns Hopkins Univ. Press, 1978), pp. 60-61, 76-78.

24. Richard Sennett, *The Fall of Public Man* (New York: Knopf, 1977).

25. Randolph, *Letters,* pp. 190-91; Hugh Blair Grigsby, Commonplace book, 1829-30, ms. volume, Grigsby papers, section 61, pp. 15-16, Virginia Historical Society.

26. See Isaac Kramnick, *Bolingbroke and His Circle: The Politics of Nostalgia in the Age of Walpole* (Cambridge: Harvard Univ. Press, 1968), pp. 11-12; Leslie Stephen, *English Literature and Society in the Eighteenth Century* (London: Gerald Duckworth, 1904), p. 35.

27. Paul Fussell, *The Rhetorical World of Augustan Humanism: Ethics and Imagery from Swift to Burke* (Oxford: At the Clarendon Press, 1965), pp. 33-35.

28. Ibid., pp. 9-10, 76.

29. Ibid., p. 65.

30. Jonathan Swift, *Gulliver's Travels,* ed. John F. Ross (New York: Holt, 1948), pp. 236, 238-39, 290-91.

31. Fussell, *Rhetorical World,* p. 39.

32. Samuel Johnson, *The Rambler,* 4 vols. (London: A Strahan, 1801), no. 155.

33. Bonamy Dobrée, *English Literature in the Early Eighteenth Century, 1700-1740* (Oxford: At the Clarendon Press, 1959), p. 447.

34. Randolph, *Letters,* p. 191; Richard Beale Davis, *A Colonial Southern Bookshelf: Reading in the Eighteenth Century* (Athens: Univ. of Georgia Press, 1979), pp. 19, 53-54; Davis, *Intellectual Life in Jefferson's Virginia, 1790-1830* (Chapel Hill: Univ. of North Carolina Press, 1964), p. 260.

35. *The Spectator,* 8 vols. (London: J. and R. Tonson and S. Draper, n.d.), no. 19.

36. St. George Tucker, "For the Old Batchellor," #12, ms. writings of St. George Tucker, Tucker-Coleman collection, Earl G. Swem Library, William and Mary College, Williamsburg, Virginia.

37. See chapter two, table 5.

38. Isaac, "Evangelical Revolt"; Wesley M. Gewehr, *The Great Awakening in Virginia, 1740-1790* (Durham: Duke Univ. Press, 1930); see, also, Donald

G. Mathews, *Religion in the Old South* (Chicago: Univ. of Chicago Press, 1977).

39. William Meade, *Old Churches, Ministers, and Families of Virginia* (Philadelphia: Lippincott, 1855), 1, 33n.

40. John Randolph, Diary "Almanack," 1824, Virginia Historical Society. The other verses were Proverbs xxv: 17, 24, 25; xix: 17, 15; xxii: 7.

41. St. George Tucker, "For the Old Batchellor," #23.

42. John D. Blair, *A Sermon on the Impetuosity and Bad Effects of Passion* (Richmond: Lynch and Southgate, 1809).

43. Meade, *Old Churches*, 2, p. 355.

44. James Moffatt, in John Tillotson, *The Golden Book of Tillotson: Selections from the Writings of Rev. John Tillotson, D.D., Archbishop of Canterbury*, ed. Moffatt (1926; reprint ed., Westport, Conn.: Greenwood Press, 1971), pp. 12, 31-32.

45. Tillotson, ibid., pp. 46, 47, 50-53, 57.

46. Meade, *Old Churches*, 2, p. 354.

47. Louis Morton, *Robert Carter of Nomini Hall: A Virginia Tobacco Planter of the Eighteenth Century* (1941; reprint ed., Charlottesville: Univ. Press of Virginia, 1964), pp. 231-35.

48. Gewehr, *Great Awakening*, pp. 138-53, 251-53.

49. Devereaux Jarratt, *Life of the Rev. Devereaux Jarratt, Abridged from an account of himself in a series of letters to the Rev. John Coleman*, by the Rt. Rev. Wm. Meade, D.D. (Richmond: Office of the Southern Churchman, [1840?]), p. 32.

50. Devereaux Jarratt, *A Sermon, Preached before the Convention of the Protestant Episcopal Church, at Richmond, in Virginia, May 3d, 1792* (3d ed., Bristol, R. I.: Dearth and Sterry, 1808), p. 14.

51. Jarratt, *Life*, p. 34.

52. Edward Baptist, Diary, 1790-1861, pp. 1, 2-3, typed copy, Virginia Historical Society.

53. In Francis L. Hawks, *Contributions to the Ecclesiastical History of the United States of America*, vol. I: *A Narrative of Events Connected with the Rise and Progress of the Protestant Episcopal Church in Virginia* (New York: Harper, 1836), p. 104.

54. Robert B. Semple, *A History of the Rise and Progress of the Baptists in Virginia*, rev. and extended by Rev. G. W. Beale (Richmond: Pitt and Dickinson, 1894), p. 38.

55. William W. Bennett, *Memorials of Methodism in Virginia, from Its Introduction to the State, in the Year 1772, to the Year 1829* (Richmond: The Author, 1871), pp. 112-15.

56. See, for example, "Campbel's [*sic*] Rhetoric," unidentified student's ms. notebook (c. 1822), William and Mary College Archives.

57. See also, and most notably, Alan E. Heimert, *Religion and the American Mind, From the Great Awakening to the Revolution* (Cambridge: Harvard Univ. Press, 1966).

58. John H. Rice, *An Illustration of the Character & Conduct of the Presbyterian Church in Virginia* (Richmond: Du-Val & Burke, 1816), pp. 13-14;

172

Charleston Farmer's Repository, June 9, 1816; Thomas Massie, Jr., to Thomas Massie, January 24, 1809, Massie family papers.

59. J.G.A. Pocock, *The Machiavellian Moment: Florentine Political Thought and the Atlantic Republican Tradition* (Princeton: Princeton Univ. Press, 1975).

60. Arthur O. Lovejoy, *Reflections on Human Nature* (Baltimore: The Johns Hopkins Press, 1961), p. 46; Merle Curti, *Human Nature in American Thought: A History* (Madison: Univ. of Wisconsin Press, 1980), pp. 106-108, 115.

61. John Gillies, *The History of Ancient Greece, Its Colonies and Conquests, from the Earliest Accounts till the Division of the Macedonian Empire in the East: Including the History of Literature, Philosophy, and the Fine Arts* (1786. Philadelphia: Joseph Marot, 1829), p. 352; Littleton W. Tazewell to John Tazewell, March 7, 1824, Tazewell family papers, Personal Papers collection, Archives Branch, Virginia State Library, Richmond.

62. Edmund Burke, *Reflections on the French Revolution* (2d ed., London: Methuen, 1923), pp. 105-106, 116.

63. *Proceedings and Debates of the Virginia State Convention of 1829-30, To Which are Subjoined, The New Constitution of Virginia, and the Votes of the People* (Richmond: Ritchie and Cook, 1830), p. 411.

64. William Halyburton to William Branch Giles, May 25, 1824, Virginia Historical Society.

65. Burke, *Reflections*, pp. 56, 117-18.

66. Ibid., pp. 55-57.

67. *Richmond Enquirer*, February 15, 1817.

68. Burke, *Reflections*, pp. 68-69.

69. Ibid., p. 65.

70. *Proceedings, 1829-30*, p. 356.

71. Halyburton to Giles, May 25, 1824.

72. See, for example, Swift, *Gulliver's Travels*, pp. 152-53; *Spectator*, no. 185.

CHAPTER SIX

Virginia Conservatism and the Rhetoric of Proslavery

The conservatism of 1829-30, because it had broad foundations in society and culture, was not limited in applicability to the issues of constitutional reform. Underlain by notions of social fragility and human imperfection, it could be used whenever conservatives needed to defend stability, inequality, and order against proposed changes in social or political life. Hence, it is not surprising, the main tenets of Virginia cultural conservatism would become the main tenets of the proslavery argument as it developed in the antebellum South. That this would happen was not, however, readily apparent in the Convention of 1829-30, mainly because slavery did not figure there as an institution to be defended. Reformers made no serious attack on slavery as such; indeed, the democratic leader Philip Doddridge even went so far as to condemn eastern spokesmen for apparently making the assumption that slavery would never thrive in the West.[1] Conservatives who spoke of slavery in the convention spoke primarily of the interests of slaveholders, not of the rightness of the institution.

So, conservatives would tie the protection of slavery into their arguments against reform, but the protection they felt it needed was mainly from a nonslaveholding majority who might seek to profit economically at the expense of the slaveholding minority rather than from abolition. Thus, when Abel P. Upshur would declare, "I have thus endeavored to prove, Mr. Chairman, that whether it be right as a general principle or not, that the property should possess an influ-

175

ence in Government, it is certainly right as to us. It is right because *our* property, so far as slaves are concerned is *peculiar*," he was less concerned for the safety of slavery than for emphasizing regional differences. He admitted, in fact, "that we have no danger to apprehend, except from oppressive and unequal taxation."[2] Other conservatives would take the same point of view, though they might be somewhat less sanguine about the dangers. John Randolph, often noted for his antislavery sentiments, could, nevertheless, use regional differences to great effect on this issue. Speaking to the majoritarian arguments of democratic reformers, Randolph declared,

> They say to us, in words the most courteous and soft, (but I am not so soft as to swallow them,) "we shall be—we will be—we must be your masters, and you shall submit." To whom do they hold this language? To dependents? weak, unprotected and incapable of defence? Or is it to the great tobacco-growing and slave-holding interest and to every other interest on this side of the Ridge? "We are numbers, you have property." I am not so obtuse, as to require any further explanation on this head. "We are numbers, you have property." Sir, I understand it perfectly.[3]

The threat to slavery thus served as one element in the conservative argument, and it was an element, too, which was raised to terrifying proportions through the figurative identification of reform goals with the horrors of "St. Domingo," but the focus was regional more than anything else.

Thus, opinions on slavery in the Convention of 1829-30 were not as sharp as they would become by the time of the Civil War. It was still possible, in 1829, to be both conservative and antislavery, or, at least, to be a conservative colonizationist. In part, this may have had something to do with the less-than-booming character of Virginia's slave-based economy at the time, as William Sumner Jenkins suggested.[4] In part, it may have had to do with the minor tradition of antislavery thought among elite Virginians. In any case, while

176

there was a link in argumentation between conservative ideology and the rejection of antislavery, it was not fully forged until after 1830, with the strengthening of abolitionist attacks on the system and, more particularly, in the reaction to Nat Turner's rebellion, which resulted in debates in the state legislature on a proposal to emancipate the slaves. Just as debates on constitutional reform had crystallized conservative ideology in Virginia in 1829-30, so would these debates on emancipation, which took place in 1831-32, force a clear statement of ideas in favor of slavery.

In many ways, the emancipation debates paralleled those on constitutional reform. Two major factors accounted for the division between proslavery and emancipationist forces, one being sectionalism—despite the lack of open conflict in 1829-30, there was a division between the slaveowning East and Piedmont and the "free-soil" West—and the other, the willingness to use the principles of the Declaration of Rights as a guide to public policy. Even the strategy adopted by proslavery legislators was similar to that used by conservatives in the convention. Identifying the emancipationists with abolitionism and urging the sanctity of property, proslavery leaders addressed themselves to the moderates in the legislature in ways designed to make waverers fear the changes proposed by spokesmen for gradual emancipation and colonization. And here, too, spokesmen for the status quo would find success, as proslavery leaders were able to marshal enough votes to defeat the emancipationist proposals in the 1831-32 legislative session. Emancipation would cease to be a significant possibility for Virginia after these debates.[5]

Much of the proslavery position in the emancipation debates virtually replicated the conservative argument from 1829-30, particularly as it focused on the justification of slavery as an institution. Few of those who argued against emancipation sought to defend slavery on principle; most agreed that such a defense was unnecessary. Slavery was a fact of Virginia life and, indeed, it had always been a fact of human history. Thus, Alexander G. Knox would ask the emancipationists, rhetorically, "to point to one solitary instance of a Government, since the institution of civil society, in which the principle of slavery was not tolerated in some form or other." And the reason this was so, according to Knox, had to do with facts about human beings, particularly facts of inequality which had to be recognized in the face of speculative assertions of natural rights and natural equality: "Fortune, genius, and physical power, constitute a difference in men; and notwithstanding nature has drawn no line of distinction between him who drives and him who rides within the coach; yet circumstances have; and these circumstances force the one to end his services to the accomodation of the other."[6] Like conservatives two years earlier, proslavery speakers sought not so much to argue principles, but, instead, sought to render principles irrelevant to discussions of policy. History and circumstances had to precede principles; policy could not derive from abstractions.

Moreover, again like conservatives in Convention, proslavery legislators predicted dire consequences from following principles in trying to formulate policy. Excoriating *"new-light* politicians" who "pushed their theory with all the ardour of new-born zeal," James H. Gholson, of Brunswick County, would claim that if one paid too close attention to natural rights as opposed to the nature of society, "the bands which bind society together would at once dissolve–the relations of husband and wife, parent and child, master and apprentice, master and servant, governor and governed, would end, and even our present deliberations would be 'most strange and unnatural.'" Referring back to a view of social relations which minimized individual autonomy in favor of reciprocity, Gholson would also charge that, "gentlemen in pursuit of their favorite theory, have adventured on the boundless ocean of *policy, expediency,* and even *speculation;* and as they have taken along with them on board, my rights and property, I hope I shall be excused if I pursue them, though the sea is rough and the voyage dangerous."[7] Here,

178

Gholson even drew on the older conservative metaphors, meant to evoke the fragility of society and the dangers of change and to connect that evocation with the arguments, offered by those who would change Virginia's way of life. Asserting, as did William Brodnax, the fundamental role of property in any political order,[8] these spokesmen for slavery, following the conservative precedent from 1829-30, would also refer to the indecencies of France to provide a warning against anyone who might meddle with the social order on behalf of principle.[9]

There was, of course, more to the proslavery argument than assertions of the sanctity of property and the rejection of arguments from principle. Proslavery Virginians were also prepared to make the comparisons between the condition of free labor and that of slaves and to assert the beneficial effects of slavery on blacks—familiar arguments in later proslavery efforts—but even here the superiority of circumstance to principle as a basis for policy was an underlying theme. The key point, in any case, is that Virginians in the 1831-32 legislative debates had a frame in which to put their defense of slavery, for they were doing little more than applying a well-established conservative tradition to the specific demands posed by the challenge of emancipation in the state.

It remained, however, for someone outside the legislature to give this proslavery framework its fullest expression. This was done in 1832 by Professor Thomas R. Dew of the College of William and Mary. His "Review of the Debates in the Virginia Legislature," reprinted as late as 1852,[10] was a seminal early statement of the Southern proslavery argument, and an important link between the conservatism of the early national period and the rhetoric of proslavery that would grow in the South in the years leading up to the Civil War.

Much that Dew wrote in defense of slavery would echo words spoken by proslavery leaders in the Virginia legislative debates. Thus, for example, his explanation for the efforts of emancipationists was fully based on traditional conservative ideals for deliberation and for political argument. Not

179

surprisingly, Dew dismissed emancipationist arguments, based on principles of natural rights, as "splendid visions" presented by "chimerical philanthropists." While he did not go as far as the conservatives of 1829-30—or the proslavery men of 1831-32—in attacking the motives of those who sought change, he went no less far in characterizing their thought as utopian and, hence, unworkable. Indeed, he would claim, their very reasons for wanting emancipation were, if not evil, still suspect. One stimulus, Dew wrote, was the relative youth of the legislators. The legislature had not been composed of men of "the longest and most tried experience," but rather of young men serving their earliest terms in office, men whose zeal for principle had not yet been tempered by experience in governing a state.[11]

Beyond that, it was a debate which had taken place in a time of feverish excitement, on the heels of Nat Turner's rebellion in Southampton. Men were too agitated, too passionate, to engage in a reasonable discussion of the issues associated with slavery and emancipation. In Dew's words, the antislavery arguments "were of a wild and intemperate character, based upon false principles, and assumptions of the most vicious and alarming kind, subversive of the rights of property and the order and tranquility of society."[12]

But Dew's real contribution to proslavery—and it is possible to see him as creating a model for virtually all the proslavery writing published after 1832—lay in the extent to which he took the scattered assertions of the positive character of slavery, many of them also clear echoes from the emancipation debates in the legislature, and put those assertions in a clear and systematic form. He did this mainly by using the central points in Virginia conservatism as it had developed prior to 1829 for his organizing principles. In particular, Dew placed great stress on the natural character of slavery, on the fundamental importance of private property in a civilized society, and, finally, on the dangers of any sort of change to a stable social and political order.

In contrast to the speculations and panic which he ascribed

180

to proponents of emancipation, Dew made much of the natural character and historical reality of slavery. Following William Blackstone, Dew represented private property in general as the product of an evolutionary process in society, and, he argued, slavery was also a product of the evolution of society from savagery to civilization.[13] In addition, and echoing the arguments of Alexander Knox in the legislative debate, Dew would assert that slavery had existed in all the great civilizations of history—the Egyptian, the Hebrew, the Greek, the Roman—and had, based on what he understood by civilization, been an intrinsic, necessary part of them all. Despite anything speculation might demand, history proved, in Dew's words, that slavery "was no *accident, the mere result of chance,* but was a *necessary and inevitable* consequence of the principles of human nature and the state of property."[14] For Dew, America was not immune from history and historical inevitabilities.

Dew could support his historical point of view, interestingly, by means of his treatment of American slavery in particular. As one who sought to defend slavery in Virginia, after all, Dew had to look not only at world history, but at the circumstances of slavery in his own country if his case were to succeed. His main strategy in this regard, consistent with his views of the historical inevitability of slavery was to reiterate the position, also prominent in revolutionary and early national times, that Virginians had not chosen to bring slaves into the New World. Indeed, it is unlikely that any abolitionist presented a more ringing indictment of the African slave trade or of the horrors of the middle passage than did Dew,[15] and he continued a long tradition of opposition to the trade in Virginia.

In part, this position of Dew's may have been an effort to deny for Virginians any moral complicity in what most people acknowledged to be an unspeakably heinous aspect of slavery. No less important, however, was that in presenting the situation as he did, Dew could emphasize the argument from circumstances that he and other proslavery Virginians

181

made. Slavery in Virginia, by 1832, was a matter of conditions, not of conscious choice, and government had to fit circumstances if it were to fulfill its proper mission. Not surprisingly, Dew turned for authority on this point to none other than Edmund Burke, noting "that circumstances give in reality to every political principle its distinguishing color and discriminating effect. The circumstances are what render every political scheme beneficial or noxious to mankind."[16]

Dew's argument from circumstances was, again, firmly rooted in the tradition conservatives had used for the Convention of 1829-30. William Sumner Jenkins rightly stressed the rejection of abstractions by proslavery ideologues, but he has only incompletely understood the origins of that rejection. It was not simply that the need to defend slavery led men to reject abstract political theory, as Jenkins said, nor was it, as Eugene D. Genovese has suggested, that they were strongly influenced by the Romantic rejection of Enlightenment rationalism.[17] Rather, their rejection of abstraction was grounded in a powerful political, cultural, and rhetorical tradition, one which could be brought to bear very effectively in order to confront a variety of political challenges argued from principle—suffrage reform and reapportionment, for instance, as well as antislavery. The weight of tradition as well as the force of immediate needs went into making this aspect of proslavery; its foundation in a respectable approach to politics made the argument acceptable.

The second key aspect of Dew's defense of slavery was based on his assertion of the fundamental importance of private property and his view, too, that the chief function of government was to protect property. Like earlier conservatives, Dew himself presented a pessimistic view of human nature. In an 1829 essay, for example, he had written that "The purpose of government was, simply, to protect men from each other and, hence, to maintain the possibility of happiness," and he left no doubt that what was most needed in society was security for property. Government's "advantages are rather negative, than positive," he had written, and because of this, it could possess no "interests hostile and paramount to the interests of the people." One need go no further with Dew's general views, for it is evident that like the conservatives in the Convention of 1829-30 (and, it should be noted, Dew supported freehold suffrage in 1829), Dew considered property, and an interest in property, to be the only proper foundation for civilized society; the protection of that property, the only function for government.[18]

In Virginia, property included slaves. Hence, in Virginia, government had no business interfering with slavery; it should serve only to protect slave property. Abolition, according to Dew, was nothing less than an attack on property, and, at the very least, it should not proceed with government sponsorship. Indeed, the chief duty of government, given the presence of emancipationist sentiment, was to insure the protection of slave property against any efforts to end the institution in Virginia.[19] The arguments for connecting government with the protection of property, so frequently asserted in 1829-30, could easily be more intensely focused on slaves and put to proslavery use by Dew in 1832.

Finally, in arguing on behalf of slavery, Dew made powerful use of the general fear of change which conservatives had also sought to evoke in 1829-30. Some of Dew's arguments in this regard were simply practical, as when he traced the potential damage emancipation would produce in the Virginia economy—a response, certainly, to those who, anticipating Hinton Rowan Helper, ascribed Virginia's economic problems to slavery. But he saw far worse than economic problems should emancipation ever take place.

One result of emancipation would be the creation of a precedent-setting policy for making property dependent on government, and not vice versa. Dew claimed to be especially appalled that antislavery Virginians had suggested asking federal assistance for easing any economic impacts of emancipation. Under such circumstances, Dew asserted, Virginia

183

would herself become dependent, and, like any orator, he painted a very gloomy picture of a state which could "no more array herself against the torrent of Federal oppression. Hitched to the car of the Federal Government, she will be so ignominiously dragged forward, a conscience-striken partner in the unholy alliance for oppression; and in that day the genuine patriot may well cast a longing, lingering look back to the days of purer principles, and 'sigh for the loss of Eden.' "[20] The imagery was almost sublime in its characterization of Virginia's potentially fallen state.

Real sublimity was, however, reserved for describing, in various places, the effects of emancipation on life in Virginia. Both "St. Domingo" and Southampton appeared in the opening pages of Dew's book—although for ostensibly different reasons. At that point, while Santo Domingo was evidence against emancipation, Southampton was simply a force that had led excited Virginians to ill-considered antislavery positions.[21] As Dew's argument advanced, however, the two would become linked in a different and more profound way. Santo Domingo was merely an early case of what would have to happen if slaves were freed to live among their former owners: "But one limited massacre is recorded in Virginia history," Dew wrote. "Let her liberate her slaves, and every year you would hear of insurrections and plots, and every day would perhaps record a murder; the melancholy tale of Southampton would not alone blacken the page of our history, and make the tender mother shed the tear of horror over her babe as she clasped it to her bosom." Indeed, as Dew declared, even talk of emancipation could turn the slave into "the midnight murderer to gain that fatal freedom whose blessings he does not comprehend."[22] Dew was not the first to bring sublime language to the description of a potential slave insurrection. James C. Bruce, of Halifax, had also done so in the legislative debates when he asserted that even talk of emancipation might cause the slaves, looking toward freedom, to attack their masters. The very debates themselves, he declared, had "excited a storm ... which will soon go abroad,

184

and be beyond the control of those who have excited it."[23] The language and imagery were familiar, and it is doubtful if any possible future could have seemed so frightening to Virginians—having just experienced the panic engendered by Nat Turner's troops—than the specter of a race war with emancipated blacks.

The sublime, as Edmund Burke had written, involved the excitement of impressions of pain, and it could be effective in oratory because passions associated with pain were most closely connected to the need for self-preservation. Once evoked, the power of the sublime was strong enough to guide men's reasonings on any issue.[24] In the defense of slavery, rhetorical theory and deep-seated white fears were mutually supportive, making for a rhetorical formula that would dominate proslavery writing into the era of the Civil War. This was the prediction of race war in the event of abolition, a prediction fully informed by a sublime imagery for characterizing the nature of blacks.

The tradition on which this characterization was based was, of course, far older than the rhetorical theory of the eighteenth century—older, even, than American colonization by Europeans.[25] It was a tradition which Dew himself would summarize by saying that, "in the free black...the animal part of man gains victory over the moral," producing either idleness or a horrible brutality.[26] It was not simply that blacks were believed to be inferior; it was that they were believed to be wholly lacking in self-discipline and, hence, to be capable of producing the worst horrors anyone could imagine. Here was a traditional imagery for blacks that was tailor-made for a rhetoric that gave an important role to the sublime.

To understand the force of this tradition more fully, however, one must also appreciate a major practical result of the debates in Virginia, stressed in Dew's argument, too. This was that these debates put to an end all talk of colonization as a device for carrying out emancipation. No one who argued for emancipation in the legislature did so on the assumption that freed blacks would remain in the state, but coupled

185

emancipation with proposals for removing the entire black population over a period of time.[27] As Dew showed, with great care and detail, the task of carrying out even the least ambitious scheme of "emancipation and deportation" would be monumental, both practically and economically, not to mention its effects on Virginia's own society and economy.[28] The point of his argument could be lost on no one. There was no easy way out of slavery, now that it had become a "circumstance" of Virginia life. Emancipation also meant the creation of a large free black population, and one could draw on a long-established tradition of racial ideas to evoke, rhetorically, the impact of such a creation on everyone.

In his predictions of racial warfare Dew brought together the conservative device of sublime language with this new evaluation of the circumstances of Virginia society—emphasizing the permanence of a black population—in order to evoke fears for the safety and security of white Virginians. But in using the language of the sublime, Dew based his evocation on the much broader sense, conveyed by such language, of how difficult it was to maintain order and stability in any social setting. The language in which racial war was predicted stressed, in its Burkean sublimity, that there was nothing unnatural or miraculous about the occurrence of the awful event foretold. Just as such natural disasters as volcanoes or earthquakes were terrible not only because of their great power but also because they represented a potential for disorder that lay just beneath the surface of an apparently orderly natural world, so too did the potential for racial holocaust exist in Virginia, no matter how stable its society appeared on the surface to be.

Sublime predictions of race war would have sent, then, a message about how one ought to look at Virginia, a message intended to confront Dew's audience with the ultimate weakness of human control in the face of a bi-racial society. Such an impression would serve not only to show the need for continued control over blacks, which only slavery could provide, but also the ease with which that control could be dis-

186

rupted, should society become careless. Constant vigilance was Dew's message, meaning that no one should act in any way that might appear to undermine the strength and structure of slave society. This demanded, above all, a unity of whites on the subjects of slavery and social order.

It would be difficult to argue that, after 1830 at least, such men as Dew wrote proslavery tracts in order to convince abolitionists that slavery, as an institution, was somehow right. It would be equally difficult to show that Dew and other proslavery writers had a great concern to assuage a Southern "guilty conscience," since, even as early as Dew wrote, there was only slight evidence of Southern guilt over slavery, despite the efforts of such men as Dew to build a circumstantial account of the institution's origins and persistence. Drew Faust's insistence that the significance of the proslavery argument "lay within ante-bellum Southern society itself" is almost certainly true, and her assigning of it to the identity problems of its framers is valuable and important.[29] One must expand Faust's view, however, by emphasizing that the proslavery argument was, foremost, a political argument; its purpose must be considered in primarily political terms.

So considered, the character of Dew's effort to evoke the need for white unity becomes clear. Just as conservatives in 1829-30 sought to create an ideological base upon which to maintain ties among themselves and from which to appeal to moderates by calling up a sense of the fragility of any apparently stable society, so too did such a writer as Dew seek unity in support of slavery. He sought to make moderates on the issues of slavery—those who might favor any apparent weakening of the existing system—recognize that there could be no moderation where slavery was concerned. Not only had Dew, following the legislative debates, established that the seemingly moderate position of favoring colonization was impossible, but as James C. Bruce had in those debates, he also used language in order to leave the final impression that any questioning of slavery, particularly from within slave society, might be the very force which would cause the entire fragile structure to disintegrate. Here was a thrust that was supported by the same foundations in political culture and social morality as those which had supported the political case against democracy and constitutional reform.

Dew's review of the Virginia debates was calmly presented, usually controlled in tone, and even ambivalent enough about the morality of slavery to build its circumstantial case for the institution's presence in Virginia. Nevertheless, the seeds for the later positive-good defense of slavery were there, and there was little in the subsequent development of proslavery thought that was more than an elaboration on the conservative tradition embodied in Dew. The rhetorical frame and the traditional notions which guided Dew's argumentation would be carried forward to the opening of the Civil War.

Although the defense of slavery took many forms in the Old South—ranging from the subtle, almost subliminal defense offered by plantation-tradition fiction to the pseudo-scientific treatises of Southern ethnologists—by far the most important form of proslavery writing was that which emphasized the social stability and the humane relationships which slavery was supposed to bring to society. This form, too, had several types, and it could be used in everything from essays on plantation management to attacks on Northern society, even to full-blown "sociologies" for the South. It was this form of argument, however, it appeared, that owed most to the tradition of which Virginia conservatism was one expression.

The argument began from an assumed pessimism about human nature and historical possibilities. Few writers were so bold in asserting their pessimism as George Fitzhugh of Virginia, who argued that any society had to be based on putting to good use "the evil passions and propensities of men,"[30] but his was a view that most proslavery writers would have accepted. Indeed, this had been a key position in the conservative tradition, as we have seen, since it asserted the neces-

188

sity of harnessed passions to any form of social stability. In any case, pessimism about humanity was important, and it could be expressed in several ways by proslavery writers.

One was that, like conservatives in the past, proslavery writers continued to assert the importance and difficulty of achieving order in society. This, of course, had been a major element in Fitzhugh's well-known attack on Northern capitalism, but his was hardly an original point of view. Thomas Cooper, as early as 1835, contrasted the stability of Southern slave society with the discontent so often manifested by the "lower classes of whites" in the North.[31] This sort of indictment of free society had a tradition that antedated proslavery. One finds evidences of it, for instance, in the writings of John Taylor of Caroline in the late eighteenth century. But it was of a piece with the more general concern about the ability of the lower classes to act with self-discipline and decency, a concern that informed elitist political ideas from colonial times through the Convention of 1829-30, whether conservatives talked about people "out of doors" or compared the consequences of suffrage reform with the excesses of the French Revolution. Southern proslavery writers rarely strayed far from the view that most men—and especially men without property—lacked the discipline and independence essential for self-government, that there were some men who were fit to rule and others who were fit only to be ruled.

This view received its fullest statement in 1858 in South Carolina Senator James Hammond's famous "Mudsill" speech:

> In all social systems there must be a class to do the mean duties, to perform the drudgery of life. That is, a class requiring but a low order of intellect and but little skill. Its requisites are vigor, docility, fidelity. Such a class you must have or you would not have that other class which leads progress, refinement, and civilization. It constitutes the very mud-sills of society and of political government... Fortunately for the South, she found a

189

race adapted to that purpose to her hand. A race inferior to herself, but eminently qualified in temper, in vigor, in docility, in capacity to stand the climate, to answer all her purposes.[32]

There was nothing in Hammond's speech that was not anticipated in the Virginia debates by, for example, Knox's assertion that circumstances made some people the servants of others, but Hammond's remarks pointed out a wrinkle that had to develop in the generally antidemocratic front of the conservative tradition, if it were to serve the purposes of proslavery argument.

For many defenders of slavery, including Hammond, one great advantage to having blacks at the bottom of society was the relative equality it allowed them to claim for whites in the South. Even Dew, writing in 1832, would make such a point.[33] Others, most notably Fitzhugh, would remain openly truer to the antidemocratic foundations of conservatism, although not without some ambiguity. In *Sociology for the South*, for instance, Fitzhugh praised the "universal" suffrage which finally arrived in Virginia in 1851 as a reform which would "draw a wider line of distinction between freemen and slaves, to elevate higher the condition of the citizen, to inspire every white man with pride of rank and position."[34] Two years later, however, praising Virginia, Fitzhugh declared himself "the friend of popular government, but only so long as conservatism is the interest of the governing class." In the South, nonfreeholders could be included, because their interests were not too distinct from those of propertyholders: "but where the pauper majority becomes so large as to disconnect the mass of them in feeling and interest from the property holding class, revolution and agrarianism are inevitable."[35]

Fitzhugh—not as eccentric as sometimes claimed—acknowledged, by this last sentence, that the basic argument had not changed. Government had to protect and was dependent upon property, including the slave property of the South. The major threat to that property had, however, changed since 1830, and no longer came from within the region. Now

190

the main threat lay outside the South in the form of Northern abolitionism. As a result, the focus of the argument also shifted somewhat. Property remained, for Fitzhugh and others, the proper foundation for government, and an argument from property rights remained basic to the defense of slavery against any and all possible threats to its existence or even to its expansion. But, by the middle of the nineteenth century, a new and no less tangible basis for government had recommended itself to many Southern ideologists, and this was the fact of race. Hence, one can understand the need Fitzhugh or Hammond–or even Dew–felt for positing a sharp line of distinction between white freemen and black slaves, and for maintaining a cultural equation which saw no role for blacks except as slaves. Under such circumstances, racial unity, no less than property ownership, made for a unity of interest among the governors. As Fitzhugh saw, so long as that unity remained intact–as a real unity of interest– then it would be an adequate, tangible foundation for a stable social and political order.

The maintenance of racial imagery was, therefore, an important part of the defense of slavery, and it took several forms consistent with the traditional conservative rhetorical frame. First, of course, was the continuing assertion of the reality of racial differences and, as in Hammond's "mudsill" speech, the peculiar fitness of blacks for slavery. This was important because it reinforced the argument that, as Hammond himself put it, Southern society drew strength "from the harmony of her political and social institutions,"[36] or, more traditionally, that the slave system was adapted to the circumstances of a biracial population.

One need not trace, here, all the details of Southern racial "science." It is enough to note that the natural fitness of blacks for slavery was asserted by virtually all defenders of slavery from William Roane, in the Virginia legislature, to Dew to Hammond and Fitzhugh. Whatever the effect of that assertion on the Southern conscience, it was even more effective when framed, as Albert T. Bledsoe did it, by connecting

191

the blacks' fitness for slavery with the argument against evaluating any social institution on the basis of abstract principles. Circumstance was the only relevant consideration: "Slavery is not the mother, but the daughter, of ignorance and degradation. It is, indeed, the legitimate offspring of that intellectual and moral debasement which, for so many thousand years, has been accumulating and growing on the African race."[37] Bledsoe, significantly, continued his argument with a passage remarkably similar to what Virginia conservatives had asserted thirty years earlier, when he presented a discussion of the political ideas of Montesquieu:

> "All men are born equal," says Montesquieu; but in the hands of such a thinker no danger need be apprehended from such an axiom. For having drank [*sic*] deeply of the true spirit of law, he was, in matters of government, ever ready to sacrifice abstract perfection to concrete utility. Neither the principle of equality, nor any other, would apply in all cases or to every subject. He was no dreamer. He was a profound thinker and a real statesman.[38]

Not theory, but the fit of polity to circumstances, had been a guiding point in conservative arguments extending back to the Renaissance. It had been a mainstay in the intellectual tradition to which Virginia conservatism had owed so much, and had been the key point in the thought of Burke, and of Montesquieu, as well. It would continue to influence Southern proslavery arguments, and racial ideas helped to make those arguments work.

One sees this strategy at work in other ways, too. For instance, proslavery writers frequently asserted that slavery had improved the condition of black Africans—made them more civilized—having done so by placing them in their highest, and most suitable, social position. Similarly, in asserting the happiness of slaves, proslavery theorists merely drew a necessary conclusion from their beliefs about social order, coupled with their usual equation of happiness with security and protection. The coherence of institutions with necessity

192

was something that would work to everyone's advantage, despite the false hopes held out by utopian schemers. Abolition was as chimerical as it was dangerous.

And it was this aspect of the argument that, again, was most suitable for expression by sublime language–by a language of terror and pain designed to evoke the need for self-preservation. Dew's 1832 prediction of the race war which would result from emancipation was repeated time and again by proslavery polemicists. Blacks and whites, it was confidently asserted, could never live together as freemen. Were emancipation to occur, Augustus Baldwin Longstreet wrote, "the whites must yield up their territory to the blacks, and move away; or the whites must put the blacks, or the blacks must put the whites, to the sword."[39] Given the mythology of African barbarism, long a part of European tradition, Longstreet quite properly made no predictions about the outcome of such a war. It remained only for the powerful orator to put such notions into truly sublime language, as William Lowndes Yancey did in his noted speech before the 1860 Democratic national convention. Pulling out all the rhetorical stops, Yancey declared *at* the Northern delegates,

> Ours is the property invaded; ours are the institutions at stake; ours is the peace that is to be destroyed; ours is the property that is to be destroyed; ours is the honor at stake–the honor of children, the honor of families, the lives, perhaps, of all–all of which rests upon what your course may ultimately make a great heaving volcano of passion and crime if you are able to consummate your designs. Bear with us, then, if we stand sternly upon what is yet a dormant volcano, and say we yield no position here until we are convinced we are wrong.[40]

Bringing together the sublime motif of race war with the classically sublime imagery of the volcano, Yancey issued a call for political action–for a Southern withdrawal from the convention–that was firmly grounded in a long conservative rhetorical and political tradition.

193

NOTES – CHAPTER SIX

1. *Proceedings and Debates of the Virginia State Convention of 1829-30. To Which are Subjoined, The New Constitution of Virginia, and the Votes of the People* (Richmond: Ritchie and Cook, 1830), p. 87.

2. Ibid., p. 75.

3. Ibid., p. 316.

4. William Sumner Jenkins, *Pro-Slavery Thought in the Old South* (1935. Gloucester, Mass.: Peter Smith, 1960), p. 81.

5. Joseph Clarke Robert, *The Road From Monticello: A Study of the Virginia Slavery Debate of 1832* (1941. New York: AMS Press, 1970), pp. v-vi, 8-9, 14, 20-21, 37-38, 40.

6. Ibid., p. 84.

7. *Richmond Enquirer*, January 21, 1832.

8. *Richmond Enquirer*, January 24, 1832.

9. Ibid. This device was most fully elaborated by B. W. Leigh, as "Appomatox," in the *Richmond Enquirer*, February 28, 1832. Significantly, Leigh not only expressed admiration for but was accused of borrowing from Edmund Burke in the composition of his essay. See, also, Robert, *Road From Monticello*, p. 44.

10. Thomas R. Dew, "Review of the Debate in the Virginia Legislature, 1831-32," in *The Pro-Slavery Argument; as Maintained by the Most Distinguished Writers of the Southern States* (1852. New York: Negro Universities Press, 1968), pp. 287-490.

11. Ibid., pp. 393, 291.

12. Ibid., p. 292.

13. Ibid., pp. 300-301.

14. Ibid., p. 324.

15. Ibid., pp. 342-44.

16. Ibid., p. 355.

17. Jenkins, *Pro-Slavery*, pp. 58-65; Eugene D. Genovese, *The World the Slaveholders Made: Two Essays in Interpretation* (New York: Pantheon, 1969), p. 156.

18. Thomas R. Dew, *Lectures on the Restrictive System, Delivered to the Senior Political Class of William and Mary College* (Richmond: Samuel Shepherd, 1829), pp. 4, 7-8, 13, 155, 179.

19. Dew, "Review," p. 387.

20. Ibid., pp. 419-20.

21. Ibid., pp. 288-89.

22. Ibid., p. 444.

23. *Richmond Enquirer*, January 26, 1832.

24. Edmund Burke, *A Philosophical Enquiry into the Origin of Our Ideas of the Sublime and Beautiful* (2d ed., 1759. New York: Garland, 1971), pp. 57-58, 95-96, 160.

25. See Winthrop D. Jordan, *White Over Black: American Attitudes Toward the Negro, 1560-1812* (Chapel Hill: Univ. of North Carolina Press, 1968).

26. Dew, "Review," pp. 429-30, 449-50.

27. Robert, *Road to Monticello*, p. 12; Jenkins, *Pro-Slavery*, pp. 88-89.

28. Dew, "Review," pp. 358-62; during the debates, the point had also been made by Rice W. Wood, of Albemarle; *Richmond Enquirer*, February 7, 1832.

29. Drew Gilpin Faust, *A Sacred Circle: The Dilemma of the Intellectual in the Old South, 1840-1860* (Baltimore: The John Hopkins Univ. Press, 1977), pp. 112-13.

30. George Fitzhugh, *Cannibals All! or, Slaves Without Masters*, ed. C. Vann Woodward (Cambridge: Harvard Univ. Press, 1960), p. 27.

31. Thomas Cooper, "Slavery," *Southern Literary Journal* 1 (1835), p. 193.

32. *Charleston, South Carolina, Mercury*, March 8, 1858.

33. Dew, "Review," p. 462.

34. George Fitzhugh, *Sociology for the South, or the Failure of Free Society* (1854. New York: Burt Franklin, n.d.), p. 255.

35. Fitzhugh, *Cannibals All*, p. 136.

36. *Charleston Mercury*, March 8, 1858.

37. Albert Taylor Bledsoe, "Liberty and Slavery: or, Slavery in the Light of Moral and Political Philosophy," in *Cotton is King, and Pro-Slavery Arguments*, ed. E. N. Elliott (1860. New York: Negro Universities Press, 1969), p. 296.

38. Ibid., p. 335.

39. Augustus Baldwin Longstreet, *A Voice from the South: Comprising Letters from Georgia to Massachusetts, and to the Southern States* (Baltimore: Western Continent Press, 1847), p. 19.

40. William Lowndes Yancey, "Speech of the Hon. William L. Yancey, of Alabama, Delivered in the National Democratic Convention, Charleston, April 28, 1860. With the Protest of the Alabama Delegation" (Charleston: Walker, Evans, 1860), p. 4.

EPILOGUE

With the close of the Civil War, the kind of conservatism espoused in the Convention of 1829-30, which had become increasingly confined to the South during the antebellum period, would assume less and less importance in American political thinking. Indeed, even before the Civil War, and even in the South, that conservatism was, arguably, in decline. As its main proponents, the proslavery polemicists, put its tenets to the cause of racial rather than social unity, they weakened the limited but strong cultural base it had in 1829-30, and the demands of maintaining a unity on grounds of color meant a sacrificing of the stands which had motivated conservative resistance to democracy. Thus, even in Virginia, the divisive freehold requirement would be laid to rest by a constitutional revision of 1851 which, in essence, gave the vote to all white adult males–the very thing for which reformers had contended in vain only two decades earlier.[1]

Still, the conservatism expressed by antebellum Southerners did not simply disappear with the close of the Civil War. To be sure, conservatism itself underwent a major transformation in the later years of the nineteenth century. In the political arena, following the lead of such spokesmen as Andrew Carnegie and William Graham Sumner, much of conservative thought came to be tied to an extreme individualism based on *laissez-faire* economic ideas and a whole-hearted defense of capitalism. Although it held to an elitism based in part on Social Darwinist ideas, this conservatism was, nevertheless, almost the antithesis of the conservatism of the antebellum South.[2] This does not mean, however, that the older tradition would disappear altogether. Instead, it remained alive, at the same time, moving increasingly into apolitical channels. Serving, mainly, as a position from which

197

to criticize urban, industrial America, this older conservatism developed into the framework for a protest thought which would represent an important minority strain in American cultural life.[3]

One sees an example of the ways in which conservatsim would serve the purposes of protest in the reaction of many Southerners, to what appeared to be the corruption of their region through the introduction of Northern businesses and Northern politics almost immediately after the Civil War. Decrying the "materiality" of Northern life,[4] some Southerners turned to the conservative tradition to launch a virulent attack on what they saw as an alien influence in the Southern setting. One of the most prominent of these was Albert T. Bledsoe, of Virginia. Bledsoe had been a proslavery writer before the Civil War, and in 1867, he founded a journal, *The Southern Review,* to publicize the continuing relevance of "Southern" values to a post-war world. In a way that conservatives in 1829-30 could have appreciated, Bledsoe laid the causes of the Civil War itself to a corrupt North, a North which had been corrupted, in particular, by an excess of democracy. Declaring that this Northern democracy could be traced to the triumph of "the radical notions and doctrines of the infidel philosophers of the 18th century," Bledsoe would also assert that "the sovereignty of the people means, in fact, the sovereignty of demagogues." That such radical notions should have been allowed to triumph, Bledsoe also attributed to a familiar cause (though with some historical inaccuracy) by noting that those who had devised the American plan of government, the Constitution, "did not know that man is a fallen being; or, if they did, they failed to comprehend the deep significance of this awful fact." Failure to recognize such facts in the future would, Bledsoe asserted, lead to still further decimation of the South.[5]

Bledsoe was a forerunner of many Southerners who brought the conservative tradition to bear in opposing social and economic change in the region. Charles Reagan Wilson, in his study of "Lost Cause" ideas in the post-Civil War South,

198

has usefully pointed out the extent to which a few Southerners, faced with the growth of industry in the region, offered jeremiads to their fellow Southerners, warning of the dangers posed by capitalism in ways that drew on the broader conservative tradition of the antebellum South. Asserting the constants of human nature, and particularly man's subjection to the drives of greed and passion, these partisans of the "Lost Cause" would consciously look back to what they conceived as an aristocratic society with its hierarchical politics in making their protest against, particularly, the partisans of a "New South." Citing the "lack of sympathy" which characterized such New South types and contrasting this with the "integrity" and "hospitality" which had distinguished antebellum "aristocrats," these protesters against social change would make a sustained effort to keep alive the political culture and social ideals that had underlain Southern ideology in the antebellum period. Still, if some of those who protested were leading men in their communities, they were but a minority of leading men, and posed little barrier to the changes that were taking place, economically and demographically, in the region.[6]

Some Americans did continue to protest what they saw as a loss of quality in American life, and, although their protests were of little political significance, they did continue to build on a tradition of cultural conservatism which carried forward many of the main themes of antebellum Southern thought. Perhaps the most significant period for this cultural conservatism in the twentieth century was during the 1920s and 1930s. Advanced by such figures as Albert J. Nock, Ralph Adams Cram, and the Southern Agrarians, including John Crowe Ransom and Robert Penn Warren, this conservatism looked to the past and, for the Agrarians, to an idealized Old South as a counter to what these figures saw as the atomization and materialism of the contemporary United States. Although the cultural conservatives were all fairly independent thinkers, there were certain central ideas which tied them together. Among these were a condemnation of democratic society and a championing of elitism, a distrust of change and of schemes for social improvement, a sense of human nature as finite and fallen, a hostility to abstract reasoning as a mode of thought, and a prizing of sociability and personal civility as a basis for society.[7] To be sure, one hundred years after the Virginia Convention of 1829-30, these cultural conservatives did not simply repeat the arguments of such men as Upshur, Leigh, or Randolph, but there was enough similarity in their words to indicate, in them, the survival of an older tradition and its ideology.

One sees the form this cultural conservatism took clearly in the works of the Southern Agrarians, those twelve Southerners who, in 1930, published a volume of essays entitled *I'll Take My Stand*. At the center of this group of conservatives were four poets—Ransom, Warren, Allen Tate, and Donald Davidson—who, in the late 1920s, became repelled by what they saw as the increasing devotion of Americans to materialism and a declining interest in the fine arts.[8] Echoing the views of Bledsoe and other opponents of the New South, these writers saw their own region becoming too "Northern" in its ready acceptance of the excesses of urban, industrial democracy, and they used *I'll Take My Stand* as a vehicle for protesting this process. Attempting, as Donald Davidson wrote, to offer "a philosophy of Southern life" that would speak to Southerners,[9] the various contributors to the volume would look to the Old South for an alternative vision of life in America.

The contributors to *I'll Take My Stand* had varied backgrounds, and their essays examined several topics. In addition to the four poets who provided leadership in the effort, contributors included the poet and critic John Gould Fletcher, psychologist Lyle Lanier, novelists Andrew Lytle and Stark Young, and the historian Frank Lawrence Owsley. Essays appeared on historical questions, on economics, on art and literature, on race, religion, and issues of manners and morals. The contributors were not in agreement on every aspect of their "agrarian" alternative to industrial democracy—

200

nor even on the nature of their antebellum Southern ideal—but they were consistent in their opposition to American society as it had become and in their perception of a need to assert their differences from it.[10]

The Southern Agrarians began with a view that, as John Gould Fletcher put it, "so long as a system is producing good results, it is useless to meddle or tinker with it."[11] But they began, as well, with a real sense that the "system" was being meddled or tinkered with by those who would introduce an industrial economy into the South. If this occurred, they were sure, then Fletcher's simple conservative principle could never be obeyed. As John Crowe Ransom wrote, "It is the character of our urbanized, anti-provincial, progressive, and mobile American life that it is in eternal flux," and he contrasted that condition with an older, "backward-looking" provincialism which, he said, "is realistic, or successfully adapted to its natural environment," and, too, "is stable, or hereditable."[12] Such a situation, according to Ransom and his fellow contributors, had obtained in the agricultural, rural antebellum South; it could not in any community dominated by urbanism or progressivism.

The attraction of the Southern past, one should note, was something more than a matter of regional chauvinism. To be sure, the Southern Agrarians had been spurred to action by the negative image of the South which had spread abroad as a result, in part, of the famous Scopes trial of 1925; they felt their region to be undeserving of the rather indiscriminate ridicule which had been heaped upon it by the Northern popular press. But most of the Agrarians had come by their Southernness late, even after years of trying to transcend what Louis D. Rubin has called "the United Daughters of the Confederacy tradition in Southern letters."[13] What made the past important to them was that looking backward not only provided them with an alternative to the reigning ideology, but an alternative which had a concrete reality. It was not an alternative which was, itself, an "innovation."

The concreteness of the Southern alternative was impor-

201

tant in the general framework of Agrarian ideas, for, like earlier conservatives, these Agrarians expressed a strong hostility to "abstractions." It would be wrong to describe them as anti-intellectuals, certainly, just as such a label would be inaccurate if applied to Virginia conservatives in 1829-30. Rather, as Ronald Lora has suggested, the conflict between these conservatives and their society was one involving two distinct modes of thought—the one qualitative, intuitive, and concrete, the other quantitative, rational, and abstract.[14] It was a conflict not unlike that which had occurred in Virginia, and from the conservative point of view, it was similarly conceived. The Agrarians attacked abstract reasoning on the grounds that its conclusions were inevitably false and that it placed unjustifiable reliance on human ability, on what Benjamin Watkins Leigh had identified in 1829-30 as "the wretched finite wisdom of man."

Perhaps the single most important example of the Agrarians' attack on abstraction appeared not in their manifesto but in John Crowe Ransom's 1930 book, *God Without Thunder.* Concerned to defend "orthodoxy" and supernaturalism against what he saw as the inroads being made by science and by liberal religion, Ransom made much of the impotence of human reasoning given the character of the world. "Nature is infinitely subtle," he wrote, "and we with our sciences are simple. We always tend to overestimate the triumphs we celebrate over nature."[15] What was true of the natural world was true of the moral, as well. According to Ransom, "The moral order is a wished-for order, which does not coincide with the actual or world order."[16] He would add, "We do not flatter the world in calling it rational or intelligible, if we remember the qualitative poverty of all our descriptive formulas."[17] Rationalism could not arrive at moral or physical truth because the human mind, being finite, lacked the subtlety and complexity ever to understand fully the world.

And Ransom shared the conservative, even Augustan view that the main cause of excessive rationalism lay in human pride and presumption. As he wrote in attacking liberal reli-

202

gion, *"The Old God was the author of evil as well as of good.* This is my orthodox version of the God of Israel at the point where it is most challenging and critical. But temperamentally it does not suit us very well today. It does not flatter that universal dream of human power which our recent science has taught us to indulge, and by which we say that evil has been overcome."[18] On the surface putting forth ideas similar to those that would be so profoundly stated in Reinhold Neibuhr's neo-orthodox thought, Ransom's view owed more to tradition than to theology, and to a stance which emphasized human history and human finitude, not divine sovereignty as such, as proper constraints on thought and ambition.

From this rather traditional perspective, Southern Agrarians—and other cultural conservatives, too—could reproach a variety of the characteristics of urban, industrial society. They could criticize its social policy for failing to recognize "the supremacy of nature and man's frailty."[19] They could criticize its democratic strivings for failing to recognize human diversity. This was a major point in Robert Penn Warren's unfortunate defense of racial segregation,[20] but the Agrarian rejection of democratic equality was not simply a justification for racism. Even among whites they urged a recognition of inequality, particularly in regard to intellect and culture.[21] The Southern Agrarians would have approved of fellow conservative Albert J. Nock's 1937 assessment of the "noble experiment" of American democratic public education that, "unfortunately, Nature recks little of the nobleness prompting any human enterprise. Perhaps it is a hard thing to say, but the truth is that Nature seems much more solicitous about her reputation for order than she is about keeping up her character for morals."[22] One could not make unequal humans equal, by experiment or by decree.

Moreover, Agrarians could criticize modern "materiality" for a similar failure to give due weight to proper, natural foundations. The Old South, at least as Agrarians conceived of it, had embodied the adjustment to nature which had to be the basis for social organization and public policy, and this

203

was because of the agricultural foundations of its economy. No society based on commerce and credit—no capitalist society—could claim such an adjustment. The psychologist Andrew Lytle made this point in a way quite reminiscent of the Virginia conservatives who glorified landed property while excoriating the "paper" economy of the North. Admitting that the Cotton Kingdom had depended on the invention of the cotton gin, "an apparatus of the Machine Age," Lytle denied that this had made the antebellum South somehow industrial: "Stocks and bonds and cities did not constitute wealth to the planter. Broad acres and increasing slaves, all tangible evidence of possession, were the great desiderata of his labors; and regardless of their price fluctuation on the world market, if they were paid for, their value remained constant in the planting states."[23] Echoing Virginia conservatives' defense of land as the proper basis for political participation, Lytle's words located the desirable character of antebellum Southern society in an economic system based on the concrete, tangible measures of wealth that were land and slaves. But, clearly, more was involved than wealth; it was also a matter of social ranking and social position. Under Lytle's scheme, position itself was based on the tangible and not on either matters of principle, as in regard to democratic notions of equality, or on artificial, paper measures.

In important ways, then, the Agrarians of the 1930s echoed the Virginia conservatives who had spoken in defense of hierarchy and property more than a century earlier. To be sure, there were major differences between the two statements of conservatism, in part because each group had very different concerns. Most obviously, that earlier conservatism had been intensely political, and it was a part of an effort to defend a way of life which was built into the economic and political structure of a state. Moreover, it was a conservatism which had strong, vital roots in the society and culture of which it was a part. The conservatism of the Agrarians, however much it seemed to propose a program for Southern society and economy, was really divorced from both realms. Its concerns and programs were themselves far less concerned with preserving a political system than they were with protesting the defects of the existing society, and particularly with that society's headlong plunge into mediocrity in thought, expression, and sensibility. That man's greatest enemy was mediocrity rather than chaos was something that would never have occurred to the Virginians of the early part of the nineteenth century.

Tocqueville

Still, for all the historical differences between the two conservatisms, there was a common foundation in seeing not only human finitude but the social nature of man as the proper source for social and political action. According to Ransom, "culture consists essentially in having and defending a delicate sensibility even while we are engaged upon the stern drive of the practical life."[24] Such a sensibility was precisely what had disappeared with the onset of industrial democracy, and here was the Agrarians' final reproach against their society. The "culture" of which Ransom spoke was nothing so much as that attuning of the mind to nature, to art, and to other people which a strong individualism could only prevent. For John Gould Fletcher, the problem could be laid to modern education and to a scientistic assumption "that because a man has been educated according to the principles of the eighteenth century, which taught him merely what might make him a reasonable being capable of reading the classics and understanding the value of a good conversation, he was thereby an uneducated man."[25] To Stark Young, as to others, the problem was one inherent in competitive capitalist society, and he contrasted his ideal with a more threatening reality when he answered critics of the South: "If the old habit of sitting back, talking hours on end, is the trouble, the same may be said of the Russian nobility, the Spanish, the French, or of any civilization whose ideal is social existence rather than production, competition, and barter."[26] It was, for Young, a question of priorities, and the priorities of industrial capitalism precluded that "social existence" which ought to be the end of human endeavors.

205

But what troubled Young most was the extent to which the South itself had become permeated with Northern ideas and values. He saw a particularly glaring example of this in an account of a visit by President Calvin Coolidge to Texas:

> At the hotel breakfast in his honor... he was asked if he had enjoyed his trip in Texas. To that effort at mere polite conversation, in favor of which there may have been some local prejudice, he replied, "I thought we had come here to eat." This, I gathered, did not appear to the company as humor, or, if to be so taken, as a boorish form indeed, and there was, the account said, some silence afterward. And yet there are Southern people, who, reading of this incident, and with the encouragement of a little journalism, may have taken all as sincerity and rugged worth—people whose fathers were gentlemen and whose servants have good manners. All this might not be worth recording, if it were not so perfect an illustration of the confusion today among Southern people who know better and were born knowing better. To these people in San Antonio the Coolidge press talk about *sincerity* and *simplicity* and *reserve* meant something very different from this they heard when the great man visited their town.[27]

To approve, even to accept such behavior as Coolidge had displayed was to dismiss wholly that sensibility to relationships with others which, to Young, had been a hallmark of the Southern tradition. Here was a political criticism which looked directly to values on social relations for its foundation.

And it was this social emphasis that may be said to tie the Agrarians most significantly to the conservative tradition of the antebellum South. If one cannot say that the ideological formulation of 1829-30 had a direct influence on the cultural conservatism of a century later, one can point to the conservative argument of 1829-30 as an early and significant synthesis of a larger political cultural tradition which would be expressed relatively intact for a long period of American history. Drawing on an intellectual heritage most notably mani-

206

fested in Edmund Burke's writings and on elite social values and ideals of order and civility, it also had roots in a view that politics, like any human endeavor, had to recognize and to control for the limitations on human possibilities for accomplishment and good. In 1829-30, such views could still play an important part in the political culture of Virginia and other parts of the United States; by the early twentieth century, this was a tradition which could serve only as a basis for protesting against a world which had become very different.

One can find elements in this cultural conservative tradition in the thought of a few more recent conservatives. Russell Kirk, for example, has made much of his own indebtedness of John Randolph. Although taking the American conservative tradition back mainly to Edmund Burke, Kirk has found benefit in his investigations of "the freedom-loving, innovation-hating Randolph," and even published a full-length study of Randolph's ideas, in which he looked closely at Randolph's performance in the Virginia Convention of 1829-30.[28] One should not make too much of this, however, because even as one can find elements of pessimism, organicism, and even a distrust of abstraction in the writings of Kirk—and of such other modern conservatives as William F. Buckley, Jr., George Will, or even the Neo-Conservatives— these elements are less central to their ideas than is their commitment to American capitalism. Theirs is more a sober, pessimistic liberalism than a genuine conservatism, and their philosophy tends to be less an alternative to American society than a presentation of what Peter Clecak has called "conservative caveats" in the face of a dominant liberalism.[29]

207

NOTES—EPILOGUE

1. Charles Henry Ambler, *Sectionalism in Virginia from 1776 to 1861* (1910; reprint ed., New York: Russell & Russell, 1964), p. 266.

2. Ronald Lora, *Conservative Minds in America* (Chicago: Rand McNally, 1971), pp. 48-49, 54-57.

3. There was an important anticapitalist strain in antebellum Southern conservatism. Eugene D. Genovese has stressed this as an element in the thought of George Fitzhugh in *The World the Slaveholders Made: Two Essays in Interpretation* (New York: Pantheon, 1969), see, esp., pp. 124-26, 127, 152, 158. This anticapitalism was not a late rationalization for slavery as an alternative to Northern society and economy. Even Virginia conservatives, in 1829-30, would disapprove of capitalism because of the way it encouraged competition and individualism, both seen to be contrary to a decent society. See, for example, Hugh Blair Grigsby, Diary, October 4-31, 1829, entry for October 15, in which Littleton W. Tazewell would assert the "constant struggle" between labor and capital as a given in capitalist society. Hugh Blair Grigsby papers, Virginia Historical Society, Richmond.

4. Charles Reagan Wilson, *Baptized in Blood: The Religion of the Lost Cause, 1865-1920* (Athens: Univ. of Georgia Press, 1980), p. 84.

5. Albert T. Bledsoe, "DeTocqueville on the Sovereignty of the People," *Southern Review* 1 (1867): 349; Bledsoe, "The Origin of the Late War," *Southern Review* 1 (1867): 269, 272.

6. Wilson, *Baptized in Blood*, pp. 79, 90-91. See, also, Paul M. Gaston, *The New South Creed: A Study in Southern Mythmaking* (1970; paperback ed. New York: Vintage, 1973), pp. 154-60.

7. For a good survey, see Robert M. Crunden, *From Self to Society, 1919-1941* (Englewood Cliffs, N.J.: Prentice-Hall, 1972), chapter 4.

8. Louis D. Rubin, Jr., "Introduction" to Twelve Southerners, *I'll Take My Stand: The South and the Agrarian Tradition* (1930. New York: Harper Torchbooks, 1962).

9. In Robert M. Crunden, ed., *The Superfluous Men: Conservative Critics of American Culture, 1900-1945* (Austin: Univ. of Texas Press, 1977), p. 197.

10. Louis D. Rubin, Jr., *The Wary Fugitives: Four Poets and the South* (Baton Rouge: Louisiana State Univ. Press, 1978), pp. 214, 218-19, 235.

11. *I'll Take My Stand*, p. 94.

12. Ibid., p. 5.

13. Rubin, "Introduction," p. vii.

14. Lora, *Conservative Minds*, p. 109.

15. John Crowe Ransom, *God Without Thunder: An Unorthodox Defense of Orthodoxy* (1930; reprint ed., Hamden, Conn.: Archon Books, 1965), p. 169.

16. Ibid., p. 47.

17. Ibid., p. 60.

18. Ibid., p. 39.

19. *I'll Take My Stand*, p. 209.

20. Ibid., pp. 246-64.

21. See Stark Young in ibid., e.g. p. 339.

22. In Crunden, ed., *Superfluous Men*, p. 61.

23. *I'll Take My Stand*, p. 208.

24. Ibid., p. 198.

25. *I'll Take My Stand*, p. 95.

26. Ibid., p. 342.

27. Ibid., p. 331-32.

28. Russell Kirk, *Randolph of Roanoke: A Study in Conservative Thought* (Chicago: Univ. of Chicago Press, 1951), 2: 135.

29. Peter Clecak, *Crooked Paths: Reflections on Socialism, Conservatism, and the Welfare State* (New York: Harper and Row, 1977), p. 117; see, also, Peter Steinfels, *The Neoconservatives: The Men Who Are Changing America's Politics* (New York: Simon and Schuster, 1979), p. 3.

INDEX

211

Cabell, Benjamin, 37
Campbell, Alexander, 34, 37, 43;
    biography of, 53-56; and Disci-
    ples of Christ, 53-56; on appor-
    tionment, 62; on aristocracy in
    Virginia, 102; on conservative
    political culture, 125; on princi-
    ples in government, 84; on
    rights, 56; on slavery, 56; on the
    passions, 78
Campbell, Edward, 37
Campbell, George, 117, 118, 120
Campbell, William, 37
Capitalism, conservative views of,
    197-98, 209 n.3
Carnegie, Andrew, 197
Carr, Dabney, 53
Carter, Landon, 144, 147, 148,
    149; family life of, 145-46; on
    social ties, 145-46, 171 n.12
Carter, Robert, 160
Carter, Robert Wormeley, 145-46
Cary, Archibald, 9, 43
Cervantes Saavedra, Miguel de,
    152
Chandler, Julian A. C., xiv, 12, 67
Change, conservative views of, 84,
    95-96, 100-101; proslavery
    views of, 183; Southern Agrar-
    ians on, 201
Chapman, Henley, 37
Christian Baptist, The, 56
Claiborne, Augustine, 36
Clay, Henry, 47
Claytor, Samuel, 37
Clecak, Peter, 208
Clopton, John B., 35, 36
Cloyd, Gordon, 37
Coalter, 36, 94, 98-99
Coffman, Samuel, 37
College of William and Mary, 43,
    47, 117, 123, 131, 179
Conservatism: and the "New
    South," 199; adapted to
    proslavery, 179, 191, 197; cul-
    tural, 170, 199-200, 207-208
Conservatism, in Virginia: cul-
    tural, 170; development of ar-

guments for, 17; main themes
    of, xv-xvi
Conservative tradition, xi, 197-
    200, 207-208
Conservatives, Virginia: as a bloc
    in the Convention of 1829-30,
    34-35; characteristics of, 38-41;
    in apportionment debate, 62-
    64; political culture of, 109-16;
    strategies in the Convention of
    1829-30, 34-35, 59, 91, 100-101,
    116, 129, 135-36; views on
    convention movement, 24-25
Constitution of 1776, Virginia, xv,
    8, 11, 19, 60; and sectionalism,
    1-2; apportionment provisions
    of, 1-2, 11; suffrage provisions
    of, 2-3, 11-14. *See also,* Conven-
    tion of 1776
Constitution of 1829-30, Virginia,
    xv, 64, 66, 68, 69
Constitutions, concepts of, 93-95
Contractarianism, 102-104
Convention of 1776, Virginia, 8-
    11, 32-33, 43
Convention of 1829-30, Virginia:
    as a public attraction, 32; blocs
    in, 34-41, 70 n.15; ideology in,
    xvii-xviii, 128-30; legislative
    approval of, 23-26; political cul-
    ture in, 128-30, 136-37; section-
    alism in, xvii, 34-41, 64-65, 68;
    slavery as an issue in, 90-92,
    175-77
Cooke, John R., 31, 35, 37, 60, 62,
    63, 64, 68, 74-75, 81, 149
Coolidge, Calvin, 206-207
Cooper, Thomas, 189
Cowper, William, 153
Cram, Ralph Adams, 200

Davidson, Donald, 200
Declaration of Rights, Virginia, 9-
    10, 19, 65, 66, 67, 84, 177
Defoe, Daniel, 152
Deliberation, conservative ideals
    for, 110-11, 113-14
Demagoguery, 114-15, 125

213

215

Passions, the: and figurative language, 130; and ideology, 128-30; and the sublime, 131; conservatives on, 74, 78-79; Federalists on, 78; in conservative political culture, 121, 123; in political argument, 130; reformers on, 78; rhetorical theory on, 121-23

Pendleton, Edmund, 118

Pendleton, Philip C., 35, 37, 118

Perrin, William K., 36

Peterson, Merrill D., xvii, 67

Piedmont, defined, 1

Pleasants, James, 36, 63-64

Pocock, J. G. A., 104, 165

Pole, J. R., xv, 19

Political culture, defined, 110

Political culture, conservative: and conservative strategy, 136-37; and ideology, 128-29; and language, 116-19; and sectionalism, 115-16, 125; in proslavery, 180; main themes of, 110-11; and the conservative tradition, 207

Political past of delegates, and voting in the Convention of 1829-30, 40

Pope, Alexander, 152, 153, 154, 156

Powell, Alfred H., 37, 83, 89, 136

Powell, Robert, 24

Prentis, Joseph, 36

Presbyterian Church, 6, 7, 164

Princeton University, 50

Principles, role in government of: conservatives on, 62, 84-87; reformers on, 19, 20, 84; proslavery writers in, 178-79, 192-93. *See also,* Experience; Reason

Proceduralism, conservative, 93

Property, concepts of, 13, 75-78, 165-66, 181, 182-83

Proslavery arguments: as adaptations of conservative arguments, xi, 179, 191, 197; forms of, 188; in the Virginia Emancipation debates of 1831-32, 177-79

Race, and racial ideas, 185, 191-93, 203

Randolph, Edmund, 11, 14, 76

Randolph, John, 32, 34, 36, 43, 50, 60, 68, 110, 130, 143, 144, 150, 153, 167, 200, 207; as orator, 47, 48, 117; biography of, 45-48; on change, 96-97; on democracy, 80; on the French Revolution, 87-88; on principles in government, 84-85, 87; on religion, 158; on rhetoric, 139 *n.*25; on slavery, 176; reading of, 152-53; social views of, 146-49

Randolph, Judith, 110

Randolph, William, 47

Ransom, John Crowe, 200; *God Without Thunder,* 202-203; on change, 201; on religion, 202-203; on social ties, 205

Rawlings, James, 24

Reason: conservative views on, 86-87, 89-90; proslavery views of, 181-82; Southern Agrarians on, 202. *See also,* Experience; Principles in government

Reflections on the Revolution in France (Burke), 166-70

Reform, evolution of arguments for, 16-20. *See also,* Apportionment; Democracy; Suffrage

Reformers: as a bloc in the Virginia Convention of 1829-30, 34-35; characteristics of, 38-41; conservative views of, 116, 121, 125-27; in apportionment debates, 61-64; in suffrage debates, 65-66; reaction to the Virginia Constitution of 1829-30, 67-69; relationship to conservative political culture, 125

Religion, in Virginia politics, 6-7, 41, 157-65

216

Taylor, Robert B., 32; on principles in government, 84; on suffrage, 65; resignation from the Virginia Convention of 1829-30, 33-34
Taylor, Samuel, 36
Taylor, William P., 36
Tazewell, John, 25, 94, 166
Tazewell, Littleton W., 32, 34, 36, 50, 53, 124; as an orator, 118; legislative opposition to reform by, 22; on change, 96; on history, 166; on reason, 119; on rhetoric, 123
Thompson, Lucas, 37, 167
Tidewater, defined, 1
Tillotson, John, 158-60
Townes, George, 36
Trezvant, James, 36
Tucker, George, xiv, 110, 156
Tucker, Henry St. George, 43, 111, 142, 144
Tucker, Nathaniel Beverly, 112, 143, 146, 150-51
Tucker, St. George, 47, 142; on apportionment, 15-16, 61; on demagoguery, 114; on family life, 143; on conservative political culture, 113; on religion, 158; on rhetoric, 124, 125; on suffrage, 15-16
Turner, Nat, 90-91, 177, 180, 185
Tyler, John, 32, 36

Upshur, Abel P., 35, 36, 43, 63, 127, 151, 200; as orator, 117; biography of, 48-52; on apportionment, 62; on parties, 111-12; on principles in government, 62, 85; on property, 76; on rights, 79-80; on slavery, 90,

156; on suffrage, 48, 50-52
Urquhart, John B., 36

Valley of Virginia, defined, 1
Venable, Richard N., 36
Virginia: Bank of, 4; colonial political system of, xiii-xv; Constitution of 1776, *see*, Constitution of 1776; Constitution of 1829-30, *see*, Constitution of 1829-30; Convention of 1776, *see*, Convention of 1776; Convention of 1829-30, *see*, Convention of 1829-30; sectionalism in, xvi, *see also*, Sectionalism; sections of, 1; University of, 53

Waddell, James Gordon, 52
Wallace, Michael, 144
Warren, Robert Penn, 200, 203
Washington, George, 98
Webster, Daniel, 57
Wickham, John, 23
Wickham, William, 22
Will, George, 208
Williams, D. Alan, xiv
Williamson, Jacob, 37
Wills, Garry, 133
Wilson, Charles Reagan, 199
Wilson, Eugenius, 37, 66
Wirt, William, 50, 151
Wordsworth, William, 153

Yale University, 50
Yancey, William Lowndes, 193-94
Young, C. H., 2
Young, Stark, 201, 206-207

Zuckerman, Michael, 171 *n*.12.

218